SUCCESSFUL
WATERFOWLING

SUCCESSFUL WATERFOWLING

ZACK TAYLOR

Fully illustrated

CROWN PUBLISHERS, INC.
NEW YORK

Library of Congress Catalog Card Number: 74-80314
Printed in the United States of America
Published simultaneously in Canada by
General Publishing Company Limited

Designed by Ruth Smerechniak
Second Printing, March, 1975

This book is dedicated to two nice ladies, neither of whom will ever read these words.

It is dedicated to the first lady because she spent so many uncomplaining hours at the edge of a duck pond. "Mommy, can we go today to the duck pond?" her four-year-old would ask. And she would sigh, grab her book, and drive the mile or so to the pond. She would read while the boy played at the edge along the stonewall dam and watched the ducks with hungry eyes. He didn't try to catch them or even feed them. He just studied them because they fascinated him, thrilled him in some inexplicable fashion. They still do.

Once upon a time an elegant officer on General Pershing's staff took to wife a winsome slip of a lass half his years, and in due course, since he was a sportsman, they went waterfowling. Years passed, and the boy at the duck pond became the son she never had. On the boy's fifteenth birthday she presented him with the shotgun acquired in her waterfowling youth and made possible his entrance into a world he had only dreamed of. He cradled the shotgun across the handlebars of his bicycle and went forth to become a hunter.

ACKNOWLEDGMENTS

So many have helped in this book. My boss, Lamar Underwood, whose inspiration it was, my ex-boss Ted Kesting, who engineered my escape from honest labor, my colleagues at *Sports Afield*— Pete Brown, John Jobson, Dave Harbour, Jack Seville, Homer Circle, Gene Hill, Jerry Robinson, and the one and only Jimmy Robinson— have all contributed directly and indirectly to my knowledge and experience. Mark Wright, Irv Diebert, and Van Jahos have been friends from boyhood, as well as steadfast companions of the chase. Tom Paugh and I met in college days and have followed the birds since we were young associate editors together. I could sneak off to go gunning in those days because of the uncomplaining friendship of another associate editor, Chet Fish, now editor of *Outdoor Life*. The hours spent reliving Sam Bonnell's and Vaughn Abbott's glorious waterfowling careers have been welcome ones. I don't deserve my own special, private shooting preserve, but thanks to George Hettich I have enjoyed one. On many a great occasion, Walter Wright has sampled it with me and shared days of magnificent shooting. Commendation must go to Mary Dillon, senior editor of *The Reader's Digest*, for her patient insistence that I learn everything there is to know about Canada geese. Andy Tanner, Frank Astambranski, Tom Marshall, and Pete McClain are waterfowl experts in their own right. All have instructed me. Members of the Fish and Wildlife Service have been generous with their time and information. Jim Carroll, Peter Anastasi, Joe Linduska, Harvey K. Nelson, and Henry Reeves have helped directly in this work. Not everyone knows that if you write a letter to a state Fish and Game Department, you get back a prompt, polite, and complete reply. At least that has been my experience, and I take this opportunity to thank those gentlemen, past, present, and future, who have responded to my requests. Special commendation must go to the unknown creator of the clam stew in the Barnegat Diner, unfailingly delicious and life sustaining on many an occasion. I also wish to express my gratitude to the Garden State Parkway Police for not sapping my economic reserves the many times when drenched trailer lights refused to function on the journey home. Lastly, no one can be a successful waterfowler without an understanding wife. Not once has Melissa remonstrated over money spent, time wasted, or a back-yard cluttered with boats. All of these people made this book possible, and I return my appreciation and affection.

CONTENTS

AUTHOR'S NOTE

My first waterfowling day occurred in 1953. We secured permission and built a blind on what I thought would be a good spot. (It would have been—fifty years before.) Decoys were procured. The pram wore its winter brown.

Old friends assembled from far places. Mark arrived with an electric blanket, thinking he had outsmarted the elements at the unheated summer house. Irv's Chevy slid in the driveway. Van arrived sniffing. Dirty weather was on its way, he said. He was right—the storm struck from the southeast. I never felt the house rock so, not even during hurricanes. The power went out, and Mark dragged rugs from the floor to stay warm.

The next day the bay was berserk. The tiny gut we had to cross to the blind looked, as Van said, "like the bloody English Channel." An oarlock broke on the pram.

The wind screamed. Waves smashed against the blind, heavy rollers crashed against the wooden box, towering sheets of spray were torn off downwind. We were wet and slightly scared. The bay was raging out of control.

No matter. Brant were migrating, "comin' on," as they say down bay. Flock after flock drove doggedly into the teeth of the gale, oblivious to us standing up to our knees on the submerged marsh. They were flying at forty to fifty miles an hour, but their ground speed was a crawl. We fired and fired, not hitting one. The lead problems were impossible to figure, the shot blown away before it could reach them. We shot until our shells were gone. Not a bird fell. We retreated—weary, sodden, beaten men.

Mark soon had the fireplace blazing. It burned driftwood. Driftwood has a scent like no other firewood—heady, tarry, with a hint of the sea. Bourbon and Scotch found their way into glasses. Guns were cleaned. We talked. Old stories were retold. The fire crackled. Outside the wind was going crazy. Tremor after tremor swept through the old house. Across the street the surf was a muffled, angry roar.

To the last of us, we realized that never again would we see such a shooting day. Never again would we see such storm fury. Never would we empty so many shell boxes to such little avail. Never again would such swarms of waterfowl pass us by.

We also knew something else. We had loved every minute of it. We were waterfowlers to the last.

ZACK TAYLOR
Christmas Day, 1973

PART ONE

THE
SPECIAL WORLD
OF WATERFOWLING

To a certain extent it's true of all hunting that killing animals isn't a requisite to the enjoyment of their study and pursuit. Of course, the more you know about an animal's preferences and peculiarities, the better you'll be able to outwit it. But the wild world is fascinating in itself. Thousands who have no hope of ever going on safari shiver at the danger of lions and tigers. We learn from the fox's craft, the elephant's wisdom, the bobcat's fury, the eagle's freedom. There is a mystique that clings to other forms of hunting. You can see grouse feathers in businessmen's hats on State Street, Chicago. Quail hunting, with its wagons, mules, and relays of dogs, gives off a heady air.

But surely the study of waterfowling surpasses all others in all it has to offer even if never a bird falls to your shot. There is first the colorful history with its arresting message. There is the awesome variety of species, each with its own specialties, and one, Canada geese, whose character is such that they are rightfully held up as models for men to emulate. And if you add to the myriad waterfowl species, their companion shorebirds—"the windbirds," one admiring author calls them—why then a lifetime is not enough to learn it all.

Mere mention of these birds whose marathon migrations exceed all others calls that mysterious subject to mind. How in the name of heaven do these birds find their way across those trackless skies? Where, indeed, do they find the stamina to do so? In one species of shorebird all the adults migrate early. Then the juveniles, not a one of whom has ever been to where they are going, take off and fly unerringly to the wintering grounds, thousands of miles away. What steers them? Ask the birds. Scientists are baffled.

Then, too, the waterfowl student finds himself in such marvelous places. Sure, you can wax poetic about a deer woods or the African veld. But dawn on the Chesapeake, sunset on the Sacramento, beat them all. The ponds, the marshes, the rivers and reservoirs add a dimension of their own.

All this is by way of saying that if all you want to do is kill ducks, you have come to the wrong place. A game farm should be your destination. It will be cheaper in the long run, the birds' flavor more consistent, your chances of success infinitely more assured. But if you admire waterfowl, even love them in that sense no one but a hunter can understand, welcome to the club. If you spend hours watching them for no reward beyond the wonder of their ways, then you are ready for the feast. If you are prepared to spend thousands of hours with no other amusement than watching the grass blow or the decoys tug at their leads, you are lucky. For many duck hunters, the season lasts seventy days or ninety days or whatever. For you, it lasts forever.

1

An Aura of Romance

There is an amazing painting on the wall of a certain Egyptian tomb. It shows a boat being pushed through reeds, and standing in the bow is a hunter armed with a boomerang. The man's arm is cocked, the boomerang about to fly. The target, neck outstretched, obviously squawking, is one of several ducks springing into flight from their hiding place.

There are differences between this scene and present-day hunting. The boat is woven out of rushes in the typical Egyptian style, and hardly anybody hunts with boomerangs any more. Yet look at the similarities that have spanned seven thousand years. Jump shooting in reeds. The excitement of the breaking birds. The thrust of pursuit. Imagine how long that Egyptian hunter trained until he gained the skill to strike down such a fast-moving target. Undoubtedly he started throwing his first boomerang when he was a boy.

When the day is over and the hunter heads home, any real differences from a modern hunter are shed completely. Beyond a shadow of a doubt, the Egyptian hunter is following his sport for the most ancient and honorable of reasons. The centuries notwithstanding, there is little difference between one hungry man facing a roast duck and another.

It seems clear from the painting of the Nile hunter that as long as there have been waterfowl, men have pursued them. The Greeks and Romans were ardent hunters and held the view that hunting helped toughen up men for soldiering. In Europe during the Middle Ages ducks were driven or lured into traps. The word *decoy* is thought to have been derived from a Dutch name for one such trap.

The early settlers in America found the Indians to be enthusiastic and skillful duck and goose hunters. Their decoys cunningly made from woven reeds and, more commonly, from the skins of ducks, can be seen in the great museum decoy collections. A favored waterfowling method of these warrior-woodsmen was to slip beneath the surface and, breathing through a hollow reed, grab the unsuspecting duck from below. Unquestionably, the Indians killed ducks on the wing with bow and arrow, as can modern archers.

A French explorer, Baron Lahontan, described a hunt in the Lake Champlain area in 1687. He set out in a canoe with thirty or forty Indians who he said were expert waterfowl hunters. In a large marsh they "made huts upon the water" out of leafy

Wavy, ragged lines of flight are the hallmark of geese—these are Atlantic brant.

branches, each blind capable of hiding three or four men. "For a decoy they have the skins of geese, bustards [swans?] and ducks dried and stuffed with hay. The two feet being made fast with two nails to a small place of light planks which float around the hut. The place being frequented by wonderful numbers of geese, ducks, bustards, teals and an infinity of other waterfowl—see the stuffed skins swimming with their heads erected as if they were alive. They repair to the same place and so give the savages an opportunity of shooting them either flying or upon the water, after which the savages get into their canows and gather them up."

The skill at which the Cree Indians of today mimic the wild calls of waterfowl and other game hints at the artistry with which any one of the wild warriors of old undoubtedly could talk ducks and geese in range long before the first white hunter touched these shores.

The early settlers in America, at least those with any leisure, took eagerly to water-fowling. In a corner of George Washington's office in Mount Vernon stands his fowling piece, a double-barreled smooth-bore flintlock, with which he hunted the canvasbacks and redheads that still swarm in the Potomac.

However, it was the coming of the railroad that opened the Golden Age of waterfowling. By the 1870s railroad and trolley lines had penetrated every nook and cranny of the country and made long-range travel easy and inexpensive. It was a time of farming. Living was hard, and labor was cheap. Every duck-shooting region contained numbers of watermen who made their living from the harvests of rivers and bays. These men had all manner of boats, large and small, that they used in their work.

The harvest of fish, clams, and oysters was largely seasonal. Spring, summer, and fall were the most productive times. With the long duck seasons coming in winter, it was natural for many of these men to turn to commercial waterfowling.

Sportsmen banded together and formed clubs. Waterfront land was cheap, and there was plenty of it. The handy watermen were available to operate the clubs during the season and to tend and look after them in the off-season. The huge buildings, looking more like hotels than duck clubs, which line the Atlantic coast-line of Currituck Sound to this day, hint at the waterfowling splendor of that glorious time. There are still plenty of duck clubs, of course, but in those days they were everywhere, and they lasted for years, with sons following in their fathers' footsteps. Club names became famous and their holdings immense. The gigantic Currituck Club currently owns some eight miles of pristine barrier beach. It is probably the nation's oldest continuously operating club, having been formed in 1857, when northern sportsmen purchased thirty-one hundred acres at a cost of a dollar an acre. The Long Point Company at Port Rowan, Ontario, held property that jutted twenty-two miles into Lake Erie. The members of Los Angeles' Bolsa Chica Club made fortunes when oil was discovered on club lands. Many of the elaborate logs of the shooting days have been preserved. They show that the toll of waterfowl was stupendous. Here is the kill for December 2, 1876, as recorded in the log of Currituck's plush Whalehead Club. "Prospects poor for tomorrow. Thermometer 49 degrees. Barometer 30. Wind light northwest," was the log entry for the previous evening. Despite this, the day's total bag was "45 canvasback, three redheads, 10 broadbill, six black ducks, 46 wigeon, two pintail, six creek ducks, two teal, nine common ducks, one shoveler, 15 geese and four swans." Imagine how club members fared on a good day!

Another common form of commercial hunting was for the waterman to turn his home into a boardinghouse for the season. The waterman and his sons and helpers would handle the hunting; the man's wife and daughters would furnish cooking and housekeeping chores. The railroad delivered the hunters.

Everything conspired to make fabulous sport possible in these halcyon times. It was an era of craftsmen, and most things were made by hand, usually locally. The watermen turned to local woodsmiths to supply the special boats, decoys, blinds, and batteries the hunting called for. Sometimes craftsman and hunter were one, but more often a man became a decoy carver or boatbuilder and seldom, if ever, hunted himself.

These craftsmen elevated decoy carving to an authentic American folk art. But if you had told these watermen they were artists, they would have scoffed at you. Yet for many, inventiveness, pride in perfect workmanship, and the stamp of individuality were quite unconsciously creating small works of art. A generation or more had to pass before their skill came to be fully appreciated. Today, experts can instantly identify not only the region from which a decoy came but also can name the man whose hands changed it from formless wood to something seemingly alive.

Combined with the handiwork of the decoy maker was the skilled hand of the boatbuilder. Each area had its own idea of what waterfowling boats should look like, and, with that individual stamp that marks all waterfowlers, almost every gunner had special preferences. In an age when every waterfront community had several boatbuilders it was easy to put these special orders into practice. The museum at Mystic Seaport, for example, has over a dozen scull designs, each distinctive. There were boats needed to live on for extended periods. Special boats were required to carry the mass of decoys—"stool" boats, they were called—and other boats carried hunters to the blinds. Some boats fulfilled that function, then served as blinds themselves.

The boat designers and builders are long gone, their names forgotten. What few examples of their handiwork that have survived the years are now in museums. Oddly, though, the origins of what is probably the most famous duckboat of all, the Barnegat Bay sneakbox, have not been lost. Why not is a story in itself.

In the 1870s a man named Nathaniel Bishop, who lived in Toms River, New Jersey, became well known by making long voyages in extremely small boats and then writing books about his adventures. In 1879, for his book *Four Months in a Sneak Box,* which described a 2600-mile trip down the Mississippi River, Bishop tracked down the name of the man who invented the craft. He found that a Captain Hazelton Seaman of West Creek Village, a tiny hamlet on Barnegat Bay, had, in "about 1836" conceived the idea of a small round-bottomed vessel that was fully decked except for a cockpit. Being a boatbuilder, Seaman had built his own proto- type and called it "the Devil's Coffin." Other baymen who used Seaman's boats to sneak up on ducks called it a sneakboat. Probably because blinds on the low Jersey coast were sunk into the marsh and called "sinkboxes" the name gradually evolved into sneakbox.

Captain Hazelton's claim to immortality must be the accolade for what must have been thousands and thousands of other duckboat designers whose names have been lost. For example, scullboaters on the Delaware River in the 1970s were still using boats built more than one hundred years before. They neither knew nor cared about the anonymous American craftsmen who built them.

It is not surprising that such times produced the most efficient duck-killing machine ever invented. Only the present-day curtain blind of Ocracoke can rival the lethal effectiveness of this device. It was called by two names—"sink box," which is descriptive, and "battery," which isn't. No one can pinpoint where the name battery came from, but it probably derived from the weaponry sense of the word, as several sinkboxes anchored in a row provided a battery of guns.

A battery wasn't very complicated. It was simply a watertight coffin about seven feet long, two feet wide, and eighteen inches deep. To hunt from one, a hunter stretched out flat to remain hidden and sat up to shoot. The box was sunk into the water, partly by the hunter's weight but mainly with iron weights, so that only an inch or two of freeboard showed at the sides. This coffin alone would be too tippy and prone to be swamped by waves, so wooden wings extended three or four feet in all directions. These lay nearly even with the water surface and gave the boxes added stability. Waves breaking on the wings roll off without sinking the box. The most startling development was that iron decoys were cast, to help weigh the boxes in the water. These were the shape of wooden decoys, but with the bodies about half size. They were appropriately painted and placed on the wings. Their number could be varied to correspond with the weights of different gunners, in order to sink the box almost to water level.

The sinkboxes were then anchored in a good spot out in open water and surrounded by decoys. A few were two-man affairs, but mostly the gunner was on his own.

You can see why it took several small ships to gun one of these contraptions. A boat had to stand by downwind or downtide from the battery, to collect the downed ducks and geese. The boxes had to be transported by boat to the gunning site, and since they were big, heavy, and unwieldy, a fairly large vessel was required, one often equipped with a block and tackle to haul the boxes on and off. If left out, they were subject to loss by theft, storm, or ice.

The boxes were dangerous. They were always prone to fill and sink and put the gunner into icy water. Often the guide boat would be off chasing a cripple, and a hunter's growing plight not noticed. And, of course, the hunter in one was almost totally unable to help himself if wind, breakdowns, or whisky prevented the man tending the box to reach it quickly. But if the sinkboxes were dangerous to men, they were deadly for ducks. Most of the dangers waterfowl face in their adult lives come from the shore. From 20 to 25 percent of a given year's crop usually dies by gunfire, and this deadly hail of lead comes almost entirely from land. Little wonder waterfowl are much less wary of anything out in open water, where they usually are safe.

The sinkbox adds to its open-water location another waterfowl attribute—low silhouette. Ducks and geese cannot identify objects as such. They respond to motion and, to some extent, to texture and shine. The sunken box concealed the man perfectly.

Sinkboxes along with a gamut of other kinds of blinds were standards in the repertory of those who carried paying sportsmen out to shoot. But the Golden Age also saw watermen who shot birds professionally for sale to markets—the market hunters.

Market hunting was acceptable and legal, though there were some limitations. Birds were shipped through regular poultry channels. One theory of how the canvasback got its name holds that the birds were shipped to Baltimore markets in canvas bags, and one hunter had written "Canvas Back" on the bag to ensure its return. Old shopping lists give an indication of the popularity of various species. Prime canvasbacks brought $7.00 a pair. "Regulars" were $5.00. Buffleheads and whistlers were $3.50. Geese were $2.00 a pair. Brant and black ducks, $1.25. At the bottom of the list were broadbills. A mere thirty cents could buy a pair of them.

To understand what happened to America's waterfowl as the century turned, you must reflect on the public attitude toward game during those years. The American Indians lived off wild creatures and knew them so intimately that the relationship was as one animal to another, rather than as man to beast. The Indians have given us some of our greatest conservation messages. They recognized that any threat to wildlife posed an equal threat to their own existence.

The white man changed that. He tried to carve a home out of the wilderness, and wild animals became a source of food for only a few Daniel Boone types. For the man trying to farm, wild animals were adversaries plain and simple. Deer ate his corn. Panthers and bears carried off his calves and shoats. Rabbits ravaged his garden. A flock of geese could descend on a field of emerging winter wheat and leave not a single green shoot. To retaliate, the farmers blasted, bombed, and trapped. They killed off the threats to their security in almost every fashion possible.

This attitude was coupled with another that was equally devastating to wildlife. People generally believed the supply of game was endless. Wipe out herds of buffalo that shook the earth? Never! Exterminate clouds of passenger pigeons that darkened the sky? Impossible! True, the ghastly tragedy of those two species shook this public attitude to the core and initiated the conservation movement. The Bureau of Biological Survey, through many name changes the present Fish and Wildlife Service, was founded in 1885. But old beliefs die slowly, especially when they suit people's desires. As the century turned most people believed—as indeed many still do believe—that all game, waterfowl included, was put before us by God, and any man smart enough to catch these creatures of God has a right as inherent as those set forth in the Declaration of Independence to shoot as many as he wants, anytime he wants.

There were some regulations. The use of a gunning light at night was abolished as early as the 1700s, though it was not the fact that ducks and geese are almost helpless in the grip of a light that caused its abolition. Its use tended to drive waterfowl out of a given area and, since most people would rather gun during the day, it was demanded that night hunting cease. Waterfowlers of the nineteenth and early twentieth century were accustomed to spring and fall seasons, and limits were regulated only by the hunter's endurance. Seasons were long, takes appallingly severe. The 1893 season on the Susquehanna flats started on November 1st. The first day's take was five thousand birds, and would have been larger "but for the calm weather." On this opening day, individual hunters killed as many as 110 birds, and 80-bird bags by a party of several hunters were common. From 1888 to 1910, 72,124 ducks, geese, and swans were killed by members of the Currituck Club alone. Carefully kept records of the nearby Swan Island Club list a total of 62,009 birds taken by members in the period between 1880 and 1910.

It had to end, of course. Game officials estimate that there were originally 400 million ducks, geese, and swans on the North American continent. By 1900 the figure was down to 200 million. But by 1913 the decline was so apparent that the first legislation was initiated to deal with migratory waterfowl on a federal basis. As incredible as it sounds today, the states bitterly fought this loss of sovereignty. They demanded in the courts that the states' right to set seasons and bags not be infringed. Mercifully, they lost.

In 1916 the U.S. and Canada signed a treaty allowing the birds to be regulated throughout their range. And in 1918 the Migratory Bird Treaty Act was signed. This prohibited all sale of waterfowl, banned spring shooting, limited the season's length to three and a half months, specified dates for seasons to open and close, and provided for bag limits of twenty-five ducks and eight geese a day.

This act—and that warden force that enforced it—gave rise to yet another aspect of waterfowling's fascinating history. Men started hunting illegally, and since they were beyond the law to begin with, they abandoned the traditional method of shooting waterfowl with a shotgun and turned to other means as deadly as they are fascinating. Homemade cannons were common.* Sometimes these were giant guns, six inches in diameter. Another form was a battery of eight or ten smaller guns mounted in fan shape. The illegal gunners usually sculled down on the birds, often at night, sometimes during the day, always blasting into large flocks. Often the market hunters took ghastly risks, braving open water in tiny boats in wild storms. The guns themselves were perilous, frequently blowing up or breaking loose in recoil and smashing back into the gunner. Use of the night light was reinstated. Waterfowl do not relate the light to human activity, and at times scullers can get close enough to reach out and grab them by the necks. The magazines of automatic shotguns were extended to the end of the barrel so the gun could hold a dozen or more shells, and the weapon resembled an over-and-under. Ducks and geese are relatively helpless before bait, which they cannot resist. The use of corn and grain to lure waterfowl within range of cannons and guns was elevated to a fine art. More insidious were the duck traps. These can be easily made out of chicken wire. Bait

---

* Market hunters were not the only ones to attack waterfowl with cannons. A retired Coast Guard officer on Cape Cod—the only man I ever saw drinking beer and eating candy at the same time—told me this supposedly true story. Some time in the '30s his cutter was stationed on the Potomac, and a great flock of geese settled in beside the ship to feed. The Coast Guardsman couldn't resist the chance for a roast-goose dinner. He dispatched a man to the engine room to gather up all the loose nuts, bolts, nails, etc., he could find, and had these rammed down the cutter's signal cannon. A blank charge was inserted and *wham*, the nuts and bolts blasted into the geese.

lures the ducks to their doom. This relentless hammering put waterfowl on the decline, but two new forces arose that engulfed them.

With the 1930s came the Great Depression. Hungry men out of work turned to waterfowl to help feed their families and perhaps earn a dollar or two. Need overwhelmed risks and illegal hunting hit an all-time high.

All game can take tremendous pursuit and still survive because the survivors get smarter and smarter. (It was said in some Chesapeake areas where birds had been night-lighted that whole flocks of ducks would leap into flight when homeowners turned on a light in a waterfront house.) What game cannot withstand is a loss of habitat, and the drought of the 1930s drove a dagger into the heart of America's duck population. The prairies of the north central U.S. and south central Canada contain only 10 percent of the total waterfowl breeding area, but the region produces 50 percent of the nation's ducks (but not geese, which breed farther north than ducks). The reason for this tremendous fertility is that the area is dotted with thousands of potholes, each one dear to a mama duck's heart. In the drought the potholes simply dried up, and a vast acreage of nursery areas ceased to exist. With the cradles emptied, duck numbers took a nose dive. The dramatic curtailment of seasons and bags documents the appalling decline. In 1929 you could kill twenty-five ducks and eight geese daily over a three-month season. In 1939 the limit was reduced to fifteen ducks and four geese. In 1935, with the drought at its height and duck numbers estimated at less than thirty million and declining fast, the season was cut to thirty days, bag limits went to ten ducks and four geese a day. By today's standards, even this is incredible. Shooting the main ducks of the prairie— canvasbacks, redheads, ruddy ducks, buffleheads— was outlawed. The Golden Age of waterfowling was gone forever.

It was a crisis and nearly everyone recognized it. The word extinction began to creep into talks about waterfowl. Serious consideration was given to closing the season entirely. The sport as a sport would come to an end. Waterfowlers knew that once the season was closed, public opinion would make it difficult if not impossible for it ever to be opened again.

Again crisis resulted in legislation. Much of the laws that we know today date from 1934, when the Duck Stamp Act was passed, and 1936, when batteries and baiting were outlawed, gunners were restricted to hunt within one hundred feet of land, the use of motorboat hunting was prohibited, gun size was restricted, and so forth. The most important provision was the inauguration of the federal duck stamp. As every waterfowler knows, this started as a one-dollar tax, with the money earmarked for the purchase of land on which waterfowl refuges would be established. This farseeing legislation is what has produced and maintained our present-day refuge system.

In 1937 a group of New York men pondered a serious question. Monies were coming in for waterfowl assistance in the U.S., but there were no Canadian funds to aid duck restoration in that country. Federal law prohibited spending public funds in a foreign country. The group formed a corporation called Ducks Unlimited and raised one hundred thousand dollars. This allowed trained biologists to set up field operations in Alberta, Saskatchewan, and Manitoba. In the early phase, what they mostly tried to do was build dams to hold water in nesting areas. Often ducks would nest in early spring, then the pond or marsh would drain and go dry. Young ducks cannot survive without water.

Ducks Unlimited's success story is a great one. Today it raises over two million dollars annually, entirely by voluntary contribution. Over two thousand nursery areas have been *constructed* by D.U. over the years, and almost two million acres of prime duck-production lands are under its watchful eye.

Thus we come to modern waterfowling. Not every young duck hunter will be interested in this tale with its sorry riches-to-rags theme. The last of the men who knew the good and the bad of the Golden Age are near their ends now. When they go, the last of the era dies with them. A dear friend, with seventy years of waterfowling behind him, comforts himself that he has no cause to complain, that he had the best of it.

It's true. Waterfowling will never again be as it was. Too many essential ingredients of the Golden Age can never be brought back. The 400 million ducks are gone. The craftsman era is history. The sun has set on readily available labor, inexpensive land, and pristine waters. Yet I've flown over the vastness of north Quebec where black ducks nest. It was empty of all but wild things. Not even Indians penetrated it. I've droned hour after hour across the James Bay and Hudson Bay region that produces our geese, scaup, and teal. It has barely been touched by man. Decades will pass while these essential nursery areas will continue to produce their cornucopia. I cannot help but hope that other Golden Ages may lie ahead. The Golden Age of Canada geese is happening today, before our eyes. Our spreading refuge system will protect waterfowl on their winter range for ages hence. Vast stretches of the subarctic nursery habitat lie far beyond man's decimating grip and seem secure for times to come. The Canada goose miracle gives us hope. Who knows what waterfowl technology of tomorrow may increase productivity or extend ranges?

Nothing lasts forever. Certainly not men. Not even worlds. But it would appear that for a very long time there will be marsh dawns and elusive targets for those who wish to seek them.

New Ways for Old Ducks

There isn't any question that the nature of waterfowling has changed radically in the last decade. Canvasbacks and redheads, the two bread-and-butter ducks of the Golden Age, have been on the closed list in various flyways for several years. Nor is the future bright for these two prized species. They nest almost solely in the heart of Canada's Prairie Provinces and are now in competition with housing developments and shopping centers—a contest they cannot win.

Elsewhere, drastically reduced bag limits are causing gunners to turn to other sports. In recent years only one mallard a day has been allowed on the Mississippi flyway. Black ducks are the preferred species on the Atlantic flyway. Two a day are the limit, and in some northern states there has been recent discussion of lowering the limit to one. With bags like this it no longer makes sense to band in elaborate and expensive duck clubs or spend hours building blinds. Who is going to take time to set out and pick up eighty to ninety decoys for a couple of ducks?

Even if you could round up enough interested members, it is all but impossible to form a duck club in these crowded days. Waterfront land everywhere is astronomical in price. Leasing land, too, calls for high expenditure. A good goose field on the East Coast rents for from fifteen hundred to two thousand dollars a season. Much marsh or river-bottom land is unprocurable anyway. State and federal agencies have gobbled up huge chunks and should and will buy more. The trend in law confronts the private hunter. Virginia marshland is public domain. No one can lease a spot and post it to keep others away.

If you are lucky enough to have your own private spot and build a hunting shack on it, you'll find it increasingly difficult to find someone to look after it, and an unattended hunting shack is all too appealing a target for young people, bored in their outboards, over the summer months. A doctor friend on the Jersey Coast had the door of his duck-hunting lodge broken into so many times he installed a steel front door. Someone chopped through the side of the house and tore the place apart.

If this hasn't happened to you, consider yourself fortunate. Two seasons ago a friend built a nifty floating blind and anchored it in a good spot off a well-used point. So far, so good. Everything was perfectly legal. The area was first come, first served. Someone who thought he had a claim to the point doused the blind with gasoline the night before the season and burned it to the waterline. I hunted with a friend in Virginia out of a stake blind. It was a big, roomy thing holding four men

Here is a houseboat that sits out on a marsh near where I used to gun. It drifted onto the marsh in a storm and a succession of inhabitants have gradually fixed it up. It's great to be on a marsh throughout the night; you can see then why the ducks don't fly much during the day. The night is full of the sounds of them feeding.

and carefully camouflaged with cedars. I noticed the fellow seemed to be going out of his way to be friendly to the watermen who used the area, and I asked him why. "Cross one of these guys in the slightest way and your blind is gone," he said. Then he recounted a list of horror stories of others who had had their blinds wrecked. A sinkbox you can shoot a hole through, and a blind must be dug up to be repaired and is useless until you do. It used to be that storms were the main hazards to elaborate wooden blinds. Now you must add vendetta. It is so easy in this day of fast outboards to open the top of the gas tank, slosh a gallon or two around, toss a match, and be away in minutes.

Every year the numbers who hunt public lands increases, partly because more good public hunting lands are being acquired, partly because every year there is less private land to hunt on. If you build a blind on public land, sooner or later you'll come out one morning and find someone sitting in it. What happens next depends on a lot of things and none of them increases your prospects of getting birds. You have no real claim. You may say it's your blind. The interloper will counter by saying it's his spot. In any case, who needs this kind of irritation? Unless you're prepared to fight for it, it's foolish to build a blind on public land.

Another worsening problem is people pressure on accessible spots. In my area, hunters stake out on good points in relay teams all night so they can be sure of being the first there at daylight. For years body-booters on the Susquehanna flats have set out at two and three o'clock in the morning, to be first in the preferred places. This was undoubtedly the reasoning of the hunter who burned up the floating blind. He felt he had as much right to gun that point as anybody. Why should he allow the one guy with the floating blind to monopolize it all season? Anyone who would burn up another man's blind is a rat, but there's a certain justification for this argument.

Then there's the subject of theft. There is a new book on duck shooting by a man who guns the Pacific Northwest. In it he discusses the pros and cons of leaving your decoys out overnight. I'm glad that for him the question is worth discussing. In most areas it would be sheer folly. They'd be stolen. When I was a boy, everyone left their decoys stored in sneakbox racks. Today such a thing is unthinkable. I don't believe that people are more dishonest today. There are simply many times more people. The few rotten apples in the barrel have become many.

Even if all the preceding were not reshaping waterfowling, another factor far more significant would be. It used to be that game was managed on a broad scale. The year's reproduction was assessed and the amount of new game, be it ducks, deer, or rabbits, was estimated. A harvest target was arrived at. Then a season was set that past experience indicated would allow hunters a kill within the harvest limits. You don't have to do much hunting to know that this concept is now as outmoded as the market hunter's cannon. All game is being managed today with extreme selectivity, and this trend is certain to accelerate. Game is being managed regionally. The deer herd on this side of the mountain can stand so much harvest; the herd on the other side can stand perhaps more, perhaps less. Where possible, game is also being managed by species. Grouse populations are high, so the season is extended. Quail are low, so seasons are reduced. Where possible, sex selectivity is enforced. No hen pheasants, for example.

Another population crisis (this one in 1947) produced the legislation that initiated regional waterfowl management. Studies were well enough along to prove that, though there is some overlap, the nation can be divided into four flyways. Accordingly, four were established—Atlantic, Mississippi, Central, and Pacific. Representatives from each state in the flyway and federal and Canadian provincial biologists constitute a Flyway Council that decides what geese and ducks we can kill and when.

The extreme variety of species of ducks, geese, and swans that inhabit the North American continent are prime targets for species management, since all are readily identifiable. In many species the sexes are apparent, and shooting can be restricted to preserve the females. As we have seen, game management has been going on for a long time, to some extent, but now the federal managers are turning to a new system of species management that's infinitely more complicated than merely saying "No more canvasbacks and redheads."

It's called the point system, and what it does is assign points to different ducks. When the points of the ducks you kill add up to one hundred you have your limit. Let's say on the Central flyway there's a poor hatch of pintails. They are made fifty-point birds. You can shoot two of them, that's all. However, on the same flyway good nesting conditions produced a bumper crop of broadbills. They are assigned ten points. You can shoot ten before quitting. You can see how this point system can be used to shift pressure. If a certain species is up in population, a bigger bag is allowed to induce hunters to let an endangered duck fly by. The nation's most sought after species is the familiar mallard, and it's easy to distinguish the green-headed male from the all-brown female. Since one male can service a number of females, it's no surprise that hen mallards usually become ninety-point ducks while the males are ten-pointers.

The point system is offered by the Fish and Wildlife Service to certain states who have the option to accept or reject it. At present fourteen have adopted it—Colorado, Florida, Illinois, Iowa, Kansas, Michigan, Montana, Nebraska, New Jersey, New Mexico, Oklahoma, South Dakota, Texas, and Wyoming.

It seems evident that the point system will continue to expand. There is a great deal of interest in states using it more broadly. It's a game biologist's dream. Hunters generally like it, as it tends to increase bags. It also has a built-in advantage that other systems lack—in most cases, birds needn't be identified in flight before you shoot. You can knock down a duck, then get out the book and see how many points you have accrued.

The system has some problems, and you can cheat on it. Provision is made to allow you to avoid an unintentional violation. Let's say you shoot a ninety-pointer. The next duck bagged is a twenty-pointer. You are over the limit, but this is allowed because you are not required to identify the birds in flight. But you have to stop shooting. A violator can lie about the sequence in which the birds were shot. He says the twenty-point duck came first. He then shoots three more twenty-pointers and tells the warden the ninety-pointer was his last duck. The warden would have to have kept the violator under surveillance the entire time to prove him wrong.

Admittedly the system has its shortcomings, its complexities not the least of them. Wags are saying that to be a waterfowler today you must be a lawyer to understand the game laws, a biologist to identify what you've shot, and a mathematician to keep score. The difficulty is that the alternative to selectivity is an across-the-board limit of so many ducks of all species. If bag limits are established on this basis, they tend to be set to protect the species with the least population, those that are most threatened. In other words, the low side calls the tune. The point system allows scarce species to be protected but turns you loose to hammer species that had the best nesting and the highest buildup. It also tends to encourage gunners to gun for species that go largely ignored.

In essence, the point system presents waterfowlers with the choice between shooting just a few of a large variety of species or taking many of a few species whose populations are high. Among hunters there is no contest in popularity between the two. Higher bags will win every time.

Even without the point system the future of waterfowling would continue to reflect the past. Scarcities of certain species will occur along with population buildups of others. In nature's design, feast can occur simultaneously with famine. When good nesting conditions produce plenty of birds, game managers open the way to harvest them. Special seasons are declared. For example, Canada geese are at all-time highs. Seasons are long, and the bag limit generous. Teal on both the Atlantic and Mississippi flyways have been objects of special open seasons. Broadbill restrictions on the Atlantic have been relaxed for several years. Conversely, in 1970 and 1971 nesting failures all but wiped out Atlantic brant. The season was closed.

All of these factors point to the need for a new kind of duck hunter. The day when you can go to the same place every gunning day and try for one kind of duck is drawing to a close. Only on the Pacific flyway, fed as it is by Alaska's boundless nursery, does it seem possible that the old ways can long endure. The successful waterfowler must meet these changing ways by adopting new techniques. First, he must be mobile. Second, he must equip himself to gun several different species.

There are a number of ways to achieve mobility. Everyone today owns a vehicle. This and a camouflage net may be all you need to gun different spots. However, I think today's waterfowler should think in terms of a boat—a special kind of outboard boat that both carries you to and from the area you want to hunt and acts as a blind when you get there. The boat does several things not all readily apparent. For one, it is a focal point. It gathers your equipment together. It serves as a blind, and can keep you warm and dry in the most arduous weather. It can be constructed to be completely locked against theft. And it's fun to fit out a little boat to suit your needs. It can be as much a companion as your retriever. But the most compelling justification for the boat is that it solves the problem of where to build a blind. It is its own versatile, mobile blind. No lease is ever required. You can gun public and private lands, anywhere there are no "posted" signs. And while you'd always seek permission to build a blind on private land, no such permission is required to drag your boat ashore and gun. You're here today and gone tomorrow. What's more, instead of sitting out in a marsh somewhere, your blind sits where it should, in your backyard. Storms won't break it up or tear it loose. No one will set it afire. The motor won't disappear. The decoys are safe. No one will ever contest you for it.

Now we come to the subject of multispecies capability. To a certain extent this requires homework: you have to get out and find where the birds are flying, and study new areas. And you will need several different kinds of decoys. You should have a few geese decoys, some puddlers (probably mallards and maybe some teal), and a set of divers. Though such a rig sounds elaborate and expensive, a combination of silhouettes, new plastic decoys, and the ease with which you can make your own decoys, puts this several-species capability within reach of all.

This, then, is the pattern of the modern waterfowler. He is mobile, ready to go. He takes the time to learn several areas. His blind sits in his backyard. He is wise in the habits of several different kinds of waterfowl. And he has armed himself with the means to draw them within range. This is the future of the sport. This is the new way to harvest old ducks.

3

Who Kills What, Where

Game biologists from the Fish and Wildlife Service keep an eagle eye glued on our ducks and geese 365 days a year. The birds are constantly being counted, computed, banded, and studied. This information is transferred to neat yellow pages and bundled into massive books for other managers to study. It's remarkable how widely this information is disseminated. Marsh acreage, broods by states, losses of cripples, unretrieved kills, and much more is all steadily calculated.

Since 1955, the populations of popular waterfowl species have been counted in Canada in May and July and again in January when the birds are on the wintering grounds. However, the Fish and Wildlife Service wishes to point out that it would be misleading to consider their counts accurate down to the last duck. There are any number of imprecisions that creep into the count, so the figures should be taken only as guidelines. Of the three annual censuses of all species—the fall flight population, the wintering population, and the breeding-ground populations—the last-mentioned population is what is generally given.

DUCK POPULATIONS

Mallards. The familiar green-headed mallard is America's most numerous and most popular duck. From a high of 14,256,000 in 1955, the total had fallen to 9,209,000 in 1973 but with three ten and eleven million years in 1970, 1971, and 1972. The eighteen-year annual average is 10,643,000. Total U.S. kill is slightly under 5,000,000. (Kill figures are a rough average of 1971 and 1972 seasons.) The Canadian kill is about 1,679,000.

Gadwall. The gadwall population has been holding fairly stable. In 1955 there 1,359,000. In 1973, 1,654,000. Average is 1,782,000. U.S. kill is about 700,000, Canadian kill, 100,000.

Wigeon. These handsome whistlers also enjoy a stable population. In 1955 there were 3,853,000. In 1973, 4,829,000. Average is 3,621,000. About 900,000 fall. Canadians take about 125,000.

Green-Winged Teal. Teal numbers have fallen somewhat. In 1955 the total population was 3,678,000. In 1973, 2,833,000. The average is 3,023,000. Harvest is over 1,000,000 in the United States, about 200,000 in Canada.

Blue-Winged Teal. This popular species is also trending down. In 1955 total population was 7,842,000. In 1973, 5,406,000. The average is 5,547,000. About 800,000 are killed. Canadian kill is approximately 125,000.

Shoveler. The 1955 total was 2,102,000. In 1973 biologists counted 1,715,000. Average is 1,846,000. Some 420,000 are shot in this country, about 50,000 in Canada.

Pintail. This popular species declined noticeably but has begun to make a comeback. In 1955 there were 11,393,000 but in the early 1960s the populations sank to seven, then four, and in 1968, three million. It has since rebuilt to 5,143,000 in 1973. Average is 6,652,000. About 1,200,000 are taken in the United States, 200,000 in Canada.

Redhead. These handsome and prized ducks are not quite holding their own. The 1955 figure was 1,325,000, and the population held steady at around the million mark until 1970 when it sank to the 700,000s and then into the 500,000s. The 1973 population was 798,000. Average is 1,090,000. United States hunters harvest around 100,000. Canadian kill is about 50,000.

Canvasback. Contrary to popular belief, cans have never been a numerous species in recent times. And, again, contrary to what most people think, populations have been holding fairly stable. A flock was observed in December, 1973, off Long Point Bay in Lake Erie that was 100 yards wide and *six miles* long, containing an estimated 30,000 to 40,000 birds. The 1955 population figure was 525,000. Lowest year was 1967, when 350,000 were counted. The 1973 figure was 730,000. The eighteen-year average is 499,000. Some 140,000 were harvested in 1971, 4,000 in 1972. Canadians take some 20,000 plus.

Scaup. The F&WS lumps both greater and lesser scaup together, and it's easy to see why bonus seasons are in order. These populations seem to be holding up as well as any. In 1955, 8,111,000 were counted. In the 1950s and '60s the figure varied between five and six million. In 1973, 7,497,000 were recorded. Average is 6,982,000. Hunters kill about 600,000 in this country, 150,000 in Canada.

Wood Duck. The preference of these ducks for heavily wooded areas make it impossible to determine their population by the aerial surveys used to count other species. The F&WS employs a system based upon band recovery and harvest data, calculating the proportion of bands returned to keep track of them. The population has remained stable at slightly over three million for the last six years. Kill has ranged between 800,000 and one million. Canadian kill is about 78,000.

Black Duck. Black ducks are not as seclusive as wood ducks and rest on open water where they can be counted. However, a portion of the population remains on ponds and streams on the wintering grounds, and estimates of this portion introduce an uncertain variable into determining the blacks' total population. For example, biologists estimate that only 25 percent of the black population can be spotted from the air in East Tennessee and Alabama, but 75 percent can be observed in Michigan and Ohio. Black-duck population estimates use aerial-survey data backed up with the determinants used to count wood ducks. The average winter population is estimated at slightly under a million and a half. About 350,000 are killed annually in this country. Canadian kill is about 300,000.

Total Duck Populations. In 1955 the total breeding population, excluding scoters, mergansers, eiders, and old squaws, was about fifty-six million. Numbers declined in the mid-1960s to approximately forty million but have been climbing to the fifty-million mark. The 1973 total was approximately forty-three million. The total United States kill is about 11,625,000. Canadian kill totals some 3,500,000.

GOOSE POPULATIONS

Canada Geese.   In 1955 there were slightly less than a million Canada geese throughout the country. This figure held stable through the 1960s when a buildup started that reached 1,500,000 birds in 1967. Since then it has climbed steadily and dramatically upward. Here are the figures for recent years: 1968—1,507,233; 1969—1,638,864; 1970—1,808,356; 1971—1,808,270; 1972—1,962,974. There are officially 1,935,000 as of 1973. Breakdown by flyways is 200,000 on the Pacific flyway, slightly more than 400,000 on the Central, some 600,000 on the Mississippi, and about 700,000 on the Atlantic. About 730,000 are harvested nationwide in the United States, 150,000 in Canada.

Blue Geese.   The total population of blue geese has been fluctuating around the 400,000 mark. There are 125,000 on the Central flyway; about 400,000 on the Mississippi and about 1,000 on the Atlantic. Total kill is 120,000.

Snow Geese.   The nationwide population of snow geese has fluctuated between roughly 700,000 and 1,000,000 since 1948. Recent approximate numbers on the flyways: 450,000 to 500,000 on the Pacific flyway; 250,000 to 300,000 on the Central; 100,000 to 200,000 on the Mississippi, and 40,000 to 70,000 on the Atlantic. About 220,000 fall in this country, 60,000 in Canada. (Canadian authorities do not separate snows and blues.)

White Fronted Geese.   Populations of this species have ranged between roughly 100,000 and 200,000 since 1948. Recent flyway rough breakdowns are: Pacific, about 100,000 (1973—51,600); Central, around 20,000; Mississippi, a buildup from the 20,000 range to the 50,000s. Some 82,000 are harvested in the United States; in Canada about 45,000 fall.

Cackling Geese.   These are found only on the Pacific flyway. The population had hovered around the 100,000 mark until 1973 when it dropped to 54,500. About 10,000 fall.

American Brant. The population of these Atlantic flyway birds fluctuated between about 150,000 and 200,000 with a kill of some 80,000, until 1972 when it dropped to 73,000 and 1973 when 41,900 were recorded. There is no present kill.

Black Brant. On the Pacific flyway brant numbers were in the 50,000 to 60,000 range until the 1960s when a decline started. Recent years have seen a fluctuating population of around 10,000. About 3,000 are harvested in the United States, 1,800 in Canada.

Swans. The nation supports a sizable swan population. About 83,000 whistling swans and 200 trumpeters use the Pacific flyway; some 100-odd trumpeters fly the Central; about 600 whistling swans are on the Mississippi; about 62,000 whistling swans winter on the Atlantic flyway.

Coot. Coot numbers are as follows: Pacific, 545,000; Central, 260,000; Mississippi, 466,000; Atlantic, 378,000. United States total approximately 1,650,000.

POND NUMBERS

Another interesting long-term statistic is the summary of the number of ponds in southern Alberta, Saskatchewan, and Manitoba—the so-called Duck Factory. In 1955 there were 7,508,000 May ponds, but this figure is misleading, for the next years saw the number drop into the two to three million range. There were 2,039,000 May ponds in 1973 and the eighteen-year average is 3,463,000. What happens to May ponds in July is also totaled. In July, 1955, the seven million ponds of May dwindled to 3,446,000. The figure has ranged between one and two million July ponds since then. The 1973 number was 1,901,000 and the average is 1,760,000. Statistics are dry stuff, but behind these numbers are the hard work and the millions of dollars spent by the Canadian government and Ducks Unlimited that enabled existing water areas to be stabilized and new ones created.

CANADIAN SANCTUARIES AND WILDLIFE AREAS

Canada offers safe resting areas for waterfowl in migratory bird sanctuaries and national wildlife areas. The sanctuaries are mostly privately owned except in the Northwest Territories, where they are owned by the Crown. There are approximately eighty sanctuaries in each of the provinces. Sizes range from .05 of a square mile to a staggering 24,240-square-mile sanctuary in Northwest Territories. Most run from three to eight square miles in size. The wildlife areas have been purchased by the government to preserve habitat for wildlife, primarily waterfowl. There are some nineteen in all, with sizes averaging from 1,500 to 4,000 acres. In addition, as in the States, there are numbers of provincial sanctuaries and privately owned sanctuaries.

U.S. WILDLIFE REFUGES

As of June, 1973, of a total of 356 U.S. wildlife refuges, 272 were reserved strictly for waterfowl and sixty-one for migratory birds of all types (plus fifteen big-game refuges, four national game ranges, and four national wildlife ranges). Total acreage of both waterfowl and migratory bird refuges is 8,303,510.9. In addition to these lands under federal control, 1,303,168 acres of wetlands known as waterfowl production areas have been secured by purchase and easement in 114 counties in North and South Dakota, Minnesota, Nebraska, and Montana.

DUCK STAMP SALES

There were 635,000 duck stamps sold in 1934-1935, when the program was inaugurated. (The following year the number dropped to 448,204, and everyone predicted waterfowling was done for.) However, sales rose to 1,000,000 in 1937-1938 and climbed rapidly during the 1940s, peaking in 1947-1948 at slightly over two million. This figure held through the 1950s with a high year in 1955-1956 of 2,369,940. In the 1960s the number of duck hunters declined drastically with a low of 1,147,212 stamps being sold in 1962-1963. Toward the end of the '60s sales began rising again. The two million mark was broken again in 1969-1970. Sales in 1970-1971 were 2,420,244, and 1971-1972 sales were a record 2,442,944.

CANADIAN REGULATIONS

The Canadian Wildlife Service, headquartered in Ottawa, maintains rigid control over waterfowl and waterfowl hunting in that country. Since 1967 every water-fowler is required to have a $2.00 (Canadian dollars) permit, and through questionnaires distributed with these permits biologists have established "one of the most sophisticated (statistically at least) wildlife survey systems in the world," so one biologist informed me. Provincial hunting licenses are also required.

Canadians enjoy an approximately ninety-day season opening September 15th, and limits are more generous than in the United States, with five or six ducks and five geese allowed daily. Whether anybody likes it or not — and most American hunters don't — Canadian waterfowlers think that since they raise most of the ducks and geese they are entitled to kill 50 percent of them. In 1967, 383,032 Canadian waterfowlers bought permits. The figure in 1972 had risen to 421,677 with Ontario leading the provinces with 131,427, followed by Alberta, with 63,309, and Quebec, with 53,982. About 15,000 Americans purchased Canadian permits.

MEXICO

Some twenty-six species of ducks and five of geese regularly winter in Mexico, mostly funneling into the country down the Pacific flyway, with a few coming through the Central. The most popular species are pintail, wigeon, and scaup. The whitefronted goose, the most popular goose, is shot mostly in northern Mexico. It is estimated that about 2,500,000 ducks and some 40,000 geese plus nearly 75,000 black brant are Mexican winter residents. Although high, often outrageous, kills are recorded by mostly American hunters, total kills are negligible due to the lack of overall hunting pressure.

THE FLYWAYS

Pacific Flyway

The huge eleven-state Pacific flyway is unquestionably the least changed of our duck-hunting areas. It is the last area to support widespread duck clubs, and much good hunting land is in private hands. Seasons are generous — ninety-three days in 1971-1972 — and bags are larger than found elsewhere — six ducks a day allowed, twelve in possession. Across most of the other flyways an average of four ducks daily is allowed (with infinite variations, of course), with eight in possession. Seasons elsewhere are fifty to sixty days. The Pacific flyway covers 825,000 square miles — roughly 25 percent of the United States — and contains some 6,200 square miles of prime waterfowl habitat. It separates into five major units; The Great Basin in the mountains of eastern California, Nevada, Utah, and Oregon; the coastal bays and river mouths that extend from Vancouver, B.C., south to Baja California; the Colorado River valley, with its many reservoirs; the Columbia River system; and finally that paradise for ducks, the Sacramento Valley.

The mallard is by far the preferred duck here. Over a third of the birds harvested in Wyoming, Montana, Idaho, and Colorado are mallards, and states with mallards amounting to a third to half the bag include Oregon, Nevada, Utah, and New Mexico. Total mallard harvest is about 1,200,000 birds. Only in California, where the pintail is king, do mallards decline in importance. Some 40 percent of all

PACIFIC FLYWAY

California ducks harvested are the handsome sprig. Pintails are important in other Pacific states as well, including Nevada, Utah, Oregon, and Arizona. The total kill is slightly under a million. Wigeon, too, are a popular species in Oregon, Washington, California, Nevada, Utah, and Arizona, where the harvest ranges around 10 percent. Total kill is under 500,000. Other 10 percent ducks are the various teals in Oregon, Washington, California, Nevada, Utah, Colorado, and New Mexico. Total kill is about 500,000.

Canada geese constitute about half the total goose bag throughout the flyway; in California, which has several other goose species, they constitute only about a third. About 200,000 fall. Lesser snow geese are an important bird in Montana and Nevada. Total bag is about 70,00. California goose shooters get a mixed bag consisting of Canadas (33 percent of the harvest), lesser snows (about 40 percent), and whitefronts (about 20 percent). Total whitefront kill is about 40,000. About 3,000 brant fall, amounting to 1 percent of harvest. Flyway states are Washington, Oregon, Idaho, Montana, Wyoming, California, Nevada, Utah, Colorado, Arizona, and New Mexico. Here are the most recent vital statistics: Duck stamp sales totaled 438,148, and 3,969,600 ducks, 151,200 coots, and 330,400 geese were bagged during 3,097,100 hunter-days afield. Those persons buying duck stamps hunted an average of 6.6 days and bagged an average of 11.1 ducks and 0.9 geese each.

Alaska is not technically part of the Pacific flyway. Mallards, pintails, and wigeon are the preferred species here with kills at 22,000, 10,000, and 12,000 respectively. Some 10,000 Canada geese and about 2,000 whitefronts are harvested. Here are Alaska's most recent statistics: duck stamp sales totaled 14,423, and 73,100 ducks, 900 coots, and 16,800 geese were bagged during 71,100 hunter-days afield. Those persons buying duck stamps for hunting hunted an average of 4.6 days and bagged an average of 6.2 ducks and 1.3 geese each.

Central Flyway

Like the Pacific flyway, the Central flyway is huge. It extends down the plains region eastward of the great mountain ranges and covers 1,115,000 square miles across ten states, accounting for more than a third of our total flyway acreage. It has seen much change in the last several decades, some of it, most notably the restoration of water, for the good. But since 45 percent of the ducks and 90 percent of the geese winter along the Texas gulf coast, loss of habitat and industrial and residential pollution have been limiting factors.

The mallard dominates the duck-hunting scene, especially in the northern states, where almost three-quarters of all ducks killed are mallards. The total Central

CENTRAL FLYWAY

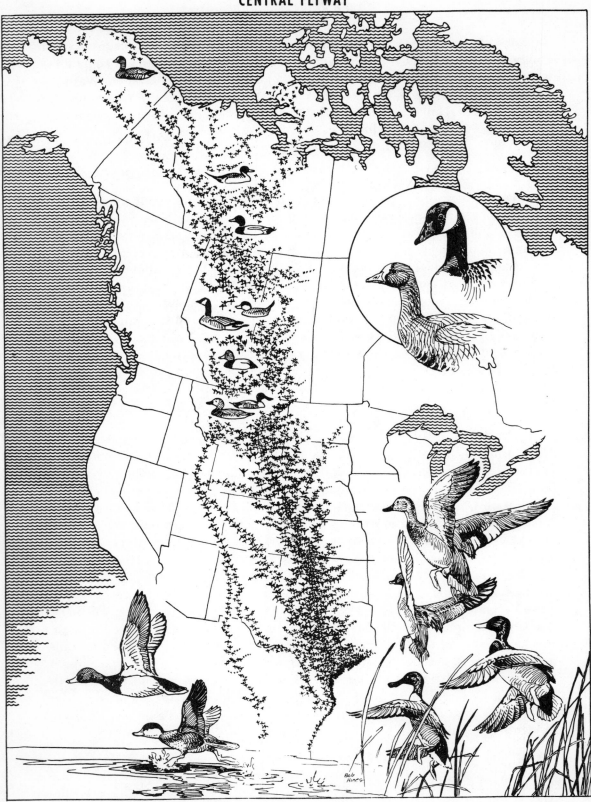

Bob Hines

UNITED STATES DEPARTMENT OF THE INTERIOR • FISH AND WILDLIFE SERVICE

INT: 4038-73

flyway kill of mallards is about one million. Only in Texas with its profusion of other waterfowl is the greenhead lessened in importance. The Central flyway's mallards nest mostly in Canada's prairie pothole region and winter on the vast grainfields of the flyway, heading south only when snow locks them from their food.

Other popular species are gadwalls, with a kill about 300,000; wigeon, with a 150,000 harvest; and pintail, with almost a million birds falling annually. The teals provide Central flyway hunters with tricky targets. About 500,000 a year are harvested. Canada geese are the most popular goose species, amounting to nearly 100 percent of the bag in Montana, Wyoming, and Colorado. About 150,000 fall. Snows are an important species in New Mexico, Texas, Nebraska, and the Dakotas. About 100,000 are harvested. Blue geese are popular in Texas, Oklahoma, Kansas, Nebraska, and the Dakotas. About 40,000 fall. The Texas marshes also produce a fair harvest of whitefronts. Some 35,000 are harvested. Recent vital statistics: Flyways states are Montana, North and South Dakota, Wyoming, Colorado, Nebraska, Kansas, Oklahoma, New Mexico, and Texas. Duck stamp sales totaled 464,635, and 2,779,200 ducks, 80,700 coots, and 413,100 geese were bagged during 3,409,800 hunter-days afield. Those persons buying duck stamps for hunting hunted an average of 7.2 days and bagged an average of 7.7 ducks and 1.0 geese each.

Mississippi Flyway
Everything about this waterfowl turnpike down the heart of America is big. The fourteen-state flyway embraces 742,000 square miles, one-fourth of the lower forty-eight states. This area contains about half of our wetlands considered suitable for waterfowl. About half the duck stamps sold in the country go on hunters' licenses in the Mississippi flyway. It is an area replete with names that set a waterfowler's heart pumping—the Lake Erie marshes, Lake Saint Clair, Minnesota's Huron wetlands. Is there a hunter who has never heard of Illinois's Horicon Refuge or of Stuttgart, Arkansas? A friend of mine guns the Louisiana marshes. He says he has many times seen the automatic lens setting on his camera change when flocks of teal literally darkened the sky.

Here again the mallards reign supreme. They amount to over half the harvest in all but Louisiana, Alabama, and Ohio. The mallard's adaptability has saved the population, for this flyway suffered much drainage of prime habitat in the 1940s and '50s. But at the same time, vast new reservoir systems were proliferating over the length of the flyway. Where these were surrounded by good grain-feeding fields, the mallards moved in. Many places claim to be the Mallard Capital of the World, but two locations with equal, indisputable claims to the title are the Illinois

MISSISSIPPI FLYWAY

UNITED STATES DEPARTMENT OF THE INTERIOR • FISH AND WILDLIFE SERVICE

River Valley and the Grand Prairie of Arkansas. Almost 2,000,000 mallards are harvested in the flyway annually.

Many other ducks also contribute important segments of the harvest in this immense flyway. Black ducks amount to between 10 and 20 percent of the bag in Tennessee, Indiana, Ohio, and Kentucky. Over 100,000 fall. The wood duck is a popular duck, totaling roughly a quarter of the harvest in Mississippi, Alabama, Indiana, and Ohio. Over a half a million are killed. The teals make up 10 percent of the bag in Louisiana, Ohio, and Missouri. About 500,000 fall. Gadwall and wigeon are popular on the flyway, with kills of around 200,000 each. Over 300,000 greater and lesser scaup fall. Ringneck ducks are another favored bird. The harvest exceeds 200,000. Pintail kills run about 100,000.

The huge numbers of Canada geese on this flyway make them an important species, but in some areas other geese are also popular. Almost 100 percent of the geese harvested in Michigan, Illinois, Ohio, Kentucky, and Tennessee are Canadas. Total flyway kill exceeds 150,000. Snows make up at least 25 percent of the bag in Minnesota, Iowa, Missouri, Louisiana, and Alabama. About 50,000 fall. Blue geese are important in Minnesota, Iowa, Indiana, Missouri, Louisiana, Mississippi, and Alabama. Total bag is around 80,000. Whitefronts extending eastward from the Central flyway give Louisiana sportsmen good shooting; almost 25 percent of the state's geese are whitefronts. Bag is about 15,000.

The flyway states are Minnesota, Wisconsin, Michigan, Ohio, Indiana, Illinois, Iowa, Missouri, Kentucky, Tennessee, Arkansas, Louisiana, Mississippi, and Alabama. Recent vital statistics are: Duck stamp sales totaled 1,003,791, and 5,461,500 ducks, 428,800 coots, and 380,600 geese were bagged during 7,177,300 hunter-days afield. Those persons buying duck stamps for hunting hunted an average of 6.7 days and bagged an average of 6.8 ducks and 0.4 geese each.

Atlantic Flyway

Once the finest waterfowling area in the world, the Atlantic flyway has now but a shadow of its former glory. The flyway covers 446,000 square miles across seventeen states, but more than eighty million people—more than a third of the country's population—make their homes there. Nonetheless, not all the glory is gone. More than half the flyway is wooded, and more than a third of the nation's wetlands is found there. About 15 percent of the nation's ducks and 20 percent of its geese winter on the Atlantic.

The mallard remains the most popular duck, but not by as great a margin as in western flyways. It exceeds 25 percent of the bag only in New York, Pennsylvania,

ATLANTIC FLYWAY

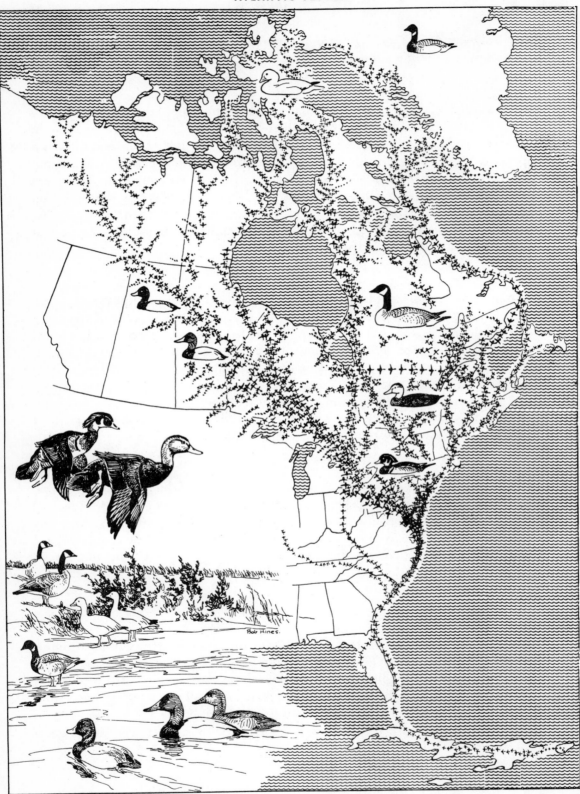

Bob Hines.

UNITED STATES DEPARTMENT OF THE INTERIOR • FISH AND WILDLIFE SERVICE

West Virginia, Delaware, and Maryland. The total flyway kill is over 350,000. Second in importance is the black duck. In the New England states, between 25 and 40 percent of the bag are blacks. The annual harvest is approximately 250,000. In New York, Pennsylvania, West Virginia, New Jersey, Delaware, and Maryland the percentage of blacks in the bag ranges between 10 and 35 percent.

The beautiful little wood duck is probably the flyway's third most popular duck. In Georgia and West Virginia half the ducks bagged are woodies, and they are a substantial part of the harvest in Virginia, North Carolina, South Carolina, Florida, New York, and Pennsylvania. Almost 300,000 are harvested. The teals, particularly green-winged teal, are important in Florida, the Carolinas, Virginia, New York, New Jersey, Maryland, and Delaware. The total bag is about 200,000. The little bufflehead is popular in New Jersey, Delaware, and Maryland. About 50,000 are taken. Scaup are shot in New York, Connecticut, Rhode Island, and Massachusetts. Harvest is some 150,000. Canadas are the only geese that can be shot legally on the flyway at present. About 220,000 fall. There is an 80,000-bird snow-goose flock that winters in Virginia and North Carolina, but no season has yet been opened. However, crop damage, always a prelude to harvest, has recently been reported. Atlantic brant were formerly an important species in New Jersey and New York. Whistling swans are legally shot in Utah, Montana, and Nevada, and there has been periodic talk of opening a swan season on the Atlantic. Pressure by bird lovers has forestalled it.

Flyway states are Maine, Vermont, New Hampshire, Massachusetts, Connecticut, Rhode Island, New York, Pennsylvania, West Virginia, New Jersey, Delaware, Maryland, Virginia, North and South Carolina, Georgia, and Florida. Recent vital statistics are: Duck stamp sales totaled 505,063, and 1,729,700 ducks, 161,400 coots, and 337,900 geese were bagged during 2,964,400 hunter-days afield. Persons buying duck stamps for hunting hunted an average of 5.7 days and bagged an average of 3.9 ducks and 0.8 geese each.

Totals for all U.S. flyways are: Duck stamp sales totaled 2,426,058, and 14,013,100 ducks, 823,000 coots, and 1,478,800 geese were bagged during 16,719,800 hunter-days afield. Persons buying duck stamps for hunting hunted an average of 6.5 days and bagged an average of 7.1 ducks and 0.7 geese each.

4

Hunting Profiles

This chapter must start with an apology, for it rests on the preposterous assertion that any one person could be aware of the infinite variations in waterfowl species throughout their range across the country. For instance, I don't think I've seen a gadwall, much less shot one. That doesn't make me much of a gadwall-hunting expert. Wood ducks have been scarce where I've hunted, and when one burst from a canal in upstate New York, I felt remorse at having destroyed a creature of such delicate beauty. And, like people, individual ducks and geese do individual things, and generalizations made for one place and time break down when put to tests elsewhere.

Yet for thirty years I've been gaming about waterfowl with other men who hunt them. I've followed the sport in the three big outdoor magazines for years and years. My shelf of waterfowl books has grown longer over the years. And my job takes me around a fair amount. Any hunter would have to have an I.Q. of zilch not to have learned something after all that. And I claim another qualification, albeit not a particularly modest one. Ernest Hemingway used to say he could go inside the minds of bears. He thought he could look at a bear and tell what it was thinking. I claim a similar understanding of waterfowl. I can generally look at a duck and know what's on its mind. Hundreds of times I've sat in blinds and had partners stiffen when birds were in the air. One glance told me they wanted no part of my decoys, that their thoughts were far away. There's a way a duck flies after it has just been shot at, faster and more directly, that can often be spotted. Young birds can often be told from older, warier adults because they project an atmosphere of innocent trust. Just last season a black duck swept in toward my decoys, and I saw it quite clearly recognize the outboard motor on the stern of the sneakbox, even though I had the motor draped with a burlap sack.

All of which isn't to say that waterfowl don't sometimes leave me shaking my head. Although they aren't quite the unpredictable creatures human beings are, they'll surprise you. They can do some odd things. I used to think I could predict when black ducks would fly, that is, trade around a lot. I *can* anticipate it to a certain extent; at least I can tell when they *should* fly, that is, when they will *usually* fly. But I've been wrong so often that now I just go and hope for the best. You never know for sure what will happen.

I particularly remember one evening of carnage. I was getting pretty good at gunning one area, so I thought, for a new challenge, I'd try gunning a nearby place that looked good. Even though the place was only a mile away, the problems were entirely different. To begin with, I threw the decoys over and they headed out to sea. The water was sixteen feet deep. I finally found some shallower water and set up in a spot that had to be good, as there was an elaborate old sink blind there from the days when a fancy duck club operated in the area.

About three-thirty in the afternoon the black ducks began coming into the marsh. In a half hour scores of birds were dropping all around me—two here, three there, but all of them put down two and three hundred yards away. Not a bird even looked at my decoys, much less came to them. Yet they didn't flare from them either. I was totally ignored. I had never seen anything like it happen before and I haven't since. To this day, I have only vague explanations for why the birds weren't all over me. I just don't know.

So after pointing out that the whole thing is hopeless to begin with and useless when finished, let's proceed:

SPEED

There are all manner of studies about the flying speeds of ducks. This species is said to go so fast, another one slower. From what I've observed, this is mostly a bunch of baloney. A duck of any of the popular species can haul freight with the best. Snow geese often take off from Canada and keep flying until they land in the Texas marshes, 2,000 miles away, making the flight in an incredible two days, at an average speed of forty-two miles an hour. Imagine what that power and stamina could do in a short shot! There is a lot of research on swans going on at present. One beeper-banded swan took off one night from the Chesapeake and put down in Lake Saint Clair (near Detroit) before dawn broke, traveling at a speed of about fifty-five miles an hour. Biologists making another migration study found that swans flew around Lake Erie rather than across it. Most birds don't like to fly over large stretches of open water, and even though you might not think it, waterfowl, in some cases, feel the same way. I once crossed Delaware Bay on a boat as a flock of Canadas on a northern migration was also making the crossing, but in the oddest fashion. Instead of the usual confident cruising at 1,500 feet, they would rise, fly slowly along for a mile or so, then sit down on the water. They'd rest for a spell, then break into flight again. Their overall speed was about the same as that of the boat I was on, about twenty mph, half their normal cruising speed. I may be wrong, but I believe that they didn't like being out there, out of sight of land, and were trying to conserve their strength, even though the mouth of the bay is only twelve miles across.

To my mind, rating species as to speed is an exercise in futility. I have observed all the popular species at speeds that must have been around sixty miles an hour, and I would bet heavy money that any of the popular speedsters could top that if something really scary, like a peregrine falcon, were after it. For example, blue-winged teal, one of the smallest, most delicate-seeming ducks, nonetheless set a migratory record every year. Their flights from Canada to South and Central America may exceed 4,000 miles! One bluewing was discovered 3,800 miles from the banding area, only a month after it was banded. Its flight average must have been 125 miles a day. It's nothing for mallards to cover 200 miles a day, day after day. The little teals look as though they are going really fast, and they are. I've timed flocks flying over the Tuckerton marshes (where a long deserted road cuts through the heart of the marsh) at over forty miles an hour in normal flight.

Canvasbacks are often said to be the fastest duck. This opinion probably came from the studies Van Campen Heilner did on duck speeds for his magnificent *Book on Duck Shooting*. As much as I admire the book and the man, I can't believe it. I've cut into flocks of cans and broadbills and have never seen the cans fly away from the broadies. There are broadbill migrations over me every season. The birds are high, often in formation, and I don't know where they come from or where they are going, but they really move. They fly in such a way that I can't put the speedometer on them, but they are certainly moving at over forty miles an hour, and I believe their speed is somewhere between fifty and sixty.

Kortright, in his monumental *The Ducks, Geese and Swans of North America*, quotes English falconers who flew peregrines at ducks and claimed that the teal always fell behind and were attacked. Far be it from me to argue with the master, but I'll have to see it to believe it. And why is it that individual differences are not considered? Suppose you could arrange such a thing as a pintail race or canvasback race. One of the birds would win, right? Another would come last, wouldn't it? Okay, then, which is faster, a speedy pintail or a slow canvasback?

AGE

Age in the wilds is another interesting question for a duck hunter to ponder. It is obviously easier to outwit a one- or two-year-old bird than a veteran of eight or nine seasons. The F&WS keeps careful track of the ratio of juvenile to adult birds by species in every flyway, as the ratio directly reflects nesting success. With mallards, you can expect to kill about one and a half young birds for every adult. Other species vary up to as much as three young ones to every adult. It is clear the first year is a dangerous one to a duck.

Banding records have shown that many ducks have lived ten years. One gallant grandma mallard returned nine times to a Nebraska nesting site. The last eggs she laid were "runt" eggs; the old gal finally reproduced out. She was known to have raised over a hundred youngsters. Despite the fact that ducks live a long time in captivity, up to twenty years or more, the best scientific guess is that the birds you shoot will be either birds of the summer's crop, or from three to five years old.

PUDDLERS AND DIVERS

Every student waterfowler knows that ducks come in two distinct types. One category is called diving ducks because they usually inhabit deep water and dive as much as twenty-five feet to get food off the bottom. The most popular divers are canvasback, redheads, and the two kinds of scaup. Diving ducks can't spring into flight but must run along the surface for a few feet to get airborne. Puddle ducks, sometimes known as river ducks, pond ducks, or puddlers, usually confine themselves to smaller water, hence the names. They use their wings against the water to spring ten to fifteen feet into the air in a lightninglike bound. Mallards, black ducks, pintails, gadwalls, shovelers, teals, wood ducks, and wigeon are the most popular puddle ducks.

THE WARY THREE

Unquestionably mallards, pintails, and black ducks are the nation's most wary ducks. Only an adult Canada goose exceeds their ability to react quickly to danger, and at times, and in some places, the duck's wild shyness even exceeds that of the lordly goose. It's seldom that you find any substantial population of geese in a place where nobody gets a crack at them. With mallards and pintails it happens all the time. For example, I know of a flock of pintails on the Chesapeake that rest in the bay during the day and feed in farm fields, sometimes at night but usually during the day. While the geese in the area tend to stay fairly close to open water, the pintails will fly many miles to feed. You could set up decoys in a given field and hope they'd come to that field that day, but this is like playing poker with each hand drawing to an inside straight. The near-hopeless prospects so discourage local hunters that few even try for them. The same situation often exists with mallards when they start feeding in grainfields. Geese will feed fairly close to a refuge, but the mallards think nothing of flying scores and scores of miles to find grazing lands. They'll get up and fly out of a refuge very high and very fast, too high to pay any attention to calls or decoys. Unless you can comb them down to where some kind of pass allows you to get up at them, or perhaps get passing shots in and out of resting areas, your gunning prospects will be about as dismal as any duck could wish for. Of course, if you can figure out their routine and be waiting for them, you're in business. Often, however, the birds quickly exhaust the food in one area and go on immediately to the next.

Black ducks and mallards are very similar species, except for the differences in color, and will crossbreed. In both species the younger birds tend to migrate earlier, and this, plus the fact that older birds sometimes have red rather than orange legs, give rise to the idea that red-legged blacks were a separate race. This notion is largely rejected by today's biologists. You'll read accounts that claim the black duck is the wariest, wildest waterfowl. In fact, even the Fish and Wildlife recognition charts say this. I'd hate to be the judge in a contest among the wary three. Certainly a pair of black ducks coming into a pond can remind you of an old lady trying to decide whether to dunk her fanny. They'll circle again and again, even when the pond is cluttered with their buddies. If they won't come in to live decoys, live action, and live calls, what will pull them?

I have the impression that mallards are slightly more susceptible to a call than either blacks or pintails. As everybody knows, mallards are easily talked in at some places, by some people—i.e., by experts. The tall, flooded timber shoots in Arkansas are legendary, and all around the Midwest calling contests for mallards are held. I never heard or saw anybody have much success calling black ducks, despite some highfaluting claims to the contrary. The same is true of pintails and wigeon. They can be somewhat influenced by calls but only that, usually, and not much more than that, ever, in most places. The Herter catalog offers eleven different kinds of calls intended for use with mallards. Some are automatic, some have adjustable pitches, some are made with special woods or reeds. The point is, there are a heck of a lot of mallard calls you can buy. The fact that they offer only one pintail and wigeon call tells a good deal about the effectiveness of calling these birds. Herter's lists nine different goose calls, which also says plenty about what a good caller can do to those dudes.

Although mallards are suckers for a call and blacks are not, blacks have their own weaknesses. In winds and during extreme cold they can't get into a decoy spread fast enough. I haven't hunted enough pintails to know when it's relatively easy to sprinkle a little sale on their tails, but I'd be surprised if there aren't conditions in which they are extremely vulnerable.

My experience leads me to think that the black duck is naturally a more wary duck than the mallard. I have the impression that pintails are too. Even as juveniles, black ducks have an inherently suspicious nature. Yet mallards have a formidable ability to wise up fast. Where I live a number of mallards are raised locally. These are half-domesticated birds that are hatched around ponds on big estates. When the season opens they are duck soup, naive and trusting, and they get cut up badly. After a couple of weeks of this, the survivors become incredibly sharp, setting up patterns of movement that prevent hunters from getting anywhere near them. You can see this same survival instinct operating with black ducks too. For example, a Canadian biologist reported to a symposium studying Atlantic flyway black ducks that 60 percent of the Quebec kill took place during the first week of the season, and half of that 60 percent were taken the first weekend of the season. After the shooting started, the birds either moved out or became too wary to decoy.

I hunted wigeon and pintails on the west coast of Mexico under ideal—if astounding—conditions. The guide would illegally flood a grain field at night. We'd chase the ducks out next morning, then set decoys and shoot the small bunches that came back. We shot the wigeon, that is. The pintails reminded me of my darker hours on the Jersey marshes trying to cope with black ducks. They were wild, fast, smart, shy, as tough as any duck I ever saw.

Anyone who takes on these three is in for hard times. Blinds and hides have to be good. One suggestion of motion and your chances, not the ducks, are dead. You can't hunt ponds or even points too often or they'll wise up. Camouflage must be perfect and calling exact. The old baymen insist that black ducks can smell a man. I sure can attest that they can hear well.

Another maddening aspect of hunting black ducks is their tendency to circle. Any of the three wary ones will come over for a look, seem to be about to sit down, then flare away and circle. At times they can be like a horse that seems to enjoy shying away from things. You have to decide whether they flared at something that won't be scary the second time around or if they did spot something amiss and have said good-by forever. When to take 'em and when not to take 'em is the waterfowler's eternal dilemma. You can be sure that no matter how extensive your experience you won't be right all the time or maybe even most of the time.

Mallards and black ducks will decoy to blocks of either species. Pintails require a decoy with white on it. Where the two species are hunted together, commonly decoys of the various species are intermingled. You don't have to separate them as you would divers and puddlers.

THE TEAL

The lovely little teal are marvelous birds, engagingly sporty and so handsome. I think the *whoosh* as a flock sails past you is one of the great sounds of waterfowling, comparable to the whistle of wings of the wary three and the distant honking of Canadas. When I hunted my pond, they would often come into the decoys so low and at such sizzling speeds that they were sitting in the decoys before I could shoot. I'd stand up, and they'd sit and give me an aghast look, as if to say, "What can this be?" Then they'd rocket off as if a gun had shot them from the water. Teal are tough to hit, almost like doves in their ability to vacate the area you just directed your shot into. They decoy well to decoys of the wary three.

WIGEON (BALDPATE)

This is another handsome duck. I can close my eyes and see a flock settling on us. Van and I had set up in the dark on an island. We had no blind but had hunkered down in high grass. Right at first light we heard the telltale whistling and in they came with feet stretched out, wings cupped, etched in memory by the rising sun. The incident happened years ago, but we still talk about it.

Not all the black ducks get away.

Wigeon will come to most decoys, but they prefer decoys with white on them. They aren't particularly wary. Flocks that have just been shot may fly a short distance and decoy to other blocks. They aren't as good to eat as the preceding puddlers. The American Ornithologists' Union has officially and just recently changed their name from widgeon to wigeon.

CANVASBACK AND REDHEADS

These two grand species are usually discussed together as they feed together, have similar habits, and live together on winter range. The hens are difficult to tell apart, even in hand, as would be the drakes without the classic Roman profile of the can. Any differences between the two species disappear almost entirely on a dinner plate. It's a rare expert who can tell them apart by taste.

Part of the canvasbacks' problems stems from their unique and little understood sex ratio. Out of one hundred births sixty will be males and forty females. This means a maximum breeding pair per hundred birds of only forty. Other waterfowl have sex ratios of about fifty-fifty. Redheads are more abundant than cans, but studies have shown that most hunters cannot distinguish between downed drake redheads and cans, much less the hens on the wing. Biologists fear that opening redhead seasons would lead to an inadvertent canvasback kill of threatening proportions. Like all the divers, these ducks seldom decoy in and sit down as the puddlers usually do. The divers more often see the decoys and swing over to take a look. If they've been shot hard, the look will usually be out of range or at extreme range. They may circle and come back in. Or they may not! Cans and redheads are nowhere near as wary as hard-hunted mallards, black ducks, or pintails, but they must be approached with respect. No sign of anything human must show, and blind camouflage must be reasonably good. Neither are particularly susceptible to calling.

THE SCAUPS

I'm ashamed to say that, though I've killed hundreds of these sporty little birds, even if my life depended on identifying which was a greater scaup and which was a lesser, I couldn't do it. They are generally called broadbills in the East, bluebills elsewhere. They don't rate too high in intelligence, and single birds are especially easy to fool. Where they feed on vegetable matter, scaup make good table birds. Unfortunately, they like mollusks and even scavenger food, and this can make them rank.

The scaups sometimes perform one of nature's oddities when landing. A flock will seem to be flying past overhead when suddenly they will fall out of the sky into your decoys. Each bird will flutter like a broken-wing cripple that's fighting to maintain altitude but can't, and drop like a shot to the water. A second before pulling a kamikaze into the drink they recover and land normally. Most of the time they bore into the decoys in a straight line, but when they fall out of the sky it is something to see.

A snowstorm always makes for great shooting, but no species is more affected by snow than broadbills. They'll fly like crazy and decoy as though your stools were magnets. They aren't particularly wary and have to be really hammered before they become point shy. I used to hunt them out of an uncamouflaged sneakbox anchored in open water. No mallard or black duck would have come within a hundred yards of it; the broadies came right in. My partner and I used to gun this boat while sitting facing the stern on either side of the centerboard. I remember when a huge flock of broadbills rose downriver from us. There must have been a thousand birds. They came sailing toward us, and the main flock went by in mid-river, out of range, but a bunch of about thirty separated out and headed for our decoys. At the last minute most of these changed course, but four ducks continued on, and, as if we had programmed it, the four separated right below us, two passing by on each side, giving us both a chance for a perfect double. Naturally, by that time we were both so excited that the boat was jumping around so we missed them. At least that's my excuse.

GEESE

BLUES AND SNOWS

The American Ornithologists' Union has finally decided that snow geese and blue geese are merely color variations of a single species. There is still a lot of disagreement about this, though, and I think it would be safe to say that most hunters in the field consider them as distinct species. These are great birds to hunt. Both are large species and (thankfully) are not as cagey as Canadas. They are superb birds on the table. Both come well to Canada decoys, though you should use some snow decoys because of the way they show up. There are snow geese on my flyway, and they are elegant things as they fly by. They tend to keep going, though. I have never seen a flock sit down on local waters or swing to any decoy spread.

CANADA GEESE

Canadas, being the magnificent creatures they are, have been profiled in a separate chapter of their own—Chapter 7.

ATLANTIC AND BLACK BRANT

These small geese are never far from salt water. In fact, they don't like to fly over land. They are extremely susceptible to decoys and calls, pathetically so at times. It's common for a flock to fly from one decoy rig to another until every last bird is killed. When they feed on eel grass their flesh is the best of all waterfowl.

You tend to remember firsts. Let me tell you of a brant first. Van and I were gunning in prime brant country out of a sinkbox. We were geared mostly for black ducks and, as I recall, didn't have any brant decoys rigged. Things were slow. Then I heard Van whisper under his breath, "Good God Almighty!" I froze, staring through the grass on the blind, and suddenly around the corner of the blind came a flock of brant, perhaps twenty birds. Before I could react, there was another small flock, then another, then the air was filled with birds. There must have been many hundreds. I distinctly remember one brant hitting a decoy as it pitched down, the only time I've ever seen *that*. Since then, I've had flocks that probably contained as many as a thousand birds come into the decoys, and believe me, it is a sight.

Thinking about brant reminds me that the damnedest things happen when you're duck hunting. The head of the state police asked me to take a pal of his, a U.S. Army general, out duck hunting. I said sure, amused to act as a guide for the first time. I set the gentleman up on my slot between two islands. We sat and waited, and then all the water ran out of the bay. At dead low tide there was usually several feet of water in the slot. Now there was none. The decoys sat in the mud. I'd go up to him and say: "You won't believe this, General, but this has never happened before." He'd give me a long, penetrating stare. I moved the boat down to deep water, and a single brant came by, looking as astonished and upset as I was that somebody apparently pulled the plug in the bay. He was sticking to the last little trickle of water that ran down the center of the slot. Man, I thought, wait till that brant spots those decoys and the security, health, and happiness they represent. Sure enough, it was like a cartoon. The brant finally saw them—it was like GLOM! You could tell the exact moment he saw them. He was flying along, the picture of gloom, and his sudden relief and glee were very evident. Poor devil, the general finished him off. The water finally came back in, I might add.

These geese were bushwacked on the Choptank in Maryland. The guide knew there would be geese in his canvasback decoys during the night, so we sneaked down a path to them at first light, and ran up on them firing.

Brant over the decoys. And not a brant decoy in sight! Brant often decoy to black duck decoys if they are set in the right spots.

You'll have noticed that I left some species out. The reason is that I want this book to meet the standards of *Sports Afield*'s late Colonel Townsend Whelen, the dean of America's outdoor writers. I knew the colonel well, and he was all that he was said to be. I admired and respected him most for his fidelity to experience. He never wrote a word that he did not know *personally* to be true. Thus, in these pages, omission is a confession of ignorance.

5

Identifying Waterfowl

A large part of the treasures of waterfowling is the wealth of handsome species, most of them incredibly swift and graceful in life, and many so richly hued in stillness that they are prized in wooden, painted, and porcelained versions, welcome additions to any living room, a must for sportsmen's dens or studies. I like to think I'm more of a practical duckhunter than what I call the Madison Avenue hunter. This is the guy who wears all the patches on his jacket and gadgets on his hat and surrounds himself with dear little duck lamps, ashtrays, and cocktail glasses—and never goes hunting. Well, I go hunting but I just looked around me as I write these words and counted eight decoys of ducks, geese, and a swan. On the wall my eyes are comforted by ten waterfowl paintings, including seven prints by Richard Bishop that, so help me, came off a calendar sent yearly to their customers in the 1930s by a Jersey coal company. When I had an artist paint me a picture of Chesapeake skipjacks I had him add strings of geese in the background to uplift the scenery. The ornamental side of the waterfowl treasury has not escaped me. I am as willing a victim as any. Only the parrots and other exotic tropical birds can compete with our waterfowl for brilliant finery.

It is impossible to be a modern waterfowler and not undertake some study of the popular species. Indeed, the laws require it. You must have some idea of what species you are shooting or you will soon run afoul of the law by shooting protected species or shooting over your limit. But, like other facets of waterfowling, learning to know your ducks and geese isn't like learning to tell whitewings from mourning doves or identifying the various quail. Some real study is required. Let's start with some technical facts.

Swans, geese, and ducks belong to the family *Anatidae*, which includes all web-footed swimming birds with broad, flat bills edged by toothlike serrations (lamellae). The family consists of 225 forms distributed throughout the world. There are nine swan species, three of which are found in this country. The world contains some thirty-five goose species, of which about fifteen are found in America. There are about one hundred species of surface-feeding, or puddle, ducks; sixteen are found regularly in this country. Of the diving ducks, forty-three forms are found worldwide, about twenty in this country.

In addition to these, there are a number of subfamilies. There are nine forms of merganser, of which three are regular visitors to our waterways. The ruddy-duck group, the members of which have their legs so far toward their tails that they are almost helpless on land, has seven forms worldwide. Of these, one is regularly found in the southern portion of this country. Ten forms of tree ducks are found, two in this country. And there are the closely related species—the coots, rails, gallinules, and so forth. Add to these the various shorebirds, some of which the waterfowler should be able to recognize since seasons open on them from time to time, and you can see that identifying waterfowl is no easy task.

My source for this information is the most complete popular book on this continent's waterfowl, *The Ducks, Geese and Swans of North America*, by Francis H. Kortright, with illustrations by T. M. Short. Both men are Canadian ornithologists. Although it appeared in print in 1948, Kortright is still considered the standard reference work for the layman student. It contains detailed studies of all the American species. Every phase of their habits and characteristics is discussed, and there are color plates depicting adult forms, young birds, and birds in molt. The book, which is still in print, is published by The Stackpole Company, Harrisburg, Pennsylvania, and copies may be ordered through any bookstore.

There are also several government publications designed to help your task of identification. "Ducks at a Distance" is available from the U.S. Government Printing Office, Washington, D.C. 20402, for thirty-five cents. It depicts in color some twenty of the most popular species, as do the free black-and-white and color pamphlets,

"Know Your Ducks—A Field Guide for Hunters," from the same source. Material from both sources has been used here. Another government book, *Waterfowl Tomorrow*, edited by my friend Dr. Joe Linduska, deals with the broader aspects of waterfowling. Its foreword says it is "about the needs of the 48 species of ducks, geese, and swans which live on the North American continent. Especially it is a book about the lands and waters that sustain these waterfowl in Canada, the United States and Mexico." And every fall *Sports Afield* magazine puts on the nation's newsstands a seventy-five-cent edition of its excellent *Know Your Ducks and Geese*. An enlarged, deluxe version can be ordered through the magazine.

Despite these aids, if you hunt ducks and geese long enough you will find species whose secrets no amount of research will unlock. Only last season I shot a duck that looked like nothing in any of my books. There are a couple of explanations for these mystery ducks. First, crossbreeds occur, and you'd have to be a trained scientist to detect them. Second, foreign species stray. The barnacle goose is one good example. Waterfowl nest at the top of the world, and sometimes they come down the "wrong" flyway. If one of these adventurers winds up in your bag, none of the easily accessible references will list it.

Let's look at the common ducks and geese and consider how you can learn to spot them from afar. In the drawings ♀ identifies the hen, ♂ the drake.

MALLARD

BLACK DUCK

MALLARDS AND BLACK DUCKS

The green head of the drake mallard is instantly identifiable at shotgun ranges. The brown hen can be confused with the darker black ducks, which are almost black-brown. Mallards are large ducks, and their white underwing is prominent in flight. Mallards in flocks are more likely than most other ducks to fly in formation. If you see ducks in a V or in line they are probably black ducks, mallards, migrating broadbills, or canvasbacks. Blacks and mallards lack the stately wingbeat of geese, but their wingbeat is purposeful. Their wing shape is pleasing, their wings large, long, and coming gracefully to a sharp point. Both ducks are wary, circling often, and they tend to fly at higher altitudes than other ducks. They typically come in with wings cupped, seldom knifing or fluttering down, though they can if they want to. Mallards often feed in fields. Blacks stick to ponds and creeks. Both ducks are fairly mute in flight. When feeding, the black hen gives off a loud, somewhat arrogant *quack, quack quack, quack*, in descending pitch, with the quacks speeding toward the end. The hen mallard gives off a loud, spontaneous *quack*. The drake has a lower-pitched *kwek-kwek*.

PINTAIL

PINTAILS

The hen is brown. The drake has a rusty brown head you can spot within range, as you can the long tail. (The female's tail is shorter.) Body is gray with a black rump. The pintail shape is the tip-off for me. They are longer in body than any other big duck, with longer necks and tails, and their wings are shorter in relation to their bodies and taper to sharper points. Their unique wings are another tip-off. They have a pronounced rake back, very much like a gull wing, and a sharp bend rather than the graceful wing bend of mallards. Pintails tend to fly in large flocks. You seldom see flocks of blacks or mallards of more than a hundred birds or so. Pintails will assemble in flocks many times this size. They are fast, graceful fliers and love to zigzag down from great heights. Like mallards they commonly feed on land in corn and grain fields. Drakes whistle; hens have a hoarse *quack*.

WIGEON

WIGEON

The most pronounced identifying characteristic of these jaunty ducks is the drake's whistle. Hens utter a loud *kaow* and a softer *qua-awk*, but anytime there are wigeon about you'll hear the whistle. The wigeon is a large bird, far larger than a teal, yet it flies in the frantically changing patterns characteristic of a teal, bunching and unbunching with whirlwind rapidity. Both sexes show their white forewing prominently.

GREEN-WINGED TEAL

BLUE-WINGED TEAL

THE TEALS

You'll have no trouble identifying the teals in hand. All are so striking, and their names so aptly describe their coloration, that to know of their existence is to be able to distinguish them. But in the air, wherever the three are found together (the cinnamon rarely strays west of the Rocky Mountains), it is well-nigh impossible to differentiate which teal they are, unless you can see their colors. In flight, the bluewing's bright blue wing patch shows clearly, as does the cinnamon's rusty head, and the greenwing's green wing patch. The teals all fly the same — very fast, with the flock constantly compacting and expanding. They also take sharp, erratic wheels and turns. They fly more like some of the sandpipers than ducks but are so much larger than any of the shorebirds that usually you can quickly tell, first, that they are ducks, then that they are teal.

Teal make a lot of noise. Often you will hear them before you see them. Their call, a quick, often repeated whistle, has been described as a titter, or as a staccato series of tiny whistles. It's a pleasant, appealing kind of call.

WOOD DUCK

WOOD DUCKS

These ducks resemble the teal in their flight, though they do a little less twisting and turning and usually fly in much smaller flocks. The teal flock averages between thirty and forty birds. Wood ducks usually gather in flocks of seven to ten. Mated pairs often fly together. Woodies are slightly larger than teal. They frequently twist their heads around, looking first one way, then another, characteristic behavior that can be seen from a good way off. The male's colors give him away. The black back, white underbelly, and noticeable white head patch are quick identification marks. The female's dark-brown hue is close to that of the female teal, but in hand, her prominent head ruff distinguishes her from the teal. You can sometimes hear the drake's *hoo-w-ett* in flight.

GADWALLS

Gadwalls are the only puddle ducks to show a patch of white on their wings. You can spot it from afar. Otherwise, the hen resembles a mallard hen. The drake has gray head, black rump, and white belly. Gadwalls are fast fliers, with quicker wingbeats than mallards or pintails. Drakes whistle and go *kack-kack*; hens *quack* like mallards but more softly, less aggressively.

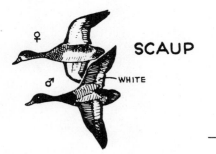

THE SCAUPS

These are the most common of the diving ducks. The drake is instantly recognizable by its starkly black neck, head, and hindquarters and grayish white body (light gray

The greater snow geese of the Atlantic flyway have the curious habit of all migrating north at the same time. They hit the St. Lawrence River about Quebec City in one splendid, pulsating flock, and then head down the St. Lawrence, feeding along the shores. *Province of Quebec Film Bureau.*

in younger birds). The little brown hen can be told in hand by the white crescent in front of her eyes; on the wing it's too small to be seen. The blue bill makes another good in-hand identification. Broadies are fairly small birds, smaller than the cans or redheads they are usually found with. They generally fly in large flocks. Bunches will break off larger flocks to decoy. Their wingbeat is almost frantically fast. They look as though they have been recently scared and are trying to get away. Both sexes are silent in flight. Feeding, the drakes *purr* like a cat, and the greater scaup drakes give off a *scaup* sound.

CANVASBACK

REDHEADS

CANVASBACK AND REDHEADS

Unless you can spot the can's sloping profile, it's difficult to distinguish between these two. The redhead hen is brown with gray wings. The canvasback hen is grayish with a brown tinge. The rust-colored heads of both make for ready identification if you can see them. Both are powerful fliers, with a rapid, powerful wingbeat that can often be recognized. On migration flights they fly in formations, usually at high altitudes. In feeding areas or when casually moving around, they don't form at all. Both species make a lot of noise when feeding but are practically mute when flying. Redheads *purr* and *meow*, sounding like a bunch of cats at night. Hens *quack* like mallards but with a higher, more screechy tone. Canvasback hens *quack* very much like mallard hens. Drakes *croak*, *peep*, and *growl*.

CANADA GEESE

Unquestionably these are the easiest of all waterfowl to identify. The formation flying, black necks, and distinctive white cheek patches can be instantly spotted. If that isn't enough, one honk gives them away. All geese tend to congregate in large, sometimes immense, flocks.

WHITE-FRONTED GEESE

In flight (especially when they're migrating) whitefronts fly in lines like the Canada's and V's and can be mistaken for them. At closer ranges you can spot the splashed black-and-white breasts that have earned them their nicknames of specklebelly and specklebreast. Like most geese, they are very vocal, repeatedly uttering a *wah-wah-wah-wah* cackle that sounds like laughter.

SNOW GEESE

You can't miss these. The stark white bodies and black wing tips are giveaways. They fly in formations like Canadas but tend to form and re-form more than Canadas usually do.

BLUE GEESE

These birds fly in formations similar to those of snow geese. They will line up in irregular lines, then change to a perfect V, then—sometimes—form in a curved line. They constantly change formation, never staying put. The Cree Indians call them "wavies." Their light brown bodies and white heads are easy to recognize. Juveniles are almost all light brown with a somewhat bluish cast. They call frequently, a ringing *ga-ga-ga-ga-ga-ga*, with a buglelike ring to it. Like Canadas, they sound somewhat like dogs barking.

BRANT

Brant also form into lines and Vs but will change a formation almost as soon as it is formed. They fly in wavy lines like blue geese. Their black heads and white throat patches are instantly identifiable. Their call is a guttural, rolling R, *whru . . . uup*, with a slight bugle at the end.

SWANS

You can't shoot swans, except in Utah, Nevada, and New Mexico, but they are fun to watch. No bird flies with a more stately dignity. Usually they are seen in family flocks of four to six birds, steadily and purposefully in line but sailing with an appearance of effortlessness through the sky. Their size, white bodies, and slow wingbeat are unmistakable. Swans are mute in flight.

There are many other popular waterfowl species, of course. The various guides will help you identify them. Kortright, however, is the only source I know that discusses *all* North American species.

PART TWO

HOW TO
HUNT DUCKS
AND GEESE SUCCESSFULLY

Now it is time to get to the root of the matter, to the heart of things. All that has gone before is merely a prelude to the light that shines for an instant when you swing your shotgun ahead of a fast-moving duck or goose, pull the trigger, and watch the bird fold in the air. This is the hunter's moment.

Yet just as waterfowling returns more than other types of hunting, it also demands more. Nobody would disagree that it is among the most difficult and taxing of all of the various forms of hunting.

The hours are ungodly. I have met only one person in my life (*Sports Afield*'s Dave Harbour) who claims to enjoy rolling out of bed at 4:00 A.M. Although early rising isn't so bad if you have a chance to become accustomed to it, the first, abrupt red-eyed arousal sends me reeling in a jet-lag-type syndrome that upsets my system for days. In a similar vein you see few vacation spas located in areas famous for ice, snow, wind, and storm. Yet these are the waterfowler's friends. There's a prayer in a Currituck Sound duck lodge. "O Lord, send us some fowl and some wind. No Lord, we have the fowl, just send us a foul wind." When blizzards and storm winds strike, other hunters curl up by the hearth. Waterfowlers go forth.

With the possible exception of hunting dangerous big game, waterfowling is unquestionably the most hazardous hunting sport. Little boats on big water in bad weather mean that sooner or later somebody is going to get killed. Every duck season men and boys die. They drown, they freeze, they get shot. So far it has never happened to me, thank God, that I've been marooned on a marsh but even waterfowling's everyday routine is fraught with peril. Every night you gun until dark, more likely than not off in the middle of nowhere. The question always nagging at the back of your mind is, What do I do if the engine doesn't start?

Hard physical effort is often involved. Building a blind is kind of fun, but it's also laborious. Digging a goose pit is no fun at all, just work. Sinking a waterproof sinkbox into a marsh can only be described as agonizing. Three of us did it a few years ago, and my back still occasionally spasms from muscles wrenched doing the job.

A yachtsman friend of mine is fond of saying that everything about a boat costs more and takes longer. The same is true of waterfowling. Merely learning to recognize the common species requires some homework. Learning to identify all the North American species demands a lifetime effort. A full study of worldwide waterfowl is mind-boggling.

Then there's the expense. An upland bird hunter needs a pair of boots and his gun. Boats cost money. To cope with the awful weather, duck hunters must outfit themselves with all kinds of expensive clothes. A decoy spread requires a substantial outlay. And all the gear takes a fearsome beating. When you're picking up decoys after dark on a frozen night with the wind howling around you, you don't treat them gently. I thought the brown marsh mud I wallow in was bad until I went to Canada and slogged through their yellow marsh mud. I believe you could paint it on the side of a house and it would stick there for years. Marsh mud doesn't add much to the appearance of anything. It doesn't add much to the life of your gear either.

If inhuman weather is the waterfowler's friend, failure is his constant companion. It follows him everywhere. As you may have gathered, I am not much of an experty expert. The reason for this does not, I assure you, stem from a false sense of modesty. It's just that on too many occasions the ducks have given me a great deal to be modest about. I have a worried feeling, which doesn't go away when I lie down, that they have not done so for the last time. There's so much that can defeat the waterfowler. The weather's wrong. The water level's too low. Or too high. (On one of the best days of goose shooting I ever had, the marsh flooded and the water came almost to the top of the sinkbox. We escaped being put out of business by a quarter inch.) Other hunters foul you up all the time. Birds are decoying and somebody lets go with a salvo. So long, birds. Or somebody downs a cripple and everybody's chances go to hell as he tramps around looking for it. I even got blizzarded out once. I was on a goose story and at dawn it started to snow. Aha, says I, this will be some shooting day. It was some day, all right. The sky fell on us. We could barely get back to town through the drifts and I found myself looking at the four walls of a hotel room at 10:00 A.M. It was just swell. Snow on the antenna conked out the TV. They closed the public library. The movie never opened. It was too early to get drunk. I wound up reading the Bible.

The only excuse for going through all this is that you've got to love it all. "You've got to love to watch the grass blow," as a friend of mine put it. It's true. You must get a kick out of just being on the marsh, content to watch the decoys bob, to see waterfowl far away, to love the look of it, the smell of it, and the sound of it. If you limit out, that's great. If you come home skunked, that's great too.

Well, perhaps not quite as great.

6

When and Where To Find Ducks

To have rabbit stew, first you must catch the rabbit. To have birds swinging into your decoys, first you must find a place where birds are plentiful. Most people don't realize that the population of waterfowl in a given area is changing constantly. This is especially true of ducks. Seasons today are set early to allow hunters a crack at teal, the earliest migrators. But major migrations of other species take place throughout the season. Migrating birds are constantly settling down to rest and feed for a day or two, then taking off. Usually you can't count on populations stabilizing until well into winter. More often, some areas will be thick with birds one week, empty the next.

To find these pockets of abundance you must resort to some kind of spy system. It's very, very smart to make friends in various duck-hunting areas. I try to strike up conversations with service-station guys. If you find one that hunts or knows hunters, you can call him on the phone and find out what's up. Another good source nobody thinks of is mailmen. They are on the road all the time and probably have a good idea about what game is moving. Game wardens expect to be queried about game populations and where to go. I doubt if there is one in the country you could call and not get a pretty savvy analysis of the situation.

Then, too, there's a new government device that helps resolve the whole question. The Fish and Wildlife Service, in cooperation with the flyway councils, state fish and game agencies, and Ducks Unlimited, is providing weekly reports on the populations of waterfowl in all the flyways. The reports "will describe the progress of fall migrations, locations of waterfowl concentrations and weather and habitat conditions associated with major waterfowl movements." The idea was started experimentally in the 1971-1972 season on the Mississippi flyway and has been expanded to all four flyways. Field reports from federal, state, and provincial headquarters are sent to regional offices in each flyway for assembly and summarization. The reports start in October and continue through January, when the birds have settled on wintering areas. Sounds almost too good to be true, doesn't it? What's more, it's free.

Once you've located a place with abundant ducks and geese, the next step is to learn the birds' habits and movements within that area. You've got to find out where they fly, where they feed, and which routes through the sky they prefer. You'll discover plenty of places that look good to you but are avoided like the plague by waterfowl. I'll never forget a day we spent building an elaborate driftwood blind on a spot I knew absolutely had to be great for brant. When the season opened we found that the brant came around a nearby point and headed toward a refuge in a straight line that took them four hundred yards off where we were. We could have gunned the blind all season and got nothing. I hadn't done my homework, so I paid the price.

On the other hand, last year I went out the first Saturday of the season. (Nowadays I usually avoid Saturday and Sunday gunning. It's too crowded. I did it for years, though, back in the somber days when I had to work for a living. I gunned Thanksgiving and New Year's Day too. I tried to gun Christmas Day but ran into heavy flack on the home front and had to stay home with the kids. Bah, humbug! After I made my escape from the office I tried to gun every day of the season for two years straight and came pretty close to doing it.)

Where was I? Oh, opening Saturday. As you might suspect, on the first Saturday on public land there were gunners everywhere. Every good spot was taken. Some years before, when the land was still privately owned, I had leased and gunned the area for almost ten years, so I knew that not only the points and a small island were good but that the whole shoreline was. We'd had blinds all along it, and the ducks came to them well. I set up my sneakbox in a spot that, unless you had studied it over several seasons, you'd never think would be any good. That black duck that flared from my motor came into this spot on this day. I missed him too.

The best way to learn how to psych out ducks and geese is to gun every day and keep your eyes open. You'll see spots—ponds, coves, island sandbars, fields, points—the birds like and use. These are the places where you set your decoys. In the chapter on decoys I describe how I pull brant with only eight decoys. That's true, but the reason—and it's the gut point—is that the decoys were located in a spot where the brant came in naturally to feed. I could have sat in the blind and shot them with no decoys! The blocks merely encouraged them a little and determined where they would sit down.

It's tough to learn an area. You have to learn water depths and discover where the hides are. You even have to learn ground levels, for you'll probably have both high-water and low-water conditions over the course of the season. And you have to observe the movement of the birds during all kinds of conditions. Frontal-type winds are usually westerly. Storm winds are usually north or northeasterly. I guarantee you that the birds will seek food and shelter in very different places, depending on how the winds blow.

Hunting pressure is a factor that enters the picture. You will be looking for the hot spots, and so will plenty of other hunters. Birds that get hammered often at the same place, stop going back to it and find other spots. Then, too, the habits of the birds may change without any help from hunters. Ducks down my way feed in the ponds until they clean them out of grasses. After that they'll decoy more readily to points and coves. In lots of places a preferred food supply will be quickly exhausted, and when that happens the birds turn to other food, and their habits change. All these things you must study and observe.

One way in which waterfowling differs from other hunting is that you can't do your homework before the season. You can locate grouse or quail before opening day, or use the bow-hunting season to see what deer are up to. Not so with ducks and geese. They arrive nearly simultaneously with the season.

At times, though, you can keep a watch on the birds after the season closes. This is a good way to learn their preferences as they calm down and go back to the spots they like best. You can study them right through the winter under a variety of conditions.

Another method is to pick somebody's brain. Find a local duck hunter and hire him as a guide, extracting vital secrets all the while. Or go out at first with a commercial guide. If you're lucky and he's dumb, he'll tell you where the hot spots are. This is a sure-fire way to get to learn a fishing area, as the guide has *got* to take you to the hot spots. But usually a waterfowl guide either owns or leases land which, of course, you can't hunt without the guide. But given a little urging, most guides can give you some idea of the wheres and hows of finding good shooting spots.

I remember a delightful man, a duckboat and decoy maker, whom I met right at the end of his life. He had a picture postcard little workshop that smelled of cedar and paint and wet retrievers, and in the center of it was a potbellied iron stove surrounded by chairs. "Anybody ever miss a duck around that stove?" I asked him. His eyes twinkled and his wrinkles deepened in a smile. "Oh, my God," he replied. "If a tenth of the ducks and geese slaughtered around that stove really were killed, the whole crew would have been exterminated years ago." If you can find a hot stove like this—and stand the carnage around it—you can also learn plenty about places and techniques. Strange story about this man's death, incidentally. Every year he had a string of unfilled orders. You had to hound him to get a boat or blocks. The year he died he had finished up all his work. He had anticipated the end.

There are only two things on the mind of a duck on the wintering ground, and both rank first in order of importance. All any duck wants to do is keep his belly full and not get shot. They're not worried about predators. Sex isn't on their minds yet. The kids are raised.

If he's smart, a duck answers the safety problem by sticking to a flock, preferably a large flock. The answer to his second problem is met in a way most people don't understand. In most places, most ducks have been turned into nocturnal feeders. When possible—i.e., when there is enough light to see to fly—they stay in safe resting areas during the day, then come into feeding areas as shadows lengthen and darkness looms.

These nocturnal habits create what have come to be called the morning flight and the evening flight. As dawn breaks, birds that are in the feeding areas leave them for their sanctuaries, which are generally in open water—big rivers, bays, or reservoirs—or in a refuge if one is handy. It might be any place where somebody won't keep blasting at them.

The morning flight varies even on normal days, when there is the usual fall or winter weather. Some mornings the birds abruptly take off. They just jump up and zoom to safety. Other mornings, for reasons I'll discuss, they seem reluctant to leave. They'll fly from one place to another, trade around seeking new feeding areas, hopefully among your decoys. This activity may last for several hours, until nine or ten A.M.

By midmorning the action has generally quieted down. Then it's dead for the rest of the day, though you may see an occasional bird or flock. These are probably birds who thought they'd found a safe place but were put on the move by some sharp-eyed hunter. The quiet period of no flights lasts until the hours between two and four P.M. By then the birds are getting hungry. Depending on several factors, they will leave the sanctuary and head out to find a nocturnal feeding ground. When they leave will depend on how hungry they are, and into the computer you must feed the fact that the colder it is the more food they require. A Canada goose needs about a half of a pound of food a day (.527 pounds in subfreezing weather, according to Hanson and Smith, 1950). A 1953 study by J. S. Jordan showed that food requirements dropped drastically in mild weather. The stage of the moon is another factor that will influence flight time. If it's a quiet night, not too cold, with a full moon set to rise at eight o'clock, the ducks will anticipate moonrise, and for the evening flight you will have the pleasure of watching the decoys bob. Yet another consideration is whether it is sunny or overcast. If it's cloudy, the ducks will realize they aren't going to get much help from moonlight, regardless of the stage of the moon. Typically, they'll try to get to their feeding grounds somewhat earlier on cloudy days. You can see that these factors, and undoubtedly many more I know nothing about, will influence the morning flight as well. The ducks will anticipate how hard or easy it will be to get back to the feeding grounds, and if they are worried about it being difficult, they'll feed longer in the morning.

This is the normal pattern and, of course, the ducks will deviate from it all over the place. Winter weather is notoriously unstable. It amounts mostly to a succession of fronts marching eastward across the country. I've never seen any studies on it, but ducks and geese are undoubtedly sensitive to barometric pressure and can make a pretty fair estimate of what to expect in the way of weather. This assessment will influence their activity, and you should do a little reflecting on this point. The first thing to consider is that their assessments aren't always correct. Ducks and geese often get caught in storms and fly into things or sit down exhausted, in somebody's barnyard. The second thing to consider is that the birds' weather predictions are largely incalculable by you. You have no way of knowing whether the ducks or geese are incorrectly forecasting what weather conditions will be and reacting accordingly.

Another thing people generally don't realize is that waterfowl live their lives in ice and snow. When they arrive on the breeding grounds, there is snow on the ground.

Nights the summer through are in the forties. Even then, when the short Arctic summer sends temperatures up, waterfowl react by molting. They shed all their feathers and grow new ones. Everything about waterfowl equips them to stay warm despite extremely frigid temperatures—their coats make the best warm-weather clothes for people. But this is why on warm, bluebird days they don't fly around much. They can't. They are exhausted by the heat. They must use as little exertion as possible.

No one will argue that fact that when weather threatens their ability to feed, waterfowl of all kinds lose their caution and become vulnerable to hunters' guns, sometimes suicidally so.

A friend of mine swears he saw this poem crudely painted on the door of an old bayman's gunning houseboat.

> First it rained
> Then it blew
> Then it frizz
> Then it snew.

The old bayman might not have been so hot in his spelling, but he knew his ducking. He's postulated perfect waterfowl conditions. He knew he was going to blow his gun barrels out in that snowstorm. Each one of those weather conditions scares hell out of ducks and geese and makes them more hungry. When a snowstorm arrives with its threat of drastically reducing the feeding grounds, or perhaps sealing food off altogether, waterfowl will be frantically seeking shelter and feeding areas. Be assured that the old bayman's decoys would be set where they appeared to offer both. Let's look at his conditions.

First it rained. Dense rain is probably the worst weather to try to gun in. The ducks can't see well through heavy rain and tend to stay put. A light rain is different. Ducks know that when it's raining, darkness will come quickly after the sun sets and the night will be too dark to fly in. The waterfowl must be active during the day. The old bayman's first condition puts the ducks on their guard.

Then it blew. What the bayman has described is a frontal condition. The rain was created by a low pressure area. It has been shoved off to the east by a cold front high. These fronts, which come one after another at the end of fall and in winter, are a duck hunter's main ally. Typically, the front passes, temperatures plummet drastically, and westerly winds blow hard for twenty-four to thirty hours. Then the temperature rises, the winds slacken, and the process begins to repeat itself. Waterfowl doesn't like anything about all this, and on a "shift off," i.e., when the wind shifts westerly and starts blowing, they'll be out seeking shelter. When the

The wind whips past a barge blind. You can tell from the angry waves that this was a prime waterfowling day. Waterfowl can't rest in heavy weather; they actually get sick if they can't find sheltered, calmer waters.

wind blows, it makes life tough for ducks that try to remain on open water. They have to fight too hard to stay in position. Rocking around in the waves makes them dizzy and fatigued. Tiring too quickly, expending vital energy that they may have trouble replacing, scares them. They seek shelter, looking for places where the waves are calm and they'll be protected from the wind. The old bayman first saw the ducks put on their guard. Now he sees them begin to tire.

Then it frizz. Ice, the presence of it, the threat of it, scares all waterfowl. Look at it from their point of view. In a severe winter, an individual duck's chances for survival are always at stake. It is a struggle merely to stay alive when they are using every available feeding area. Now suppose you deny them a substantial percentage of their range or even threaten to. (The time just before a big storm can offer you some excellent shooting.) Remember, as temperatures are falling, the duck's energy requirements are increasing, so the ducks, who are barely able to keep themselves alive at best, are now going to be severely handicapped. Why shouldn't they be terrified? Lakes, ponds, potholes, streams, bays, and reservoirs for feeding purposes are going to be frozen over. Ducks migrate south while the daylight hours are diminishing. When the days begin to lengthen after December 21st, their instincts no longer permit additional southern migration. Instead they will stay put and wait it out. Many times, in many places, during prolonged icing conditions thousands of ducks starve. You can tell these birds, incidentally. If approached, they will fly only a few hundred yards and sit down again.

Game departments sometimes get criticized for not providing supplementary feeding when these crisis conditions strike. If you study the enormousness of the problem, you will see that they really can't. In the first place, they would have to anticipate the crisis and stockpile grain which if not used would be useless. Second, the distribution problem is unthinkable. Grain would have to be scattered over miles throughout the state. Third, every state game department is pushing its budget to the limit. There aren't funds for such a tremendously expensive undertaking. Even if these factors could be resolved, the project could easily backfire. Wild animals that get accustomed to supplementary feedings find it difficult or impossible to revert to fending for themselves.

Then it snew. After watching the birds annoyed with rain, harassed with wind, and scared by ice, the old bayman now delivers the *coup de grace.* Ice has deprived them of their watery feeding grounds. Now the fields are sealed off with a carpet of snow. If it's a windy snowstorm, the birds will seek food and shelter. If the snow falls gently, the birds will still forage frantically in an attempt to stuff as much food into themselves as possible.

Ice and cold and snow strike terror in the hearts of ducks and, to a certain extent, geese as well. Their need for food is increasing, their ability to get it decreasing. All of these weather conditions, even the suggestion of them, increase waterfowls' need for security. Your decoys never looked better to them. All ducks and geese shed their wariness in relief at the sight of a sheltered flock. Mallards, pintails, and blacks that will drive you crazy in calm, warm weather pitch in then without hesitation. I've heard of baymen using gallon oil cans painted flat black to decoy black ducks or even turning over chunks of marsh with a shovel and setting the black-looking blobs on the ice of a pond. Would they work? Given the old bayman's conditions they would. Put out tin cans in normal weather and the ducks would laugh at you.

Of course, this foul, fowl weather will create problems for you, too. Ice can put you out of business. You simply can't get a boat through it. Drifting ice may make it impossible to keep decoys in position. The storm may drive all the water out of your favorite shooting ground or put your blind three feet under the water or wash it away. But if you're a modern waterfowler, you won't be too handicapped because adaptability and mobility are the keys to your success. If you're shot down one place, you can find another.

There are some other weather conditions that affect waterfowl:

Fog.   This has an effect similar to that of rain. Ground fog will bother you but not the birds who fly above it. A thick, dense fog that has altitude will tend to cause the birds to stay put, as the lack of visibility frightens them. But a light fog is good. It decreases their eagle eye and you have the overcast condition and certainty of an early, dark night.

Thunderstorms.   When winter warm fronts come through, they come accompanied by thunderstorms. The ducks and geese don't like the rumbling and the fireworks any more than you do. They will be active, trying to find shelter and the security of being with their pals. One afternoon in my coffin box I could have shot every brant on the bay. They'd come in. I'd shoot and, of course, frighten them away. The flocks would sit on the water, looking at the decoys. They could stand it only for a half hour or so. Then they'd come in again. It hailed and spit snow, the sky turned black, and it rained in torrents. I held the hatch cover over my head in the heavy rain and laughed at what a spectacle I would have made if there had been anyone crazy enough to be out there with me.

The Changing Season.   Every hunting season is like a life. It opens full of youth and innocence, grows to maturity, and becomes wintry and dour at the end. The modern waterfowler must be prepared for these changes. You must note those points and ponds that the birds learn will always threaten them. If the populations move or change, you must know about it and act accordingly. All the birds will increase in wariness. You should probably set out more decoys late in the season than you do when the season is young (I don't). But you certainly must pay attention to the visibility of your hide, keep the grass on your blind in top shape, and see that the decoys don't get the paint knocked off.

Then the season closes, and I always feel a sense of relief. I eagerly look forward to the season's opening and enjoy the heck out of following the birds, but I'm always glad when the hunting ends. Enough is enough. The birds need the chance to live without harassment and fear. They need the opportunity to recoup and regroup, and so do I.

The pressing business for them comes in summer. While they do their thing on the northern breeding grounds I play with my boats. Finally the leaves start to turn, and we're both ready for another round.

7

Models for Men

Down the flyways they come. We pause in what we are doing—tending April's garden or raking October's leaves—to watch the great V beat steadily across the sky. Often they pass in the night, and the honking of the flock can be heard in the darkness overhead, one of the most haunting sounds in nature. It seems to cry, *Earthling, we are wild and free. You can only dream of the far places. We are on our way.*

At one time or another Canada geese visit every state except Hawaii. Their majestic size, distinctive flight formation, and buglelike call make them our most readily identifiable waterfowl. Romance clings to them as to no other bird. "They represent the 'wild' in wildlife," a biologist friend told me. This symbolic essence is probably why a Canada was chosen to be pictured on all our Federal Wildlife Refuge signs.

When you visit the refuges these days and see Canada geese by the tens and tens of thousands, it is hard to believe that only twenty-five years ago reliable waterfowl authorities were grimly predicting eventual extinction of the species. Today, with a total population of nearly two million, there are more geese in North America than there were when the continent was first settled. Even more important, state and federal biologists have succeeded, through modern conservation methods, in reintroducing breeding flocks of Canada geese into regions vacated by the species a century or more ago. "It's one of the greatest conservation success stories ever," says Joe Linduska, deputy director of the Fish and Wildlife Service, "ranking with such wildlife triumphs as the introduction of the ringneck pheasant and re-establishment of our wild turkey flocks."

This kind of conservation rests squarely on knowledge of wildlife, its habits and preferred habitat. The Canada goose triumph was preceded by years of failure. It wasn't until biologists hit upon a single curious facet of the Canada's admirable nature that populations started upward. They discovered that young Canada goslings, if released as soon as they are able to fend for themselves, will return year after year to the area of that initial release. Ducks will not. Other kinds of geese will not. Like the Canada goslings they will live and grow during the warm months, but come fall they will migrate, intermingle with other waterfowl on the wintering grounds, then return with the flock to their traditional breeding grounds. Released mature Canadas do the same. But Canada goslings, almost like salmon, unerringly return to the place they first experienced life.

The biologists knew that literally countless unused areas fulfilled the Canada's relatively modest environmental requirements for open water, feeding fields within fifteen miles, and undisturbed nesting sites. In the late 1950s wholesale experimentation began. What happened in Colorado is typical.

Even though the state had had no wintering goose population in over a century, a test was initiated on College Lake, fifty miles north of Denver. Knowing that nest sites were lacking, the biologists created artificial structures they hoped the geese would use. In 1957 thirty-one goslings were released. They thrived but did not nest. The next year twenty-three more birds were put out. They stayed healthy but still made no nests. More birds were released in 1959 with the same dismal results. "We were a discouraged group," remembers project leader Jack Grieb. "Here we were spending all this money with nothing to show for it. But in the spring of 1960 our resident manager called me in great excitement to report breeding activity. When a Canada gets romantic there isn't any mistaking it. By the end of that month the ganders were no prouder than we were of the fourteen tiny balls of fluff on College Lake."

When Canada geese find a secure field, they pitch in in seemingly endless waves, flock after flock parachuting down with effortless grace.

More birds were planted in 1961, and twenty goslings were hatched that year. When stocking was stopped the following year, natural young-bird production went over the hundred mark. "The flock then numbered over five hundred birds and we found breeding pairs moving from College Lake into other suitable areas. There were nests on lakes and marshes all over Larimer County," reports Grieb. "Five similar projects are underway now. Best of all, we had nearly ten thousand Canadas flying around Colorado last winter."

A canvassing of state conservation departments turns up similarly spectacular results almost everywhere. Breeding flocks of Canada geese have been successfully introduced on sixteen National Wildlife Refuges in the North Central states alone, according to regional biologist Herbert Dill. "Ten years ago virtually no Canadas were nesting in the St. Lawrence vicinity. Last year we had some six hundred goslings there," says C. H. D. Clarke, chief of Ontario's Fish and Wildlife Branch. A recent census shows Michigan now has 7,765 geese and "thousands of people from Detroit view and photograph the Kensington Park flock every weekend," notes Edward Mikula, waterfowl specialist. The Tennessee Valley Authority, in cooperation with state agencies, is developing a captive-production unit at the Buffalo Spring Game Farm near Rutledge, Tennessee, and goslings from it are being released in reservoirs throughout the Tennessee Valley. Dr. Harvey K. Nelson, director of the Northern Prairie Research Center in Jamestown, North Dakota, is interested in giant Canadas, huge birds that may weigh twenty-five pounds or more. He notes that Saskatchewan is producing giant Canadas for release throughout the province, and there are already a number of successful local breeding flocks. North Dakota too is establishing giant honker flocks. Almost nine hundred goslings were released in the state in the summer of 1972. Even dusty Arizona has a honker population measured in thousands.

The effort to manipulate the wild Canada goose's nature in his own behalf has prompted intensive reinvestigation of the birds themselves. Astonishingly, the Canada goose's character, long romanticized beyond belief, has emerged unscathed under scientific scrutiny. Increased knowledge of the kinds of lives they lead simply makes the student admire them the more. Canadas *do* mate for life and display what can only be interpreted as love and tenderness toward each other. They *are* faithful and affectionate parents. They are wise enough to select experienced leaders and follow their advice. And they live together in notable peace and harmony. Fights are almost unknown. Kortright opens his chapter on Canadas by saying, "Sagacity, wariness and fidelity are characteristic of the Canada goose which, collectively, are possessed in the same degree by no other bird. The Canada in many respects may serve as a model for man."

These models for men are clearly family-minded. Even huge flocks are built up of family units that tend to stay together until the parents nest again in the spring. Either one of a pair may take another mate in the event of the death of one, but if both goose and gander stay healthy, the union appears to be for life. And every flock includes solitary older birds who, it is believed, have lost mates and are unwilling to mate again. Canadas may even mate on the love-at-first-sight principle. When live decoys were legal, farmers would attempt to strengthen semidomestic flocks with broken-wing wild birds. If the goose found no mate in the home flock, it was an accepted practice to make the rounds of neighbors' flocks until sooner or later the cripple would make a cry and rush to the side of a mate it had never seen before and would leave only at death. Like many birds, geese go through an elaborate precopulation ritual, but Indians of the Canadian breeding grounds report a far tenderer association among the northern flocks. Yearling birds arrive in pairs in the spring and stay together during the summer but never mate. The Indians say they are "just sweethearts." The following year they will raise a brood.

Ornithologist E.W. Nelson describes the suicidal fidelity Canadas of both sexes frequently display. "When one bird from a flock is shot, a single bird will often be seen to leave its companions at once and come circling about uttering loud calls. If the fallen bird is only wounded, its mate will invariably join it and may even allow itself to be approached and shot without attempting to escape."

Although I never saw this happen with a Canada—I did with a wood duck, though—one of the most extraordinary things I've ever witnessed came about with a pair of Canadas. I was gunning my pond. Just at dusk I saw them come in low over the marsh and pitch in heavily in a big creek not far away. From the way they flew, and since there was a man in a white-hulled fishing boat right next to where they landed, I assumed one of the birds was hurt.

Back at the launch ramp I was standing in the blackness listening to the sounds of the marsh when the white-hulled boat pulled in. I helped the man haul out, then asked him about the geese. He confirmed my observation that the one bird seemed in bad shape.

To realize what was happening, you have to know something about waterfowl and their habits. The healthy goose was keeping its mate out in open water during the day and bringing it into the marsh to feed at night. The main goose migration had been over for several weeks. That meant that these two were coming down the flyway in short hops—the only kind the wounded bird could manage.

The healthy bird was taking risks that by its own level of perception could only be described as enormous. To leave the security of the flock, with its multiple eyes and senses, put the two in grave peril. To lag behind while winter deepened increased the chances of ice and snow or fierce winter storms threatening them. Finally, the healthy goose could see the man in the fishing boat and had no way of knowing whether he'd shoot. Yet when its mate could fly no farther, the goose accepted the risk without faltering. Scientists have a fancy word for attributing human emotions to animals, but if courage is recognizing danger and coolly facing it, that is exactly what the bird I saw was doing. I've called them the confident Canadas. They are also the courageous Canadas.

And look at what having its mate stand by meant to the wounded bird in terms of survival. The healthy bird remained ever alert, its senses not dulled by pain and weakness. It could make the life-or-death decisions of when and where to fly unimpaired. On the Atlantic marshes seagulls, themselves perilously close to starvation, tear wounded ducks apart. Elsewhere, foxes or raccoons do the job. No seagull or fox would approach the crippled goose with its mate ready to rush to its defense. Just the encouragement alone, the comfort of having a partner, could help it succeed in the struggle for life.

Hunters are the first to pay homage to the Canada's encompassing intelligence. Going on a wild goose chase has not become synonymous with failure without reason, and there have been many occasions when the goose proved more than a match for the hunter. One scientist estimates the Canada's eyesight as equal to man's aided by an eight-power telescope. Although it is clear that the gander is boss in the family unit, when families form into flocks, by some unknown process one bird takes over leadership and the others defer to its judgment. Since the watch gander assumes no special place in the flock, it is impossible to distinguish, and scientists can only guess at the range of its authority and merely surmise that it is always a male. "Give the watch gander a gun, and he'd get the hunter every time" is an old goose-hunter's lament.

When the flock leader falls, the flock flares from the gunfire in normal fashion but then, finding itself leaderless, sets up a tremendous clamor of calling and honking. Confusion reigns. Instead of staying together, flock members fly every which way and can even be seduced again over the decoys, which would never happen with the watch gander alive. Finally, by some mysterious process, another assumes leadership. The flock reassembles. The frantic calling subsides and, before your eyes, discipline and purpose are restored and the birds move on.

Exactly how birds can communicate such complicated concepts baffles scientists. A study of calls used by Canada geese turned up at least fifteen different ones, including a loud love snort the male reserves only for his mate. Wild Canadas hiss at danger and grunt at their goslings, who in turn peep back. There is a unique snorelike postcopulation cry, a scream of pain, and an oddly disturbing distress call. You'll imitate the *ga, ga, ga, ga* gurgle of the feed call and commonly use the buglelike *ar-oonk* to attract a flock's attention. A study team observed this characteristic call used in at least five different situations and suspected that innuendos too slight for the human ear to detect could well extend its meanings to the extent of making it a language system by itself. Geese "honk" to warn away territorial intruders, to greet their mates at long distance, to hail another flock, and to signal alarm. We generally hear wild geese before we see them, because the call is apparently also used to supplement sight in keeping the flock together, providing a continuous audible signal that each member of the family contributes to.

The cooperative behavior of a Canada flock is demonstrated in other ways. Since the big birds have their legs positioned in the center of their bodies, they are not clumsy on land as ducks are and do most of their feeding there. Watch a flock as it grazes in a field or marsh. One or two birds, posted sentinels, will always stand, necks erect, alert for danger. Others take their place from time to time while the sentinels feed. Geese fly in the distinct V so that each breaks a path through the air for the other. Notice how they shift off the most taxing number-one position. In high winds you can sometimes spot a bird out of line, flying not behind, but alongside another. This is a parent encouraging a tired young bird by its calls and presence. Two of the nation's most eminent waterfowl scientists have reported in the government publication *Waterfowl Tomorrow* that "one often sees [on the breeding grounds] large flocks made up of many broods attended by no more than a half a dozen adult geese. Now and then other geese replace these 'babysitters' so they can join adults elsewhere. Should a person intrude, however, there is bedlam as the youngsters scatter and adult geese appear from all directions to reclaim their offspring."

Canadas will set up housekeeping almost anywhere a site satisfies certain critical requirements. The couple needs about twenty square feet of territory with a good clear view in all directions and some water nearby in which to rear the goslings. They will nest in old automobile tires and on roofs of sheds. One biologist spotted a nest eighty feet up in a tree. "I worried about how the goslings would get down," he said. "But when the time came they floated down like falling leaves." Fortunately, though preferring isolation, Canadas domesticate easily and will nest near human habitation if, with characteristic sagacity, they determine that the humans mean them no harm. Both sexes share the incubating chores and are somewhat careless of the nest. However, about thirty days after the eggs are laid, the peeping of the emerging goslings draws the male to his mate's side, and from that moment on nothing may approach the nest. Even game breeders, who can lift the female off her eggs — the first hatch is usually incubated artificially; the geese then lay again — stay well away after the goslings hatch.

An enraged Canada goose is a formidable creature. Each wing has a knobby "spur" corresponding roughly to the human elbow. Equipped with sufficient muscle power to cruise comfortably hour after hour at forty miles an hour and able to reach sixty if pressed, these strong wings are dangerous weapons as the renowned John James Audubon discovered. "Whenever I visited the nest of a courageous gander," he recorded in his journal, "it seemed to look upon me with utter contempt. It would stand in a stately attitude until I reached to within a few yards of the nest when it would lower its head and shaking it as if it were dislocated from the neck it would open its wings and launch into the air, flying directly at me. So daring was this fine fellow that in two instances he struck me a blow with his wings on the right arm which for an instant I thought was broken." After the attack the gander would rush back to the mate, rub necks with her and stand by, according to Audubon.

My friend Dr. George Halazon, professor of wildlife management at Kansas State University, was watching tiny goslings "pipping" through the shell in Wisconsin's vast Horicon Marsh when a skunk emerged from the grass and went for the helpless babies. The gander immediately attacked, hissing and making short rushes, but the skunk kept on. "Finally the gander was desperate," recounts Professor Halazon. "He sent the skunk reeling with a blow from his wing. The skunk regained his feet, turned and sprayed but the gander ignored the horrible attack and charged again and again, hitting the skunk with such violence I thought he might kill it. The skunk finally turned and fled."

Both parents take over child rearing, yet even the tiny goslings give a hint of the courage and resourcefulness that will be theirs at maturity. In the first week of life, common seagulls pose a deadly threat. They can swoop down and pick up a tiny chick before the parents can fend them off. In his book, *Honker*, C. S. Williams tells of coming across a California gull attacking a bunch of two- or three-day-old goslings. The gull tried to dive-bomb one after another, but the little fellows would wait until the last moment, then pop safely under the water. Soon the gull tired of the unrewarding effort and left.

The youngsters grow quickly and some fifty-odd days after birth follow their parents into the air for the first time. All summer long the parents have led the gangly youngsters on practice flights, but as the Arctic winter moves closer, the flights become longer and more frequent. The goose families move slowly over the vast stretches of treeless muskeg toward "staging areas" along the shores of large bodies of water. Resting in open water during the day and moving inland to feed during the afternoon or night, family joins family, building into large flocks. Other migratory fowl of the area behave similarly, and day after day flocks take off on the long journey south. Many migratory birds fly hundreds of miles nonstop to their destination. Not so the Canadas. They meander down some nine distinct highways in the sky, seldom if ever crossing from one to another. Navigating by little-understood instincts, the Canadas cruise easily at 120 wingbeats a minute to wherever their leader finds the necessary food and safety. They will stay in areas for weeks if weather and fancy suit them, at times filling park lakes or grazing on football fields, moving in with civilization as if to make us poor stay-at-homes envious of their Gypsy freedom. In fact, in Westchester County, New York, one harassed game warden every fall has the task of shooing flocks out of three or four swimming pools.

People wonder how they dare set up residence in such exposed places, and the answer is that they know from past experience where they will be safe. Scientists know from banding returns that twenty- and twenty-five-year-old birds are common. I talked recently with an former market hunter in Currituck, North Carolina, with his onetime hunting flock at his heels. Every one of the birds was at least thirty-five years old, and one, he said, he knew for a fact was fifty. The combination of strength, intelligence, and experience makes the geese confident of their safety. We see them more often in fall as they meander down the flyways, taking their time. With parental duties on their minds, their spring flight north is more purposeful and direct.

However, the minute the fall hunting season opens and guns start popping the wise Canada leaders waste no time in getting flocks to the safety of a federal refuge. The geese will congregate in astounding and, at times, aggravating numbers. Federal biologists have sometimes tried to move flocks from crowded refuges to empty ones, mostly with little success. They've bombed the geese, buzzed them with airplanes, withheld food, increased hunting pressure. The Canadas aren't about to be pushed around.

About three out of four of all geese killed are juveniles, since their lack of experience makes them most susceptible to hunter's decoys and calls. In fact, when live decoys were permitted, "Judas" geese would call to the wild flocks and sometimes hunters would see the juveniles, like unruly children, fly to the tempting sound while their parents honked futile warnings.

Wildlife biologists recognize eleven different varieties of Canadas, including two West Coast species that are no bigger than ducks. All retain the black neck and head with the unmistakable white throat patch. The most numerous are "common" Canada geese, well-proportioned birds averaging about nine pounds. Oddly enough, although rumors existed for years of a giant Canada strain twice as big as this, only recently have scientists verified their existence.

In 1962 Dr. Harold Hanson, a research biologist with the Illinois Natural Survey, was invited to band, weigh, and measure a trapped sample of birds from a flock of large geese wintering in the city park of Rochester, Minnesota. "On that memorable day," writes Dr. Hanson, "work proceeded smoothly except it was obvious our scales were faulty. We were getting impossible weights. To test the scales I bought a five-pound bag of sugar and a ten-pound bag of flour. Our 'impossible weights' were correct. A giant race of geese was living as a distinct and separate entity in the Mississippi flyway."

The giant Canadas are widely distributed now, especially west of the Mississippi. With a body a fourth to a third larger than regular Canadas, the giant bird has a long swanlike neck and proportionately longer wings, a white rather than gray breast, and often a white forehead patch. These birds call less frequently than other Canadas, and their flight is slower and usually at a lower altitude.

No doubt the large size of the common Canada goose contributes to the myths and legends surrounding it. To the Indians of old the wild goose was much more than a giant bird. It was a god and, as such, called upon for wisdom and counsel. Even to the northern Indians of today the Canada goose assumes an importance that cannot be fully gauged in ordinary terms. Quite literally, Canadas can mean the difference between life and death to them.

Impelled by the spring mating urge, the geese desert the wintering ground in April, and their great stamina carries them almost without pause to nesting areas on the subarctic tundra. The north is at its cruelest then. The months of bitter cold have sapped the strength of the Indian inhabitants. They have tightened their belts long before. Now survival depends on what little game is abroad. If game fails, as happens often, the Indians must leave their trapping camps in the bush and strike out for the isolated settlements. Yet when the first warming trend sets in, even this may be impossible. Wet snow clings to snowshoes, preventing land travel. It may be days or weeks before the unfrozen river highways will carry canoes. Until then, the Indian families are prisoners in their tents. Even in good times, the threat of starvation is never far away.

Into this dangerous situation every spring come the Canada geese. Arriving before rivers and lakes thaw, they are the first real food available throughout the north. And never in their life cycle are the sagacious geese more vulnerable. The need for open-water sanctuaries seems forgotten. The mating urge destroys the mutual-defense system of the flock. Pairs wander extensively, investigating nesting sites, and many who seek mates for the first time are supremely eager for any response to their calls. No hunter knows these calls better than the Indians. Their guns boom again and again.

In a few weeks it is over. Waters open, other game emerges, and food is plentiful. The Indians will not bother the geese again until fall. Then like millions of other hunters they will hunt more for sport than food.

The Confident Canadas

It starts with partner's hiss. You open your eyes. A flock of four Canada geese is 150 yards out. They are swinging in to your decoys. Their wings are full and curved as they parachute to lose altitude.

"I see 'em," you whisper softly. You don't want your partner to call you. He is a motionless lump hunched in the grass that surrounds your blind. Neither of you will move anything but your eyes until the guns fly to your shoulders. The geese are looming larger. There is no sound. You remember the old goose hunter's rule that the big birds aren't in range until you can make out their eyes. You are a long way from seeing their eyes. You wait.

Whatever it was that brought these geese out of the sky where thousands before ignored you, you will never know. But they are certainly in your grasp. Nothing will alarm them now. Your three cardboard Canada decoys stand erect on shore. Your set of fifteen black ducks is perfect. A decoy maker with magic in his hands picked up pine blocks and something uncannily close to live ducks sprang from his hand. His masterpieces bob and dip in the waves as the Canada flock sails steadily toward their doom.

A touch of pride tinges your thoughts. For you too have passed this test. You left the blind for a nap, but you chose a position where long rows of seaweed conceal you. You didn't start or jump at your partner's alerting hiss. Only your eyelids moved. Best of all, across your waist, cradled in your hands, is your 16-gauge Parker. It is a small gun, but it will speak with deadly effect. Your fingers tighten on its stock.

Boom! Boom! "What the hell is that?" you cry. *Boom! Boom! Boom! Boom!* The geese are flaring away, honking raucously at the treachery and deceit, their majestic dignity ruffled.

You leap to your feet. Partner is out of the blind. A man with his two sons in a blind 250 yards away has opened up on your geese. He has frightened them away. He has ruined your one chance in ten years.

Clouds of steam issue from your ears as you march toward the distant blind. Later, you don't like to think of the things you said. There were a number of ways you could have made the point that the geese were at least three hundred yards away from them, that they were decoying to your decoys, and that only an ignorant so-and-so of questionable ancestry, indifferent intelligence, and woeful sportsmanship would pull such a trick. Blackbeard would blush at the invective you fling down upon this infamy. The three cower in their blind like white mice before a lion's wrath. Their contriteness gives you no pleasure. The greedy bastards would do the same thing again if they had the chance. To hell with them. You spin on your heel and stalk away.

The rest of the day you sit in the blind. There is no pleasure there for you, the black taste stays with you for days. Years later you can recall the incident only with anger.

The seasons pass. Brant you kill in profusion. An Arctic adventure produces blues and snows. Many ducks fall. But the wary and confident Canadas elude you.

You study these birds. You begin to admire them. More than that. The wavering V of a Canada flock against the sky is a symbol to all men of what is wild and free.

These are regular Canada geese, not giant Canadas, but you can still see the size of them. The goose on the right will weigh fifteen pounds.

Their cry in the night sends shivers down the spine of every earthbound stargazer. Something more than admiration grows as you learn of their steadfast fidelity, their encompassing parental devotion, their astounding wisdom, their great courage.

You go to Easton, Maryland, Canada goose capital of the world, to do a picture story of a professional goose-hunting operation. The sports sit in a pit blind. When the guide hollers "Now!" they leap to their feet. The sky around them is full of Canadas. They fire, and the birds fall. "Come on, Zack," the guide urges. "Get in the blind and kill a couple." You shake your head. Not these birds. This is between you and them. No intermediaries.

The hunter in you hungers. In midsummer you prepare. You add eighteen geese half-bodies to your five water decoys and two field decoys. The paint job doesn't suit you. Madison Mitchell, the famous decoy carver from Havre de Grace, has made you a half-life-size Canada goose lamp. It goes to your workshop as a guide. Every feather and touch of color is reproduced. A mail-order house sends a record, and the sound of honking geese pervades the house until wife and children flee. The sixteen-gauge double is retired in favor of a choke-equipped, automatic twelve-gauge. The senses quicken, the hunting cat's nails grow sharp, it licks its whiskers.

"Tow Island is where a whole flock of Canadas live," Pat, a sometime guide, tells you. "There's sand there. They need that. And it's open, far away. Geese don't like to be near people. Scare's 'em." He scratches his head. "I recollect there's an old pit blind on the island right next to Tow. Be about right there." His finger stabs at your chart. "Don't know what shape she's in, or even if she's there, for that. You're welcome, if you want. You should get geese there. You'll get 'em there if you get 'em anyplace."

The blind is old and busted. You haul materials and tools to the marsh—sheets of plywood and caulking compound for patches, sod shovels to replace the grassy slopes, galvanized nails, saws, hammers, axes. You slop mud out of the blind, the viscous, foul-smelling black ooze of the bay. You could offer a man fifty dollars an hour to clean a sinkbox, and he'd laugh at you. You clench your jaw, shovel mud into buckets, hand the buckets to your partner, who pours the ooze back in the bay.

Before season you haunt the marsh. Striped-bass fishing is your excuse. The real reason is goose watching. You want to watch where they go, where they rest, where they feed.

The season opens, and your vaunted hopes fall to the ground. It is a comedy of errors. The geese easily outwit you. Flocks desert your island and seem to be landing in another area. You go there and frantically place your decoys. The geese are back where your blind is. It is a beginner's mistake! A tailwind is forecast. You set up before dawn. The spread is perfection itself. Not a bird mars the unbroken horizon all day. (You later learn that a tailwind reduces wing lift and actually makes flying harder. Ignorance of the law is no excuse. Ignorance of the law kills no Canadas.)

Then there is another day that will live in infamy, only this time there is no one to swear at but yourself.

You believe the radio weather report. It says low tide has passed. You have a job to do. You do it and return. The radio is wrong. The tide has fallen further. Your boat is aground, and you can't budge it. You sit high and dry in the middle of a mud flat while the inevitable happens. It is the day of the biggest migration ever. Geese are everywhere, at times so close you grab your gun in desperation. Flocks sit down behind you, to your right, to your left. The blind site, a half mile away, is the resting area of a particularly large and succulent-looking bunch. You never take the decoys out of the boat. Long after dark the tide turns and sets you free. The cat slinks home, the laughter of the mice ringing in its ears.

The season is slipping by. The weather chills. Most of the geese have migrated, but you are at it again. Three of you are in another blind, a blind that would be better for ducks, but your rig is out, your geese are set. There is a small sandy beach near the blind, and you set the water decoys off it. The field decoys go on the shore. You check it out from the boat and it looks good — like a flock had landed and were climbing into the marsh to feed.

A flock appears, still miles away. You keep down and blow the calls. They pass majestically by. They don't slow down. They don't lose altitude. They look your way and pass majestically by.

A single appears. Surely you can decoy it. You call and call, and the single responds. It knows its vulnerability and longs for the safety of a flock. Through the blind grass you can see it studying the decoys, listening intently. It flies by 150 yards away and never returns. Nobody did anything wrong. It was just too wary for you.

Another flock passes. Then another. Nobody does anything wrong. It is merely that they are Canada geese, confident Canada geese. You know Canada populations are building up all over the country, and the reason why is becoming nauseatingly apparent. The cat's whiskers droop, its nails grow dull, its step feeble and lame.

Another flock appears, and from the beginning you sense a difference. These birds are low. They seem weary. You call and call. With stately wingbeats they come across the marsh, straight toward you. You call and call again, but they remain mostly silent, now and again honking softly. Now every wise eye is on your location. Perhaps for decades these birds have listened to men's calls, studied men's decoys, kept clear of his blinds, made mockery of men's cunning.

Now every wise old eye is upon you. You are against the mark. You are about to pass or fail waterfowling's ultimate test.

About a hundred and fifty yards out the flock rises. You bite your lip. There are too many, maybe twenty birds. The fewer eyes the better. They sweep upward, all together as if by command, and you know the reason and shrink from their scrutiny. They gain altitude and slow to take a longer look. They are making the decision to come closer or pass by. This is when a decoy askew or the sun glinting off an empty shell spells failure, when the slightest movement is fatal.

They sweep down low on the water a hundred yards out. You can make out their white cheek patches as they veer off to your right, then slip out of your sight. "Where are they?" you whisper frantically. "Don't know. Can't see 'em," your partner hisses back. He pauses but a second to speak and continues calling. No one has moved more than an eyelid since the birds appeared perhaps ten minutes before.

Suddenly the flock reappears, inches from the water, gliding in. You realize they have circled to land into the wind. They are too low to see much. Partner is hunched over, calling. He can't see. The middle man is a guest, a newcomer. His instructions are simple: Go into a catatonic stupor until further notice. He is bent over, head down, hand on gun, motionless. He is a man thirty-five years old. He has shot deer, bear, and wild turkey, but his hand is shaking. You're not surprised; your own hand is shaking.

You study them through the half-inch slit between your hatbrim and the top of the blind. You want them in as close as possible, of course, but will they sit down? That would be the time to take them, when they hang with feet out, almost motionless in the air. They start to lift up again. Will they circle again and then sit down in the decoys? No, they'll see something if they circle again.

Okay, we'll take 'em, come what may, you decide. They are at extreme range, maybe as close as sixty yards, maybe as far away as eighty. It's hard to tell. "Get ready," you growl. With all their speed on, they can flare as you stand up and be out of range in a split second, but a split second is time enough. You long ago decided your gunning strategy. You are going to pick a bird and get as much lead up toward it as fast as you can.

The birds are lifting off the water now, lifting and turning, maybe sixty yards out, and you can see their eyes clearly. Their wingbeat picks up, and a few begin to honk. The range is long, terribly long, fifty yards if it's an inch. You see several birds with necks sharply outstretched, hollering frantically, and it is clear that *Danger!* is what they are crying. "Let's go, boys," you shout, "It's now or never." You had meant to give the word quietly, and your shout surprises you.

You throw your gun to your shoulder as the flock veers away. There is one bird at the end. You pick a point over and in front of him and pull the trigger, *bam, bam, bam,* as quickly as possible. You want as many No. 4s up around that bird as you can get. The bird collapses in the air, instantly dead, and falls heavily. There is a smack as it hits the water. Your partners empty their guns to no avail. The range was too great. Canadas can take heavy blows without flinching, and their feathers turn shot easily.

The rest is anticlimactic. A decoy line is broken, and you sit on the boat behind the blind fixing it. Your two partners start calling. As you watch, another Canada flock flies past, lowering to look, but not decoying. Shots ring out and another Canada falls from the sky. The new man got him. He was aiming at the first bird and the fourth fell, he admits. He is sheepish, properly chastened by his awesome good fortune.

The cat licks its whiskers. The cat naps in its chair. Its belly is full of Canada goose. You are something of a waterfowl connoisseur, but you have never tasted anything comparable to your goose. Mild, moist, dark meat, it is neither too fat nor too lean. How easily it slides down your gullet! Two of you find it hard to stop eating the corn-fed, grain-fattened goose. It is too good. But the satiety will not last. The hunter's hunger will return. Next season, you vow, more Canadas will fall.

9

The Funnel of the Flyways

Only a handful of hunters get to experience the fabulous waterfowling of the northern tundra breeding grounds. Of that small group, yet a smaller number experience the right combination of weather and fowl to produce what must be considered the absolutely best waterfowling on the North American continent. That lot has fallen to me. I have described it in the adventure that follows. As with the preceding chapter, this is exactly as it happened.

You start complaining — silently — about your slipping suspenders, about the blisters on your heels, about your cased gun jumping like a flag in the breeze.

Most of all you complain about the wind smashing into you. Each gust comes as a blow. Without it, you'd be sitting in a canoe now, enjoying the three-mile ride to the blind. But the swollen river at your side is an angry expanse of breakers. You've come 1,500 miles to hunt the delta of Ontario's mighty Albany, and the last three miles are the roughest. You tread grimly on, concentrating only on putting one foot in front of the other. And you keep up your silent complaints.

You can't complain about a lack of waterfowl. They are everywhere. Ducks and geese fill the air. You identify a flock of Canadas beating over, ignoring your little band. A pair of black ducks flashes by with the wind under their tails. A wavy line of birds sideslips across the wind. They seem to be strong birds, and big. Most are gray, but a few are snowy white, identifying them instantly as snow geese. Your foot trips and you fall heavily on one knee. No more rubbernecking, you vow. You fix your eyes on the heels of the man in front and try to forget your blisters.

You are walking into the vortex of a giant migratory funnel. All of northern Canada is the gigantic cone. The flyways are the spout. This is the narrow band of spongy, nutrient-rich muskeg that rims James Bay. Throughout September the flocks pitch into it, fattening up for the long migration. Their numbers are staggering. Birds in the millions are congregated in an area several miles wide and reaching maybe a hundred miles up both sides of the bay. You are hiking across it now.

Two weeks from now a storm like this might send them south. They'd put the wind to work. Flock after flock would head down the spout, most down the Mississippi flyway, a few down the Central, some down the Atlantic. But the shortening hours of daylight have not tripped their inner signal as yet. Now they are like waterfowl anywhere in a storm—unhappy, restless, constantly on the move, seeking shelter.

Abruptly the heels in front of you stop and you bump into the man. "Look dere," he says. There are five of you, three white hunters and two Cree guides named Moses and Lawrence. Your friends are as tired as you, grateful for the break, but Moses and Lawrence aren't even warmed up. You know they have many times walked like this for weeks. The thought is faintly disquieting.

A gigantic flock of snow geese is rising from the muskeg that stretches out of sight before you. Bunch after bunch climbs into the air. You silently count. "How many?" asks one of your friends. "I figure between two thousand and twenty-five hundred," you reply. "Maybe as few as fifteen hundred. What do you make it?" You agree on two thousand. On an impulse you turn to the Indians. "How many?" you ask. Moses grins. His teeth are strong, straight, and white. "Many," he answers. "Bery many."

Patches of water bush are found along the rivers of the James Bay marsh, and the Indians cut this and carry it to the area they want to shoot. It looks like a burden but this Indian's pack is child's play to him. He could easily walk 40 miles with it and feel no strain.

You can see here how the Indian arranges the brush to conceal the men. I added to his burden by having him make me a little blind so I could take these photographs and still be concealed. Although it looks cloudy here, this was a day of broken sunlight and not too many geese were on the move. But there are so many birds and they are so susceptible, having forgotten last year's caution, that they come to the calls and decoys of white wings.

This is the tundra of James Bay, somewhat farther north than the popular hunting area at the southern tip of the bay near Moosonee. The bay is probably several miles distant across the flat, treeless plain. I noticed rocks all over the area. It was the first time I ever saw rocks on a marsh. Where do they come from? Ice floes in the winter slide miles into the marsh, dropping the rocks they have picked up along the rocky Hudson Bay and James Bay shores.

He and Lawrence talk quickly together. Their language is fast and unmusical, a gutteral burst of *ah*s, *ug*s, and *eg*s. Moses turns. "We get in ditch ober dere," he says, pointing with his chin. "Not far." He grins. Abruptly he and Lawrence set off.

You watch them stride across the marsh. You've been told that when white men carry a canoe, it bobs. Not so when the Indians carry it. The canoe stays level. Even though both men wear hip boots, their gait is graceful, with toes pointed straight ahead, feet hardly lifting. It is as though their body weight didn't shift from foot to foot but remained half on each. The thought strikes you that their walk is more animal than human, but you immediately reject it as uncomplimentary. Yet the fact remains. It is a tireless, mile-eating, effortless glide. You remember seeing a movie in which a leopard slid down a tree and into the bush in one liquid motion. The way Moses and Lawrence walk across the marsh has that same quality.

By the time the three of you reach the creek the Indians have done their work. Sticks are cut and the white wings of snow geese stuck on them. These, along with birds shot down, will be the decoys. The marsh is dotted with small stands of willow bush. Lawrence's axe cuts at them. The willow branches are jammed into the earth to hide you. This is the blind. You sit on the side of the ditch, groveling in the yellow mud. One of your pals calls out, "Well, here we are up the well-known creek again without a paddle." You laugh. Lawrence laughs too. Even if an Indian can't speak English he knows the white man's cuss words. "Which way will the birds come from?" you ask him. Lawrence is tall, broad-shouldered, limber-hipped, lean-legged, and ramrod straight. Moses has the broad-nosed, flat Indian face. Lawrence's features are those of a deeply tanned white man. He sports a Charlie Chan moustache. Now his features are animated and warm. Later, back at the camp, in the waning daylight with the hood of his jacket up, his face will take on a wild look — somber, impassive, slightly frightening. Now he considers your question carefully, probably having to translate it. "From every way," he answers.

Abruptly he throws himself behind the willows, cups his hand to his mouth, and starts calling. Moses too starts calling. A flock of snows is downwind. The geese look in your direction. As fast as the wind will let them, they strain to come to the friendly voices.

The calling of these Crees is famous. The calls are high-pitched, much like the distant sound of a small dog barking. Both voices reverberate with the tingling goose bugle sound. The calls seem to vary while the sound remains the same.

One thing is certain — both men are working hard, yelling as loud as they can, putting real lung-power behind each call. *"Coo, coo, coo,"* they scream. *"Car, car, car. Kirt, kirt, kook, kook, kook. Koink, koink, koink."* A steady cacophony of sound.

The birds beat steadily upwind, blues mostly, but with several gleaming-white snows among them. As they draw closer the three of you hunch down. The Indians are out of sight in a willow bush. Suddenly their voices change. *"Nnnn. Ga, ga, ga, ga, ga. Nnnn, ga, ga, ga, ga,"* one cries. It is a gutteral, nasal gurgle, a feeding or recognition call. You hear the birds answering, gurgling back. The other Indian starts a low, seductive whistle, such as a lover might use to signal a rendezvous — soft, musical, reassuring, even tender.

"Shoot now," Lawrence shouts. You leap to your feet. Three guns bark. A bird falls. One bird from a fusillade! The Indians laugh. They are dead shots.

"Canabas! Canabas!" Moses shouts. (His mispronunciation will become a joke in which he seems to take great delight.) But now you are alert to the gray birds two hundred yards away. The Indians imitate their call. Their shouts carry out to the interested but wary geese. They answer back but turn away. No matter. Moses has spotted more snows. The two yell at them and again you leap to your feet and fire. "Dere! Dere!" Lawrence shouts. You turn, half slipping. Two snows sweep down. You fire, and a bird folds. You pull on the next bird, then pull again. The bird flies on.

As you watch, the two thousand-bird flock rises again, now less than five hundred yards from you. Two birds crumple and fall, then a third. An Indian is hunting beneath them. You see him jump up after his birds.

The flock is breaking into smaller bunches, groups of twenty to thirty, many pairs, a few singles. Some turn and sweep over you, flying as though the Furies are after them. The three of you fire, reload, and fire again. You are through one box of shells. Birds are in the air over you as you frantically rip into a new box, fumbling with stiff fingers.

The flocks wheel out of sight, and the Indians bob away to retrieve the downed game. They never lose a bird. It's incredible to watch them stalking the spot where they marked a bird down. Tenderly turning back the grass, thinking as the cripple does, whistling softly, sending out some ancient hunter's message until the cripple replies in its wounded voice and the Indian completes the kill.

There is a stark reason for this hunter's skill—survival. The men who guide you today live in what anthropologists term a "survival culture." They live from day to day, making no plans, building no reserves, dependent on game. If the game fails— or if the hunter fails—the Indians starve when winter makes them prisoners in the desolate land. Indeed, the camp you stay at is sponsored by the Province of Ontario in the hope of turning it over to a leader like Moses or Lawrence to run and thus bring jobs and money to the tribe. But sometimes the Indians are deep in the bush, or planes cannot fly, or the Indian is old or hurt or sick.

Suddenly the Indians are calling again. A flock works wearily upwind. They are standing almost still in the gale, sliding sideways. "Shoot now!" Lawrence cries. You blaze away, not bothering to stand. Before they are gone another flock heaves into view, then another. You realize it is the two-thousand-bird flock coming back to their resting spot. They are all flying over you, as the Indians knew they would.

You miss and miss and miss. The birds are high. The lead problem is fantastic. The others are shooting and missing and hollering. Occasionally a bird falls, more often than not a bird other than the one being shot at. "It can't be happening," you think. Unbelievably, you are fumbling for another box of shells, your last.

More birds come over. "Okay," you say to yourself, "I will be calm. I will be scientific." You lead ahead and to the right. No good. You lead just to the right. No better. You glance at Lawrence. He is laughing at you. There is no need for him to call. You shake your head, then you laugh too. Another bunch beats a slow, crabwise path over your head. You fire three times and don't part a feather. One man is out of shells. You pass a handful down.

"I give up," one of your companions cries out. "You try." He hands the gun to Moses. Grinning broadly, Moses blasts away with the rest of you but does no better. (He admits later that if they were his own shells he wouldn't have shot. The lead problem is unsolvable.) A flock goes over. "Shoot now!" Lawrence yells. You leap up and see them over the gun barrel, the size of bees, way out of range. "Waddaya mean, shoot now!" you yell at Lawrence, scandalized. He is bent over with laughter. He holds his stomach at the great joke. You are getting so excited you are ready to shoot at anything. It is a great joke, you decide. You call him something and he laughs the harder. You laugh too, partly at him, partly at yourself.

The action slows down. You have three shells left, the others have three between them. Recalling the hunt later, you mention that the birds were over you for two hours. Your friends hoot. More like twenty minutes, they claim. Only then do you realize how excited you were.

Another flock swings into view. Lawrence calls to them. They aren't any closer or moving any easier than the others. To hell with it, you think, and stand and swing on the last bird. To your infinite surprise, he folds and falls. You pull the gun past the next bird forward and fire, busting him good. A double. Having burned three boxes of shells with maybe three or four geese to show for it, you suddenly get the range. You have a shell left, but you pass it down the line. Moses folds a duck in a fast passing shot and grins from ear to ear.

The Indians are counting the birds. There are twelve geese and as many ducks. Among the three of you you've used up every bit of ammunition. It's never happened before to any of you. You laugh about it, tell each other about this or that shot, while the Indians gather their wing-decoys and load the birds on their backs.

The wind is at your back on the walk home. It blows you back to the camp alongside the dark river that stretches halfway across Canada. There will be goose for dinner in the Indian camp as well as your own. You will sit around after dinner, and Moses and Lawrence and a few Indian pals will join in when drinks get passed around. You'll kid Moses about his "Canaba" geese, and he'll kid you about your shooting.

Then the lantern light starts to fade. You say goodnight and watch the Indians slip away into the darkness, walking flat and fast, slipping over the earth like predatory animals bedding down. Tomorrow will be another hunt.

10

Successful Goose Shooting

Unquestionably, geese pose waterfowling's greatest challenge. The Canada's prowess at matching wits with man is legendary. So highly touted are their reputations that many would-be goose hunters are discouraged before they start. The birds are bigger, so everything else about goose shooting is magnified. More decoys are needed and, being larger, they cost more. Farm land must be bought or leased, and it must be farmed in ways that legally attract the birds. Goose guns must be bigger, and goose blinds better. And goose shooters are a clannish, closed lot. Duck shooting, even on bluebird days, usually provides some kind of action. Anyone contesting the lordly Canada can expect his audacity to be met with failure many times, perhaps more often than not.

It would be specious to pretend that the Canada's reputation is not well deserved. Brand as untrue any suggestion that you can enjoy first-rate goose shooting in prime areas without having to buy your way in. You pay, and the costs are not inconsiderable.

Against these dismal realities must be balanced two encouraging notes. Public hunting areas for geese abound, and for all their wariness, geese have moments of vulnerability. In fact, geese are sometimes easy to fool. They can be surprised. Hungry or tired or threatened with hunger or exposure, they will decoy willingly. Electronic calls of feeding geese so unerringly lead them to their doom that such devices—but not the voice imitations thereof—have been banned. Their astonishing trait is one every refuge pass shooter knows. Under certain conditions geese will throw caution to the winds and, apparently paying no heed to hunters below, will fly at altitudes well within gun ranges, ignoring their fellows peeling out of formation in nose dives.

What applies to Canada geese also goes for other goose species but in lesser, sometimes vastly lesser degrees. The common Canada goose stands at the pinnacle of wisdom and wariness; all other goose species fall in behind. Even the lesser Canada strains are markedly less wary. Blue, snow, and whitefronted geese cannot compare in wariness to the masters, and the brant of both coastlines are at times almost too easy to decoy and kill.

Game in abundance, population buildups, long seasons, increasing bag limits—all these point toward success. There is no reason why any waterfowler can't start orienting himself toward these matchless birds. For, as we'll see, you can become a goose shooter—a Canada goose shooter—without spending an arm and a leg. In fact, all you really need, besides a magnum shotgun, are a few smiles from Lady Luck to surround a few of these sagacious denizens with wild rice and sweet peas on a happily regular basis.

The first, easiest (and most underhanded) way to become a goose shooter is to be in the right place during the opening moments and days of the season. While some geese species fly purposefully to wintering grounds the lordly Canada comes down the flyways in leisurely fashion. Staying just ahead of cold weather, the flocks fan out, taking up residence in farmers' fields, on reservoirs, even in city parks. They will stay as long as there is food, and their habits can be studied and predicted. If they are accustomed to feeding in a certain field on opening day, you can be in that field, concealed in a crude blind with a handful of decoys, and stand a fine chance of getting a crack at the flock.

Those first few days of the season the odds are briefly with the hunters. Young geese are confused by the hunting. Flocks are broken up, the young get separated, and a

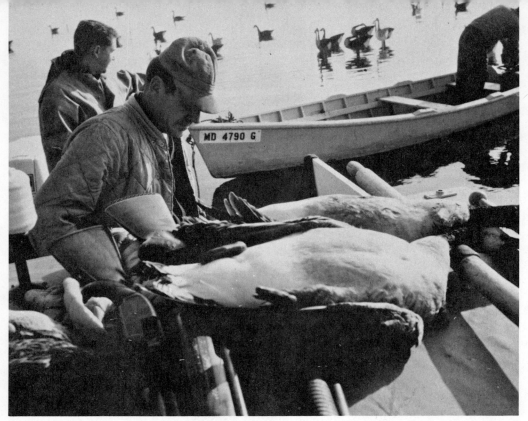

A body booting rig on the Susquehanna flats. You can see it pays off; the boat behind is an old scull boat used to carry extra decoys.

lone bird is extremely susceptible to your decoys or calls. This shooting ends abruptly, but for several days a blind with a reasonable number of decoys — two dozen, say — will produce thrills and chills aplenty and, with any luck, meat on the table.

However, the fun won't last long. Soon after the gunfire begins, flock leaders hightail it to safety. The flock usually picks up and goes — at 1,500 feet at forty miles an hour — until the leaders recognize from long experience the waters and feeding areas of one of the vast waterfowl refuges scattered the length of every flyway. It may be a state refuge or even one of the many private refuges, but more probably it will be one of the federal tracts bought over the years with your duck-stamp money. Once the geese land in the refuge they stay there. This leads to the second salient fact of goose hunting: If you want to shoot geese on any regular and sustained basis, get thee close to a refuge. Federal banding studies on a Missouri refuge indicated that some 84.5 percent of all band returns came from geese shot in the immediate vicinity of a major refuge. Since only major refuges were included in the study, geese killed near smaller state or private refuges probably brought the figure even higher. If you've got a local flock of Canadas in residence on some nearby reservoir (which can happen), consider yourself lucky. You don't have to join the crowd that will be found in, around, and near any refuge holding sizable numbers of geese.

Federal refuges are attracting huge concentrations of geese, "short-stopping" them, in the view of some southern hunters, in areas too far to the north. Various methods for dealing with the problem have been attempted, mostly without success. One thing that emerges from experiments is that the amount of food grown on a refuge has a direct ratio to the surrounding goose kill. If you've got 100,000 birds setting up housekeeping, the food budget will be immense. As soon as the refuge fields are eaten bare, the birds leave and forage in fields in and around the area. This makes them susceptible to your wiles. The more they feed abroad, the more cracks you have at them and the more geese are killed.

This is no place to go into the short-stop controversy, but it should be noted that every refuge manager is performing a tricky balancing act. If he doesn't provide refuge food, the geese tear the hell out of farmers' crops, and the farmers howl. With too much food, the geese don't migrate south or leave the refuge, and hunters are up in arms. If there's too little food on the refuge, the geese are forced out again and again, and overharvesting results. Then the game department clamps the season shut, and everybody howls.

If geese would fly long distances from refuges, as ducks will, it would spread the wealth (but make it harder to hunt them). They don't, however. About twenty miles is usually as far as they'll go to forage. And though geese share the ducks' inclination for morning and afternoon flights (when they can't fly at night), dawn and dusk foraging expeditions are nowhere near as important to geese as to ducks. Geese are more like gentlemen of leisure. They arise late. And they retire early. I was in Easton recently, on the night before goose season opened, and heard the guides telling the parties to be ready at 4:45 A.M. I stepped out of my motel room to be greeted by a fusillade of shots and to see geese everywhere reacting in astonishment that their favorite fields were attacking them. The hour was 8:00 o'clock.

Since in most places you must hunt within range of a refuge, you'll very quickly learn the next major fundamental of successful goose shooting. Every suitable field in and around any major refuge will be locked up tight — posted. And merely asking the farmer's permission will not gain you access. He will have been solicited so often that a positive value will be put on the field. The geese are one of his cash crops, and he'll expect to be paid for allowing blinds on his land. If you've found an exception, consider yourself favored.

What the outsider who can't buy his way into potential goose shooting must do is utilize the public shooting areas that are required by law in and around most refuges. Sometimes blinds are available where decoys can be set out. More commonly, hunters will be assigned positions by means of lottery arrangements.

These positions, some good, some bad, will allow pass shots at the birds as they trade in and out of the refuge.

This pass shooting is mostly luck. It's a matter of luck where you are placed. Chance will decide where the geese fly. It's (partly) luck how high they fly. At the range most shooters try for them, it's something beyond luck when occasionally a bird falls; it's more in the nature of a miracle.

However, under certain conditions you can very much improve your pass-shooting chances. Some days the geese fly low, and some days they don't fly at all during the day, and it is possible to tell with some certainty how they will behave. For example, right now you can tell exactly when you should *not* go goose hunting in the fall of 1980.

Dave Harbour made an exhaustive fifty-six-day study of goose habits on a Colorado refuge. The study documented what experienced goose shooters already knew.

On moonlight nights geese, like ducks, can see well enough to feel safe when flying at night. During the season, most goose species became highly nocturnal in their habits and feed at night, when guns are lawfully silent. They spend the daylight hours within the safe confines of the refuge. How much moonlight is enough to send them flying will depend somewhat on cloud conditions. If it rains, for example, chances are geese won't night-fly even with a full moon. But generally, in planning any waterfowling trip, it is best to utilize the dark-of-the-moon phases—from the last quarter of the old moon to the first quarter of the new.

Harbour documented the times of the flights in the dark-moon periods. Flights out of the refuge generally came from 8:00 to 9:00 A.M. By eleven o'clock or so, the flocks were coming back to the refuge. By 2:30 P.M. flocks began to take off again, and on normal days were back in the refuge by three-thirty or four o'clock.

The Harbour study also revealed a second basic rule of all waterfowling. Always hunt in unusual weather. Snow and rain storms, extreme cold, fog, and high winds all put waterfowl on the move. Let's take a look at each condition and see how geese react to it.

Waterfowl don't like thick fog. They can get lost in it. All waterfowl will, if possible, sit tight until any dense fog clears. (Harbour found ground fog drove the geese up.

A passing shot — and a Canada out of the sky. The range here is about 45 to fifty yards. Note the lack of concealment. When geese are on their way somewhere, they often couldn't care less about hunters below.

A typical big bag of the Quebec north. These are all honkers except for a black duck and either a teal or a wigeon. Notice the Canadian Imperial shells. You take your gun to the north, where everything moves by airplane (except for the train to Moosonee) but buy the shells there.   *Rainier photograph.*

They'd fly to clear weather above the fog.) Most times, though, a day of moderate fog will work for you. The geese may move less, but when they do fly they will probably stay low enough to keep the ground in sight, since they follow landmarks, just like early airplane pilots. Another aspect of fog that's in your favor is that the cottony sky robs geese of their binocularlike eyesight. They may not see you until it's too late. The fog's windless silence can also make them extremely susceptible to calling.

Ice and frozen fields make feeding much more difficult, and the birds will attempt to feed more as the temperature drops.

Hard, driving rain is the worse possible weather for any waterfowling. A mild rain or showers won't bother geese one way or another, but a real pelter very likely makes them stick right where they are, probably because of decreased visibility.

Storms of all kinds, if not too violent, are the best times to hunt ducks and geese. Snow, or the threat of snow, puts the birds on the prowl. Dave Harbour found that on snow days the geese left the refuge early and remained out all day, trading from field to field, eating as much as they could stuff into themselves. If a storm of blizzard proportions with gale winds and above sweeps in, the birds won't attempt to fly. They'll try to feed in advance, then stick to the refuge until things abate. After a long storm with heavy snow, look for the geese to trade, searching for undrifted fields to feed in. Winter frontal storms are excellent gunning times. The ominous dark lines, the thunder, and the snow and hail squalls spook ducks and geese as much as they do humans. In such conditions the birds will fly about, hoping to find sanctuary and security.

Weather in all its forms (the more extreme and unusual the better) is the goose shooter's main weapon. Similarly, those high winds that spell *finis* to most hunting and fishing are great times for goose shooting. The birds will seek shelter and are extremely edgy, often trading a lot. Harbour's study also made it clear that geese fly lower in high winds, probably because wind velocities are lower at ground level than higher up.

If the geese are trading, your chances of decoying them are obviously better. And weather aids the pass shooter too. At certain times Canadas almost totally abandon their wariness. They are headed where they are headed, and getting there occupies their minds totally. They will react to hunters only by flying over them faster. If you anticipate bad weather conditions and luck out on days like these, you'll score consistently higher than hunters who take whatever weather comes.

Although pass shooting is probably the commonest form of goose shooting, it is by no means the only way. The crudest method is to bushwhack them. It is highly effective. Locate a flock in a field and stalk them Indian style. You'll need a rise or some other concealment between you and the honkers. At least one bird will be posted as sentinel at all times. You can spot the sentinel because his long neck will be extended. And being as smart as they are, geese don't settle in very close to cover from which danger can spring. The accepted bushwhacking technique is to crawl as close as possible, leap to your feet, and race toward the flock. It takes Canadas a moment to get going, and a short sprint can slice a few yards off the range before you deliver your broadside. Under these conditions, geese would be easy to kill with a rifle but federal law prohibits this.

Shooting geese over decoys is the most exciting method. The spectacle of a flock of geese setting their wings and pitching down into a field is one of the wonders of nature. The birds are so graceful and dignified as they curve their wings and parachute to earth. When the hunting dimension is added to this, the thrill is supreme. Here they come to *your* decoys. *You* have outsmarted them. Soon they will be in range. It is unquestionably waterfowling's finest hour. Even the lesser geese, the blues and snows and brant, make an impressive sight as they turn majestically into the wind and settle down on your blocks.

All that has gone before applies as much to the field shooter as to the pass shooter. You'll hunt the refuges in bad weather if possible. You don't want large flock concentrations. If 25,000 geese are feeding in a field two miles from your blind, what chance do your handful of decoys have?

Guides at Remington Farms, a goose shooter's Valhalla on Maryland's Eastern Shore, have put out as many as five hundred decoys in an attempt to influence part of the estimated 25,000 Canadas that winter on the farm. Forget it. Neither calls nor decoys worked. The geese ignored them. The only ruse that pulled them out of the sky was electronic tapes of geese gurgling over feed. These they found to be deadly. They are illegal, however.

Weather tends to break down the size of the flocks, and the smaller the flock the more easily the geese can be charmed by your spread.

Although commercial guides sometimes set out from four hundred to eight hundred decoys, consider what they are attempting to do. They are trying to lure the smartest waterfowl known *again and again* into the same trap. Even then, they will shift locations if possible, usually gunning one field for several days, then shifting to another.

The individual shooter has no such problems. I have a week of early season Canada-goose shooting. At least 99.5 percent of the geese fly past me as though my spread isn't there. I have a crack at the remaining half percent, and on a few occasions I could have killed my limit several times over. My Canada spread consists of fifteen full-bodied land decoys and six water decoys. I arrange them to look as though the flock has landed on the water (which is what they would do on a coastal marsh) and some have strolled ashore to graze. I hunt afternoons every day, usually in beautiful November weather, unfortunately, and consider myself fortunate to kill geese on two days out of the six-day open season.

If I set 150 decoys, I'd undoubtedly kill more geese but not many more, I think. I get a chance only with migrating flocks that are tired or hungry enough to want to sit down at that particular moment. My spread gives them an excuse. It's a one in a thousand proposition. I score once in a while because many thousands of birds are looking me over.

If I had a season-long crack at geese I'd spring for sixty to eighty decoys, mixing full bodies with silhouettes. Decoying blues, snows, and whitefronts is easier. These birds aren't as wary, and the white shows well. Silhouettes are so easy to make out of plywood painted flat white that a good spread is little trouble to assemble. But newspapers, pieces of white bed sheets, Clorox bottles, and wings stuck in sod clumps with paper-cup heads all serve as decoys for these species. On coastal brant I formerly set a dozen decoys but found I could reduce the number to eight. (I painted the extras as Canadas.) Many, many times flocks of 75 to 150 brant have decoyed to those eight decoys.

Everything said about hunting ducks from a blind applies also to Canada geese, only more so. There must be no motion, no visible faces, raw earth, nor spent shells. Calling is of infinitely more importance where geese are concerned than it is with most ducks. All geese are highly tuned to the calls of others. I can damn near stop a brant in the sky with a call. I can call them with just my voice but prefer using a regular goose call. I gurgle a rolling-*r whrup* in the beginning, then at the end of a rising pitch I do more blowing than gurgling to finish with a slight bugle. The sound is something like an Indian war whoop.

For Canadas I use the regular calls. I can do several and fiddle around until I find a nice middle-range tone. Then I call as loud as I can to every flock I see. If I am with a knowledgeable partner, both of us call, loudly and often, repeating the familiar *huuuuuuroooonk* again and again. I start it low and make the bugle ring. I'll call as soon as the birds are close enough to have any chance of hearing, aiming the call at them and calling at the top of my lungs. Then, as the geese get close, I'll call more

A James Bay blue goose is about to join his ancestors. The range is about 55 yards, well within the shooting capability of the 12-gauge over and under.

Up on the tundra, showing off a snow goose. You can see the 1100 with polychoke. This is also the coat with the edible buttons. Eveyone asks me how you eat the buttons; I suppose you boil them in water—but I really don't know. I can't imagine how I mustered a smile. My borrowed boots were about three sizes too small.

softly and less often, aiming the call at my feet to disguise the location of the sound as the birds decoy.

Although it is true that many commercial goose guides do not use the call at all, or use it very little, I think that every goose shooter should practice with a call and use it in the field. Even pass shooters can sometimes lure birds closer to their station by judicious calling. Juveniles are extremely susceptible, and all geese are so gregarious that even the old ganders will listen, probably to scoff at our amateur attempts, but they listen!

Certainly the commonest goose-shooting error, after not keeping still, is shooting before the birds are within killable distance. The fact that they are so much larger than ducks throws everyone's judgment off. Also, their slow glide to decoys sometimes becomes too exciting to bear, and you leap to your feet and slam away.

An old adage says that you can't kill a Canada unless you can see its eye. If you can see the eye, take him. Beyond that range, hold fire and hope the next bunch comes over closer. In the chapter on guns we'll discuss some long-range techniques. If you use these, you'll never see the bird's eye, but if you do go to these extremes, you should have enough experience to estimate ranges with accuracy.

11

Boat Designs

I once made a major duckboat survey. Every Saturday for a whole season I parked beside a tollbooth on a popular highway that leads to gunning areas in my state and observed what kinds of boats hunters were teaming up with in their attack on the waterfowl. The results of the study were astonishing. Any kind of boat you could possibly conceive of — and some you couldn't — was in service as a duckboat. There were many sneakboxes and little johnboats expressly designed for waterfowl work, of course, but what surprised me were the other kinds of craft pressed into service. Canoes! Inflatables! Sailboats! All manner of punts and prams. Then there were the nonboats. These were things that probably floated but were so weird in shape or building material that they couldn't be dignified by being called a real boat. Besides the diversity, another thing that impressed me was the number of relatively large boats. I saw plenty of twelve- and fourteen-foot aluminums being used, and there were many outboard runabouts in the fourteen- to sixteen-foot class, some painted like duckboats, may left in their summer colors. Some of these bigger boats were obviously used only to haul hunters to and from hunting areas, but others appeared to be used as hunting boats as well. These varied in how expertly they were disguised. Just the other day I received some photographs from a Long Island gunner who has camouflaged his thirteen-foot Boston Whaler so well that it is, in effect, a portable blind. Two men sit on the bottom, facing the side. The boat is beautifully grassed over the deck, with the ends of the grass coming down low to the water to conceal the sides. With a really good job like this you can fool even the wary three at times.

Double-duty duckboats like this are great. Certainly I've put many such vessels to work. I had a little seven-foot pram that I used as a tender on my bugeye in the off-season and took, suitably painted, to the marsh in season. I've spoken of my sneakbox. In summer she sported a sail, and I could have raced her if I'd wanted to. My beloved stool boat I found abandoned and dredged it out of the river. It was sunk, holed, and had a double bottom and huge oak stringers where an inboard engine had been installed. "You'll never be able to make that old tub float," my partner said with disgust. I sawed the stringers into pieces to make the frame for a decoy box, patched the holes, removed the double bottom and fiber-glassed the original cedar bottom. We used the boat hard for a dozen years. Never once did I fail to cheerily remind him of his prediction that it would never float again. Summers I used it offshore, fishing for blues and stripers. (I finally wrecked the boat by running it up on the spikes of an old sunken barge. Some boating expert!)

Many of the vessels of my survey must have been desperation duckboats. A canoe has no place on a duck marsh. It would do for a creek float, sure, but in the open water of the coast it would be dangerous, unwieldy, almost totally unsuited. The guys using one did so because they couldn't or wouldn't spend the $250 to $300 necessary to build or buy a real duckboat. They were probably like many waterfowlers, casual adherents in nice weather. When people gun is their business, of course, but they are never going to reach waterfowls' Hall of Fame with this approach. The modern waterfowler needs a boat—the right kind of boat. Before we get into exactly what that is, let's discuss some overall types—live-aboard boats, access craft, and actual hunting boats.

Living-Aboard Boats are relatively rare nowadays. When I was a boy every marsh was dotted with little houseboats, and before my time the practice was even more prevalent. Every waterfowler worth the name had his houseboat tucked up some creek or thoroughfare. He'd hole up in the ducking area for days at a time. When modern houseboats made their appearance I thought more guys would use them for waterfowling headquarters. After all, it's a great experience to live in waterfowl country. The sounds of the night are a thrilling blend of wingbeats, calls, and cries. You can sleep later and still be in the blind before daylight. And it's pleasant to be

With a big 25 hp outboard on it, the Zackbox gets me to the blind fast and can carry three men and gear without trouble. I must have been gunning out of the boat and thrown some grass on the deck for camouflage.

able to head back to the nearby boat, and warmth and coziness, a cup of coffee or a bowl of hot soup. But a houseboat is expensive and poses troubles and problems. The first December storms often approach hurricane strength, and towing a houseboat is a tedious job. Nonetheless, plenty of duck hunters used to consider the rewards justified the bother.

Probably the best way to procure a headquarters like this would be to shop for a used houseboat. In outboard versions they are comparatively reasonable. Or you might find one whose engines and outdrive are shot. You can rip out the engine and glass over the outdrive opening if you wanted to use the boat strictly for waterfowling. A relatively small outboard, a nine-and-a-half-horsepower motor on a twelve-foot aluminum, say, will tow a big houseboat at five to seven miles an hour. If you look for an older boat, and plan to use it in salt water, steer clear of steel hulls. Fiber glass or aluminum will stand up better.

Another kind of live-aboard boat might be considered. It's called a cabin johnboat and would have wide application in many parts of the country where someone wanted a headquarters on the water at a reasonable price.

For a while I used this little Grumman Cartopper for an access boat. It was twelve feet long and only weighed 97 pounds. I was shooting the pump in those days.

The boats, the dawns, the rippling waters, and the sunsets form as much a part of the romance of waterfowling as the hunt itself.

Access Boats. In some places you can drive or walk to where you want to gun, but more often than not, if you want to get out beyond the crowd, you must travel some distance. Almost any kind of a boat will do as an access boat, since you will be parking it far enough from the shooting area so it won't scare the ducks. The little aluminums are fine. They don't draw much water and are light enough to be slid over mud flats or sandbars if need be.

There are plenty of boats that do double duty as both access boats and hunting boats. The most improbable I ever heard about was a twenty-four-foot Bertram that a guy camouflaged with burlap nets. He shot broadbills in Long Island Sound from it. I think it might work, especially if you got the boat among some rocks or against an island where the background would soften the bulky silhouette. We've already seen that the thirteen-foot Boston Whaler can be made into a gunning barge. Its sides are relatively low, and camouflaging the boat doesn't hamper its ability to run to shooting areas. You can drape a camouflage net around a little aluminum, a canoe, or a pram and sprinkle some grass around to help slide the boat up a gut, guzzle, or ditch.

Hunting Boats. There are all sorts of specialty craft designed for hunting. Some of these, such as the sneakbox, can also be considered access boats. Others, such as the coffin box, are strictly to be towed to your spot at the beginning of the season and towed out when the season closes. I am partial to these little specialty craft. They are the modern equivalent of the market men's gear of old—part of the color of the sport.

The Perfect Duckboat. There are all sorts of places and all sorts of ways to shoot ducks and geese, and I don't know all of them. But I think that a boat that gets you to the shooting grounds and hides you when there (while holding the elements at bay) is essential to today's waterfowling. The perfect duck-hunting boat should meet the following requirements:

A full deck with a hatch to cover the cockpit is essential for several reasons. First, you can leave the boat out and not worry about snow or rain filling it. Second, the hatch can be locked to protect stored decoys from theft. Third, a deck makes the boat more seaworthy. With a canvas shield forward, like that on sneakboxes, and a three-inch cockpit coaming you can take bad seas over the bow or stern and still survive. Fourth, a deck keeps you warm and dry. A fully decked boat with a small heater in the bow or under the transom you can gun really severe weather in comfort.

ZT and the Zackbox at work. The forward hatch is for decoys. You can see my anchor rig on the bow. This is the little gut out of which all the water ran.

This is how you can utilize a slot and gun. The Zackbox that I'm in here is a fairly large boat. When the tide sinks down enough so the far bank hides the boat hull, I can gun right out of it. Tall grass on the right hides me from that angle.

The old-timers stuck a square of painted canvas in under the afterdeck, to serve as a blanket and rain shield in bad weather. One of the most severe days I ever gunned was weathered in a coffin box. The wind was blowing a steady forty miles an hour and gusting to fifty, and the temperature was between ten and twenty degrees. It was a nice sunny day but a real socker with the wind-chill factor down in the storm cellar. We punched No. 10 tin cans around the bottom, set them on old license plates, charged them with charcoal, and stayed as cozy as anything. Talk about weather making ducks seek security! If I'd put a black-duck decoy on my head, they would have pitched in to my shoulders.

You lie out flat in a boat. Sitting up with your elbows on the deck is comfortable and lets you see a long way, but when the wings start whistling overhead you must withdraw into your shell, hat low over your eyes and only the tip of your nose showing.

Every effort should be made to keep the perfect duckboat light. Weight should not exceed 150 pounds for a one-man boat. You want the weight light enough so you can drag the boat to good hides.

Trailerability is a must. If you gun with others, it is not too hard to rig racks so that two or three one-man boats can be trailed. Some trail one boat and cartop another.

There are two reasons why your duckboat should be equipped with oars. First, it is easy to set and pick up decoys when you can row. Second, that night when the motor doesn't start. . . .

The boat's profile should be as low as possible. This means keeping the sides low and curving the deck. This last is important, as the slope of the sides throws the grass out and down, to further hide the hull.

The color must be drab. Most waterfowlers paint the boat light brown with flat paint—so-called duckboat brown—but I have seen boats painted dark brown (almost black), gray, and (for gunning in ice) white. If you gun around ice, you can use the scullboater's trick of putting sheets on the boat and throwing water on them to freeze in place. State numbering requirements pose problems. To be legal most places, numbers and yearly stickers have to show and be permanently attached. The only thing you can do is to mount them as required and conceal them with burlap strips when gunning. If you feel artistic, add camouflage spots made up by mixing darker and lighter paint. This is as good a place as any to go into the "to grass or not to grass" argument. I think any boat or blind is better grassed up, but plenty of guys don't bother. They let the duckboat drown go it along, and the ducks usually don't seem to mind.

The perfect duckboat should be able to go through ice without damage. Aluminum and fiber glass boats are unharmed by any kind of ice, but wood boats must be protected at the waterline. If you use sheets of wood, they must be replaced as ice chews them away. It's best to use sheets of galvanized steel tacked above the waterline so as to glaze the water or skim just below it. Probably the best thing to do, if you adapt or build a wood boat, is to fiber-glass the bottom and bring the glass six inches or so up the sides. The fiber glass protects the wood from ice and eliminates the possibility of leaks.

Now none of these things says anything about hull form. The old sneakboxes and their cousins, the Long Island scooters, were round-bottomed displacement hulls. They rowed beautifully and could be sailed, but they wouldn't go fast—six to seven miles an hour tops. You'll want a boat that will plane, and the simplest planing bottom is a flat bottom, and since this is also good for shallow water and for sliding over the mud and grass, this is the best duckboat hull. (My sneakbox has a round bottom flattened to plane aft, but don't ask me where to buy one like it. A fire put the company that built it out of business.) This flat-bottomed planing hull will be cranky to row but (hopefully) all you'll need the oars for is decoy work.

A project I started (and never finished) was to take a twelve-foot wood-and-canvas runabout and create a masterpiece to meet the highest duckboat requirements. I stripped the canvas, refastened the tacks, and sawed the sides to lower the profile. Decked and fiber-glassed, it would have been a great duckboat, as it was so light. You could take the seats out of a little aluminum boat and saw down the sides with a hacksaw blade in a saber saw, then bolt a wood stringer along the edge to create a new gunwale. Wood keying should be built into this gunwale. Make the deck carlings strong, as you will take a lot of lateral strength out of her when you remove the seats. Although you would probably build any of the following designs out of plywood, because it's the easiest material to work with, a plan I've thought about would be to find a light twelve- to fourteen-foot rowboat, then remove the thwarts, lower the sides, and add the deck. This saves all the work of building a hull. The trouble with this scheme is that the rowboat would probably be painted and you'd have to sand the paint off to fiber-glass it for ice work or use expensive epoxy resin.

CABIN JOHNBOAT

This boat may be the ugly duckling of the boating world, but it turns into a swan when you go into the cabin. Inside it's a mansion! Here you'll find honestly livable quarters that two husky men can occupy over an extended period of time. That's not the only time the swanlike beauty appears. When you look at the vessel's price tag you'll feel as comfortable as you will in her heated cabin on a chill night. She's cheap. For years this kind of boat was always the least expensive and most livable design for the money. It still is.

A boat like this could take me to my duck blind before daybreak. Then I'd gun until midmorning when things slow down. About this time, I'd want a second breakfast. I'd go back to the boat, cook up a storm, then stretch out for a snooze. About 2:00 or 3:00 P.M. I'd be back in the blind. If I felt like it, and things looked good, I would pull her into a creek, anchor fore and aft, and spend the night.

I call this boat a gunning garvey. A garvey is like a johnboat but with a little more grace. It's basically a wall-sided, flat-bottom vessel with a sled bow—the cheapest kind of vessel to build in 1875 or 1975. The old baymen would build a house on their garveys big enough to live in for the duck season. Along the Mississippi and the southern waterways of the country it would be called a cabin johnboat.

There are plenty of cabin boats around, to be sure, but few have space for spending a night or two, to say nothing of permanent living aboard. For this you need headroom, a really decent place to cook and eat, and bunks long and wide enough to allow some tossing and turning. All these things are designed into the ugly duckling.

You can't buy this houseboat today as she sits. The boats that come closest to it are the cabin johnboats offered by Monark, Polar Craft, and others. In the twenty-foot versions, they sell at around $900 without power. I'd estimate the basic boat shell of this houseboat could be sold for perhaps half as much. I've built the boat so you can use the largest johnboat in production as a stock model. She's twenty-six feet, built by Ouachita, and costs about $750 for the beefed-up commercial hull that you'd want for this boat. If you're willing to do without some cockpit space and/or the dinette-heater area, you could easily build the boat on the twenty-foot commercial hull that almost all johnboat firms offer at a cost of about $600.

If you start with one of these hulls and build the design as you see it out of plywood,

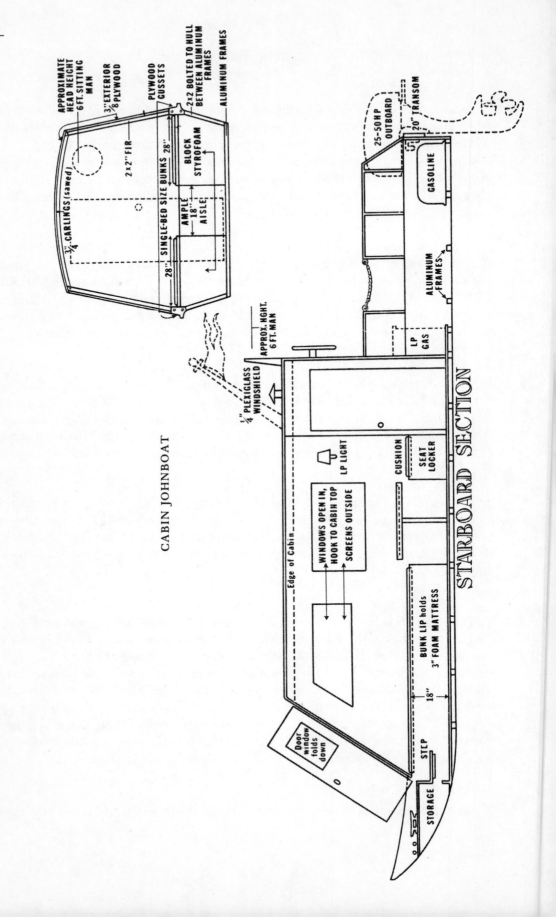

CABIN JOHNBOAT

APPROXIMATE HEAD HEIGHT 6 FT. SITTING MAN

$\frac{3}{8}$" EXTERIOR PLYWOOD

2 x 2" FIR

$\frac{3}{4}$ CARLINGS (sawed)

PLYWOOD GUSSETS

2 x 2 BOLTED TO HULL BETWEEN ALUMINUM FRAMES

ALUMINUM FRAMES

SINGLE-BED SIZE BUNKS 28"

BLOCK STYROFOAM

28"

AMPLE 18" AISLE

APPROX. HGHT. 6 FT. MAN

$\frac{1}{4}$" PLEXIGLASS WINDSHIELD

25-50 HP OUTBOARD

20" TRANSOM

GASOLINE

ALUMINUM FRAMES

LP GAS

Edge of Cabin

WINDOWS OPEN IN, HOOK TO CABIN TOP SCREENS OUTSIDE

LP LIGHT

CUSHION

SEAT LOCKER

Door window folds down

BUNK LIP holds 3" FOAM MATTRESS

18"

STEP

STORAGE

STARBOARD SECTION

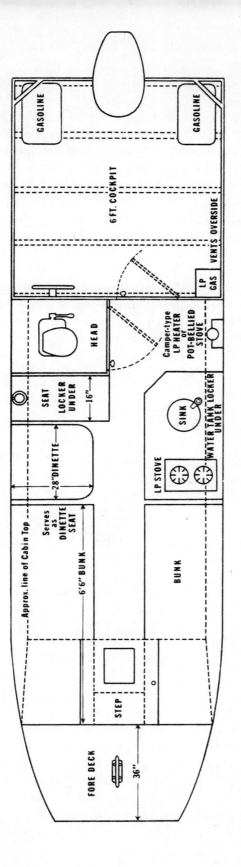

I see no reason why, with some judicious purchasing, you couldn't have it, with all equipment mentioned, including power, for less than $3,000. And at that price it will be neither a toy nor a poor performer. In fact, it will be fast. The eighteen-foot aluminum-cabin johnboat has been clocked at 22.7 miles per hour driven by a Merc 35. A 50 drives her at 30.9 with four on board. I'd expect this boat, as designed, to plane with a 25 horsepower at 10 to 12 miles per hour, reach 15-18 miles per hour with a 33 horsepower and hit 25 miles per hour or more with a 50-55 horsepower. Prices on these motors are $510, $650, and $1,000. Although the boat is clumsy-looking and will be subject to windage problems, the flat johnboat hull is stable, and the weight of the cabin will sink the hull only an inch or two.

There should be no skimping on the size of things if you are to be comfortable aboard a boat. A seat less than 15 inches high will cramp your legs after a while. A bunk should be 28 inches wide and 6 feet 3 inches long or you won't rest easy. This boat has what is called sitting headroom. You go into the cabin and sit down, and things are arranged so you can cook, wash, etc., from a sitting position without moving around. And with almost five feet of headroom, you don't have to crawl on your knees when you do move around.

The cabin johnboat has no frills, no fancy stuff, but it is comfortable and livable for long periods and in all weather. Maintenance is at a minimum, enjoyment is maximum.

HOW TO BUILD A CABIN JOHNBOAT

Until some manufacturer starts offering at least a shell of these boats in all-aluminum, the only way you can get one is to build it yourself. But don't suppose that you can build the hull more cheaply than you can buy an aluminum hull. By the time you fiber-glass it, the cost will be as great as the commercial aluminum — not counting the time involved. And the wood hull is inferior to the nonrotting aluminum.

What you'll have to do is go to a dealer for one of the companies or write them directly and order the hull. Few dealers will stock 20- and 22-footers anyway. You'll want a commercial model because they're slightly more rugged. Order it without seats but with a net deck, that is, a forward deck that slopes toward the bow and contains scuppers (holes) to drain water over the side. This will be your forward deck. The hull will weigh 450-475 pounds. Transom is 20 inches.

It would be preferable to build the boat with side decks, but the beam of the stock boats—76 inches—doesn't permit this and still enable you to build 28-inch bunks and leave enough space to comfortably traverse the aisle between. If you were starting the boat from scratch, you could give the hull more freeboard and slightly more beam and carry the sheer of the forward deck up higher. With side decks she'd be handsome, but the stock hull will more than suffice.

Bolt 2 X 2-inch fir stringers about twelve inches long to the hull sides between every frame and at each end of the cabin. Use 1/4- or 3/16-inch stainless-steel bolts and washers for this. Any other material will corrode the aluminum. For other fastenings, galvanized iron is okay. Then add the uprights. You can make them straight, but angling them in as shown improves appearance without robbing usable space. The uprights butt to the frames and are held securely with plywood gussets on each side. Fasten these temporarily with galvanized screws. When everything is fair, remove and glue with Weldwood glue at temperatures above seventy degrees.

To attain a pleasing curve, saw the cabin carlings, drawing the curve with a long, bendy batten. Use 3/4-inch spruce, sweet pine, or fir for the carlings. Smooth and round the underneaths so it won't hurt so much when you crack your head on them. Bolt carlings to the ends of the uprights.

Plank the cabin sides and top with 3/8-inch exterior plywood screwed and glued to uprights and carlings. Use 2 X 2-inch stock at corners. Cut windows, build doors.

The cabin entrance hatch does not show on the plans. The best way to build this is directly in the center of the cabin. Make it a large hatch. This prevents a full windshield unless you want to get tricky and build a windshield that the hatch can slide under. The generous hatch allows you to slide it back and give headroom in the aftercabin area. It makes a nice place to stand in, leaning on the cabintop, thinking uplifting thoughts.

When the cabin is complete, fiber-glass all edges using Dynel, which can be tacked in place and the resin painted on afterward.

Cabin Sole

Most aluminum johnboat hulls are framed with 2 X 2-inch aluminum frames. They aren't pleasant to walk on but are tolerable in the cockpit. The cabin sole (floor)

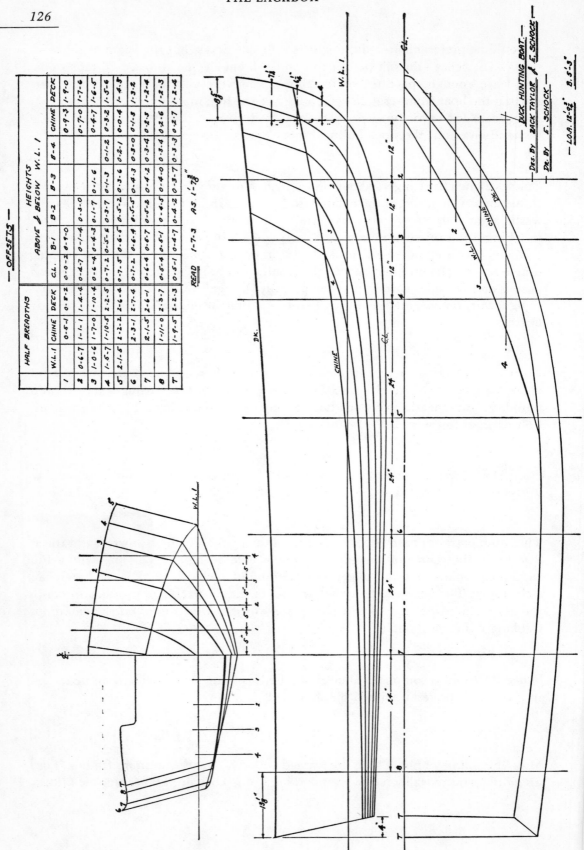

— OFFSETS —

	HALF BREADTHS			HEIGHTS ABOVE & BELOW W.L.1					
W.L.1	CHINE	DECK	C.L.	B-1	B-2	B-3	B-4	CHINE	DECK
1		0-5-1	0-8-2	0-0-2	0-9-0				0-9-3	1-9-0
2	0-6-7	1-1-1	1-4-4	0-4-7	0-1-4	0-3-0			0-7-0	1-7-6
3	1-0-6	1-7-0	1-10-4	0-6-4	0-4-3	0-1-7	0-1-6		0-4-7	1-6-5
4	1-5-7	1-10-5	1-2-5	0-7-2	0-5-6	0-3-7	0-1-3		0-3-2	1-5-6
5	2-1-6	1-2-2-1	1-6-4	0-7-5	0-6-6	0-5-2	0-3-6	0-1-2	0-0-4	1-4-5
6	2-3-1	1-2-6-4	1-7-4	0-7-1	0-6-4	0-5-5	0-4-3	0-2-1	0-0-3	1-3-2
7	2-1-5	1-6-1	0-6-4	0-6-7	0-5-8	0-4-2	0-3-0	0-1-3	1-2-4
8	1-11-0	2-3-7	0-5-4	0-5-1	0-4-5	0-4-0	0-3-4	0-2-3	1-2-3
T	1-9-5	2-2-3	0-5-1	0-4-7	0-4-2	0-3-7	0-3-0	0-2-7	1-2-4

READ 1-7-3 AS 1-7⅜"

— DUCK HUNTING BOAT —
— Des. By ZACK TAYLOR & E. SCHOCK —
— Dr. By E. SCHOCK —
— L.O.A. 12'-2½"   B. 5'-3" —

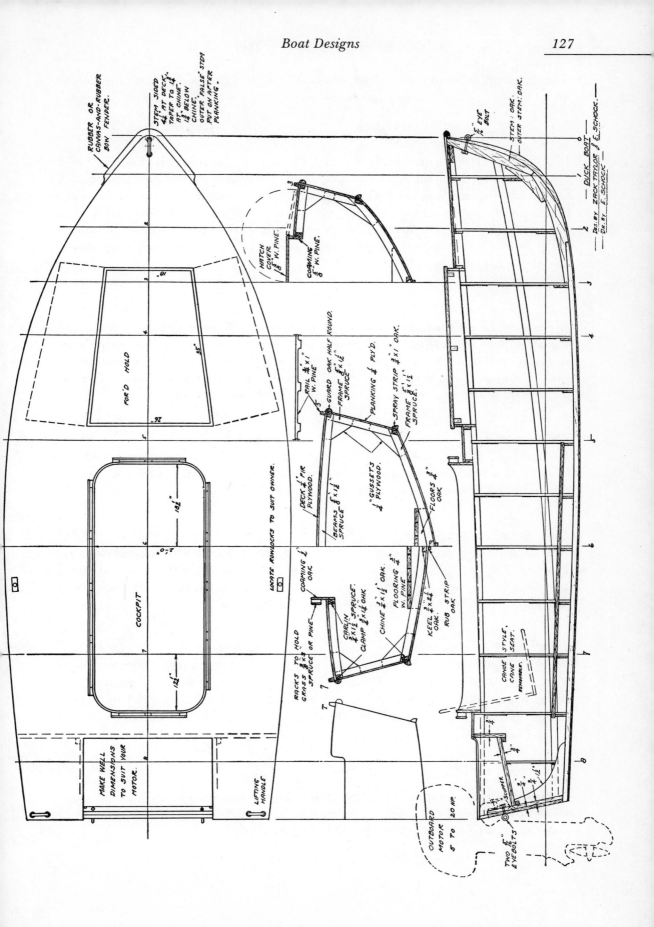

should be covered with plywood laid on the frames. This is not only comfortable but keeps things dry if water gets into the boat.

Flotation

Johnboats are made with Styrofoam-block flotation under the seats. You can build flotation in under the bunks as shown or leave it out and use the area for storage. Coast of Styrofoam to float 1,600 pounds, ample for this boat, is about one hundred dollars, and there is room for it. I'd be inclined to leave it out. Most fiber glass cruisers do. But I'd have plenty of life preservers around. It is a good idea to build a watertight bulkhead at the end of the cabin as high as you'd care to step over. Bunks are plywood with 3-inch foam with vinyl covers.

Doors and Windows

If you are going to use the boat in hot weather, you'll want good-size doors and windows. If you plan to use it in cold weather, cut down on size or storm-strip them. Actually, with today's trailer heaters, you could heat any cabin. I'd be inclined to make her as light and bright as I could. I'd heat her with an LP gas trailer heater or a catalytic heater or two. No carbon-monoxide danger with catalytics.

Head

No problem with the head. You can use several kinds, including a bucket. (Always works.) If a marine head is used, remember to bolt it with stainless bolts. Use neoprene seals to prevent weeping.

Sink, Stove, Icebox

Any LP stove is great—inexpensive, safe, and plenty hot. Self-contained sinks are available. Water is such a convenience you shouldn't do without it. I'd use a portable icebox on a platform high enough to drain over the side. They are cheap and good. A locker under the sink might work for this.

Lighting

Good LP lights are available through trailer-supply houses. Also there are many battery-powered lamps. If you plan to use an electric-start outboard motor, your battery can probably handle cabin lighting demands, if supplemented by battery lamps. If you use too much juice, there is no problem, as the outboard can be started manually.

Canvas Top

A canvas top for sun and rain protection turns the cockpit area into living space. Glass for large windows should be safety glass or Plexiglas. The cockpit rail can be omitted if you don't mind the risk of falling overboard.

Calling All Manufacturers

What's really needed is for some manufacturer to build this boat using aluminum throughout, caring not one whit about appearance or style and keeping everything as simple and inexpensive as possible. Even if he offered only the shell, it wouldn't be difficult to fabricate the interior, and the aluminum sides and top would be stronger, lighter, and cheaper. I'll take the first one, paint her duckboat brown, and name her the *Black Duck*. Then just try to reach me on the telephone when the ducks are flying or the fish are running.

THE ZACKBOX

Right up to the time manufacturers began turning out high-horsepower outboards that were cheap, light, and utterly dependable, the Barnegat sneakbox was the grandest duck-hunting machine ever made. I'll admit it is downright uppity, even for a know-it-all boating editor, to knock a boat that did its job so perfectly for 138 years. But the truth is, the critter is obsolete.

What is sorely wanting is a blend of the old and new. Today's duck hunter needs the planing hull of the runabout, and he is cheerfully willing to sacrifice the sneakbox's sailing and rowing ability to get it. Yet who wants to sacrifice the unique and wholly magnificent features that made sneakboxes the finest duckboats ever?

The Zackbox can do everything essential the boats of old could do, and it adds a wrinkle or two of its own. The boat you see here was a three-man effort. Edson Schock designed the hull, I specified the lethal (to ducks) features, and Zack McClendon, president of Monark Boats, built her. (He calls it a Zackbox, incidentally.) Several seasons' hard use has convinced me it is a sweetheart. One old-timer looked my boat over sagely, frowned, thumped the aluminum hull, ran his hand over the 9½-hp Johnson with mouth turned down, and grunted at the sight of the decoy compartment. I expected the worst, but he turned to me beaming. "That's a neat little rig," he said. It sure is.

The Zackbox is a complicated craft that deserves proper boatbuilding techniques. The plans here show all the information you need. The section on how to build a sailboat will teach you how to take off the Table of Offsets (if the process isn't evident)· and the lines should be lofted. The scullboat section also describes that process in detail.

PLYWOOD SNEAKBOX

The traditional sneakbox is a hard boat to build, probably beyond the scope of an amateur. You have to steam-bend oak frames and fit each plank. Plywood construction is much simpler. Yet you can't duplicate the box's lovely roundness with plywood, as the material bends only one way. Years ago when I worked as an associate editor for *Sports Afield* my days were enlivened when Harry Megargee, a fellow Jersey waterfowler, would drop in my office and soon birds were falling all over the place. Mr. Megargee was by then retired and pursuing his hobby of designing and building little boats strictly as a labor of love. We put out a *Boatbuilding Annual* in those days, and this was a convenient outlet for his talents. His assignment was to design a boat for plywood building that retained all the virtues of a traditional box. This was the marvelous result.

The Wigeon is not a true sneakbox, for old baymen will tell you that these boats should have "clean-swept chines," meaning that the bottom and crowned deck timbers as well as the curve of the chine are all arcs of circles. Our boat is a modified sneakbox with dead-rise sides and a V bottom. It is designed for simplicity of construction with plywood, which cannot be bent into the compound curves inherent in a true sneakbox.

Because it employs plywood, which requires careful alignment, the plan calls for "setting up" substantial 2″ X 4″ stringers on which molds are located. The boat is built bottom up and then turned over to construct the deck.

The setup plan has legs at a convenient height from the floor, but if you have a substantial pair of horses, the legs may be dispensed with. By all means, build the setup form accurately and make sure that it is square at the four corners before nailing the diagonal crossbraces. Note that the stern transom and the bow assembly are the only pieces in the setup that remain in the finished boat. Lay off the indicated distances for each mold and nail the mold braces in place to receive them. The molds are cut from second 1″ planks such as 7″ wide shelving. Be sure, however, that the lumber selected for both molds and setup stringers is not warped, for your success depends upon these forms being accurately sized, aligned, and placed. Fasten molds to the mold braces with screws so that they may be easily removed at the proper time.

Note on the plans that the line where the side planks and deck meet (the deck line) is a straight line running fore and aft. Always keep this in mind, as it is an essential reference line. At the deckline, cut notches in each mold that will take 7/8″ X 1″

strips extending from bow to stern on both sides. These must form a straight line, and if they do not, molds must be corrected. When the side planks are in position, these strips are used to scribe the deckline on the planks.

Note that the angle the sides make with the vertical is the same for all the molds and for the stern transom as well. It is a diagonal in the ratio of 1:4. I suggest that you make a very accurate pattern cut at this angle to be used in making all molds. For convenience in attaching clamps to hold side planks, nail a 1″ X 1″ batten to the end of each mold.

A stern transom is formed from 7/8″ spruce or pine. At the deck, its curvature is the arc of a circle whose diameter is 4′9″. To draw this and other curves, make your own beam compass from a 1″ X 1/2″ batten, 5′ long, with a pencil stub set in one end and a brad driven in as a pivot at the proper radial distance.

Having laid this arc off and drawn the cord, which is 35″, draw the side angles with your 1:4 pattern. The angle of the V bottom is 1½:8, and this should be laid off directly on the transom, as indicated on the detail plan. After the transom has been shaped, glue and screw pieces of 1″ X 1″ oak flush along the ends, and also the 1″ X 1″ X 6″ oak strip to which the keel is fastened so that the keel will be flush with the transom. Like the molds, the transom is set at a right angle to the setup stringers and is temporarily fastened to the braces with screws.

Bow assembly is shown in precise detail on the plan. Rough out the nosepieces, but leave out final shape-up until ribs and deck frames are in place, after which you can determine with a straightedge just how much trimming is needed. Temporarily screw bow assembly to the setup form, making sure that it is properly aligned. Now you are ready to start actual construction. You will need two 3/4″ side planks, 8″ wide and 12′ long. My preference would be white cedar boat boards, but clear spruce or pine is good. Start by clamping the planks at the stern by applying pressure at the opposite end with a rope tourniquet. Proceeding from the stern, clamp both planks to opposite sides of each mold. As you go toward the bow, spring the boards gradually with the tourniquet until they are flush with the bow assembly. In this way you will avoid unequal pressure that might pull your molds slightly out of line. Now clamp 1″ X ½″ battens 12′ long along the molds at the chine lines, and draw these lines on the side planks. Scribe the decklines as indicated above. Saw the planks to shape, allowing at least 1/8″ top and bottom to be planed down. The planks should be identical. Now clamp them together and plane down to exact size. Reclamp them to the molds, using the same procedure outlined above. At the stern the planks are permanently glued and screwed to the transom, and at the bow, glued and bolted to the assembly.

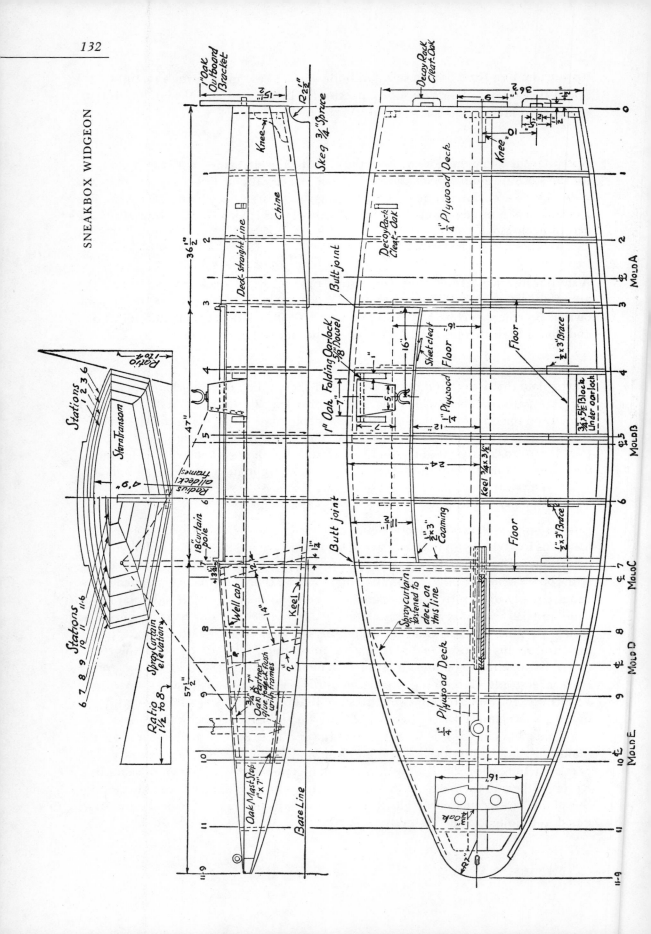

SNEAKBOX WIDGEON

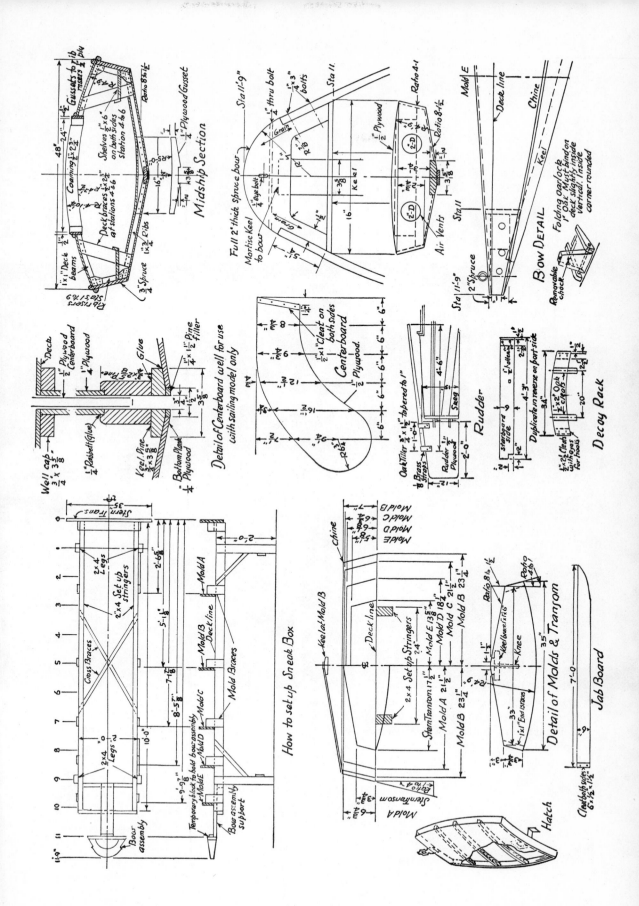

Midship Section

Bow Detail

Detail of Centerboard well for use with sailing model only

Centerboard

Rudder

Decoy Rack

How to set up Sneak Box

Detail of Molds & Transom

Jab Board

Hatch

These boys demonstrate how to take a black duck. They have the sneakboxes in a tide pond and all the water has run out. No matter, the ducks will come in anyway, although not as well as the decoys lose their animation. Notice how the boats are carefully grassed. Shortly after I took this photograph, a family of geese came into the pond and the boys downed three.

The bottom frames or ribs are 1" deep, 3/4" wide cedar or spruce and joined at the center with 3/8" plywood gusset which is dimensioned on the detail sketch of the midship section. These rib assemblies are identical as to angle (1½ : 8) and vary only in length. Using a sheet of plywood (the piece you will use for the floor is okay), lay off a baseline 4' long and bisect it at right angles with a centerline. At the ends of the baseline draw 4½" perpendiculars. From the centerline draw the two lines that subtend the right angles whose sides are 24" and 4½" (ratio 8:1½). On these lines, which form an obtuse angle, nail 3/4" X 1½" battens. At their junction, with its ends touching the battens, center and nail a block 3 5/8" X ½" that is 1¼" thick.

If you examine the detailed midship section, the above will be quite clear. This arrangement will provide you with a jig upon which to construct all the ribs. The ribs are mortised so that when laid along the battens they fit the keel block on the jig. Nail them temporarily in place and lay a gusset on them. Drill three screw holes on each side of the keel block, glue the gusset to the ribs, and screw it in place with 3/4" No. 6 screws. Put gussets on both sides of the ribs. Make ten ribs to be installed at stations 1 to 10 inclusive, and each long enough to span the boat at its particular station. Ribs and deck frames are connected at stations 1 to 10 with 3/4" to 1" rib risers (see midship section) and joined by small 1/4" plywood gussets glued and screwed (only one gusset to each joint). Each rib riser is attached to the side planks with glue and two 1½" No. 7 screws.

Set up one rib at station 6 and brace it firmly from the setup stringers in a vertical position, making sure that it is absolutely square across the boat with the keel notch exactly at the center. Prepare the keel, which is 3/4" X 3 5/8" pine or spruce, and bevel it as indicated. Fasten it permanently at the stern transom, bend it into the notch on station-6 rib, and clamp it temporarily there and to the bow assembly. Working forward from the stern, set all ribs. They must go in place without forcing the keel out of line fore and aft. If additional arch in the keel is necessary, simply loosen clamps at station 6 and bow. After securely fastening all ribs to the rib risers, glue the keel to the ribs. Next glue and screw to the center of the keel a ¼" X 1½" pine strip against which the bottom planks butt.

With ribs and keel in place, use a batten laid along the ribs as a guide in trimming the bottom of the bow assembly so that planking will fit snugly. Bevel the sides to conform to the rib angle. Temporarily attach a 2' X 12" sheet of ¼" marine plywood to the ribs. Lay the stern end of this sheet flush with the outside of the stern transom. The sheet is roughly marked along the keel and cut to shape and then carefully planed to fit along the keel exactly. With a few screws, temporarily fasten the sheet in place and scribe the line of the chine on it (where side plank meets the bottom sheet). Cut to this line, allowing at least ¼" to be planed down when the sheet is permanently installed. This sheet will serve as a pattern for the opposite side. Both are carefully fitted and glued to the planks, keel, and ribs. Space 3/4" No. 6 screws 2" apart along side planks and keel, and 4" apart on ribs. It is recommended that a hard-setting resorcinol resin glue be used. If you plan to use an outboard with more than 3 hp, then use 3/8" plywood on the bottom. Then the thickness of the strip along the keel between the bottom planks must be increased to 3/8". Fiber-glass bottom if desired.

The boat is now turned over to be decked, and the setup form is removed. All deck frames are sawed on a 4' 9" outside radius using the beam compass. Have the grain run tangent to the frame at the center. Frames are cut from a 3/4" plank and are made 1¼" deep. They are set flush with the sides at stations 1 to 10 and rest on the rib risers, to which they are fastened with gussets as described above. Before you permanently fasten deck frames, set them temporarily and check for alignment. Lay a straightedge at the center of the frames from station 7 to the bow and one from station 3 to the stern transom. If your side planks have been properly shaped, each group of frames will be in perfect line. If not, you must correct the side planks to bring them into line. Bevel the side planks to conform to the curve of the frames. Also at this point trim any excess off deck level of the bow assembly, so that the deck fits it. Note that at stations 3 and 7 the frames are double where the deck is butt joined. If you plan a centerboard well, do not install frame 8 until the well cap is in place.

Although the finished boat will not have frames across the cockpit, install full frames from side to side at stations 4, 5, and 6. Leave them until you are ready to install the side decks from stations 3 to 7 and braces supporting the deck are in place. Temporarily nail a longitudinal strip to deck frames 3 to 7 close to those points where coaming will be installed. This will prevent lateral movement of the frames. Cut away frames 4, 5, and 6. On each side screw-fasten a strip ½" X 1½" extending from frames 3 to 7, its top flush with the deck frames. We will call these strips "cockpit liner." Glue the side decks and screw them to the side planks, cockpit liner, and frames with 3/4" No. 6 screws. Save cutaway frames and use to construct a hatch.

Before going any further, let us consider several optional uses of the boat. If you plan to use her entirely with an outboard motor, you may dispense with the centerboard and well, mast hole and step, and rudder and sails. By all means retain the oarlocks and buy a stout pair of 7' ash oars, both for safety and convenience. Should you decide to depend on your own brawn and the little winter sail for reaching when the wind blows fair, the centerboard and well are not essential. You can omit the summer sail and rudder as well. Steering is done with an oar by all web-footed baymen. There's a trick to this. Kneeling on the floor, put an oar over the lee side and scull her head around until the sail fills. As she gains way, the tendency of the oar is to come out of water. To prevent this, turn the blade from a vertical position through about 30°. The forward motion of the boat will then keep the oar under water. You must learn to do this with one hand, as you will need the other to tend sheet.

Finally, you may wish to use Wigeon as an all-purpose boat that you will share with your family, and then you will shoot the works and build with all appurtenances.

The sneakbox is a safe and seaworthy boat for children learning to sail. Witness the hundreds of one-design Perrines, named after their builder, Samuel Perrine of Barnegat, New Jersey. Many of today's top skippers learned the rudiments of racing in these little sneakboxes.

As the drawings show, Harry rigged her with a sprit, which is a good way to utilize a short heavy mast and much lighter sprit to keep the center of gravity low and thus reduce the possibility of a capsize, a disaster in winter weather. The lateen rigs of the Sunfish and Sailfish (which accomplish the same thing) were not common when we designed the boat, and several builders of this boat recently utilized the readily available Sunfish/Sailfish sails with excellent results.

If you decide to install a centerboard, which is essential if you want to sail her, refer to the detail drawing on the plan, and build the well before you put on the forward deck. Cut a 3/4″ slot in the center of the keel and carefully fit the head ledges, making the mortised end extend through the keel to be sawed off flush with the bottom. Ribs and gussets at stations 7 and 8 must be cut through to take bed logs.

The well cap extends from station 7 to 9 flush with deck frames. It is 3/4″ X 3 5/8″ pine, and here again head ledges are mortised into it. Frame 8 should not be placed until the well cap is in and then is cut and mortised to it. The well slot through the cap is 1½″ wide to permit the 3/8″ plywood sides of the well to come through and butt against the deck. Start the well from the bottom, planing the bed logs to conform exactly to the curve of the keel. Rabbet their upper edge to receive the 3/8″ plywood sides, which are carried up through the cap.

Use plenty of soft-setting marine glue where bed logs meet the keel and on other parts of the well. Secure bed logs to keel with 2″ No. 10 screws on 3″ centers. Paint the inside of well as it is constructed. Before decking, install mast step partner, which is flush with top of frames, reinforcing blocks under oarlocks, and bolt on outboard bracket. If you use sail only, attach a riser 1″ X 1″ to carry lag screws to hang rudder. If you plan to use both motor and sail, make a detachable oak outboard bracket slightly tapered to drop into metal channels and forked to slip over the rudder riser. Just above the fork, insert a 1/4" galvanized bolt on either side of the bracket.

Bow and stern decks are 1/4" plywood, and after careful fitting are glued and screwed to the side planks on 2" centers and to frames on 6" centers, all with 3/4" No. 6 screws.

Next install coaming around cockpit, oarlocks, 1/2" quarter-round trim around coaming, 1" half-round rail, 1" half-round gunwale, brackets and cleats for the decoy rack, skeg, and, of course, the spray curtain.

Usually sneakbox oarlocks are made to fold down against the deck to get them out of sight. The inboard bottom side of the oarlock block is quarter-rounded so that it will fold inboard. The fit must be so close that the upright block jams slightly inside the vertical position and is held there by a small chock wedged into a deck cleat and a notch in the oarlock itself. Folding oarlocks are not too important. They may be solidly bolted to the deck if preferred.

The decoy rack should need no explanation. It is made of 1/2" X 6" siding. Two cleats on the stern portion fit into sockets fastened to the stern transom. At the forward end the sides fit behind the oarlocks, and near the stern engage the end of a cleat on each side, and finally hooks and eyes fasten them to the stern piece.

The rack is the handiest method of stacking decoys I know. It will accommodate thirty to forty stools, sloped on their tails. If anchors are dropped from side to side in regular order, the decoys may be put out without fouling anchors or liens, provided you unload them in the reverse order.

The three deck frames (4, 5, and 6) cut out to make the cockpit are used to frame a hatch. Cut two hatch ends 1/2" X 2" to fit the outside of the coaming ends and on the same curve. Temporarily fasten these in place and spring two pieces 1/2" X 2" around the cockpit side and fasten them to the hatch ends. Next notch the saved pieces of the deck frames (4, 5, and 6) halfway through to fit over the coaming, and glue and screw them to the hatch sides at intervals. Over all, glue and screw a piece of 1/4" plywood to complete the hatch. At the stern end of the underside of the finished hatch, fasten a Z-shaped metal bracket that will slide snugly under the deck. At the bow, fasten a hasp with staple on the deck so that a padlock will protect your gear stowed inside. The hatch is left ashore when afloat.

The midships section shows 1/2″ X 6″ shelves on both sides extending from stations 4 to 6. These are not essential but are very handy to store shells, lunch, duck calls, and other small bits of gear.

Of vital importance to the hunter going to windward in cold weather is the spray curtain. With this gadget your sneakbox will shed water like a duck. Heavy seas rolling over the bow will part on the curtain and wash to either side. Start with a 1″ curtain pole, 18″ long. With this held upright at the center of the coaming, measure the distance to the top of one oarlock and double this. You will need a piece of ten-ounce tan canvas approximately 3′ X 7½′. Cut the long dimensions of the canvas exactly to your measured distance and sew a hem in one edge to take a 1/4″ cotton rope. At the center of the hem sew a 3″ triangular gusset and next to the hem place a grommet which takes the pointed end of the curtain pole. Put brass screw eyes at the oarlock corners and fasten the rope ends to them. With the pole in place, draw the center of the canvas taut to a point a few inches aft of the mast hole. Turn the canvas under and fasten to the deck. With surplus material turned under all around, tack to deck on curve, as shown on the plan, and also down the side of the oarlock. When completed, cut off surplus material from the inside.

Here a word about propelling the boat with oars. They should be stout 7′ ash. Baymen always row a sneakbox seated on the floor so that when the curtain is up no spray bothers them. The position when pursuing crippled ducks, if it is not blowing too hard, is to face the bow while kneeling at the stern and to push the boat forward with the oars while keeping the swimming duck continuously under observation.

If you build with a centerboard well, you will find a "jab board" a great convenience. It is simply a 1″ X 6″ board, 7′ long, pointed on one end, with a cleat at the other to serve as a handhold, that is thrust down the well into the bottom of the bay to hold the boat when setting out decoys.

GUNNING JOHNBOAT

This is the classic duckboat. Flat-bottom construction, sled bow, curved deck, and general construction methods give all you need to revamp to suit your own requirements. This little boat was designed for pond work, but you can enlarge as you see fit, beefing up specifications as you increase in size. You want to come in around 12 or 13 feet for a one-man boat, 14 or 15 for a two-man. If you prefer a

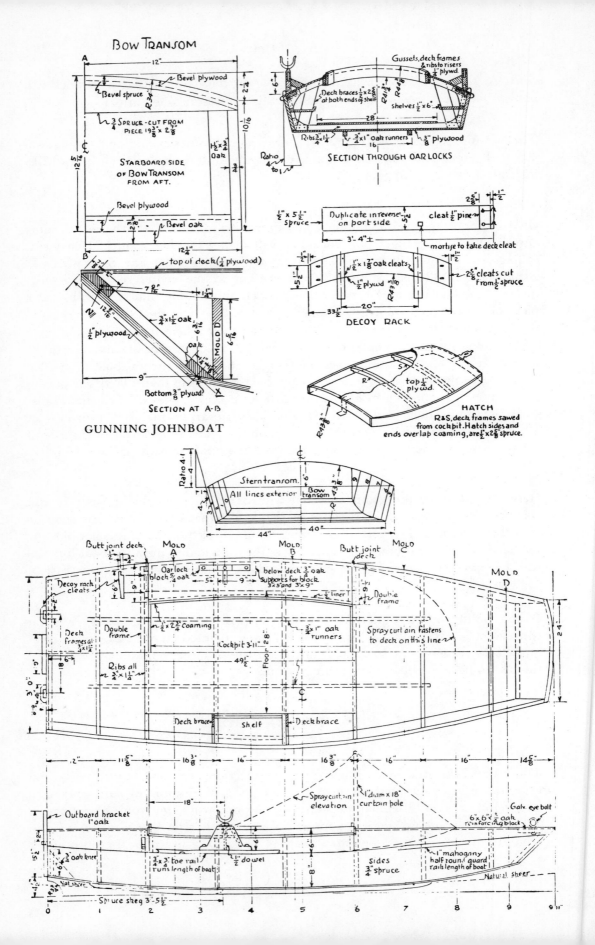

GUNNING JOHNBOAT

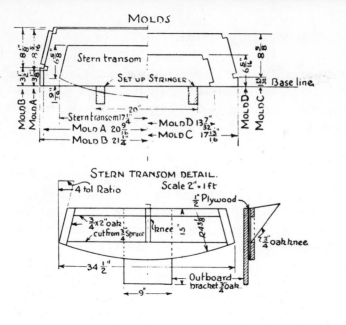

STERN TRANSOM DETAIL.
Scale 2"=1ft

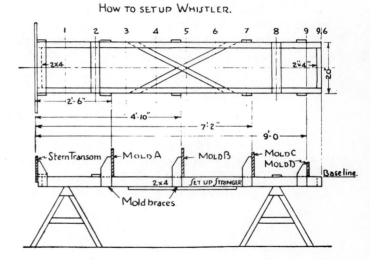

HOW TO SET UP WHISTLER.

sharp bow, which is slightly more seaworthy though it extends length without adding usable space, redraw the bow to bring the planks together and back with a stem piece as used in the scullboat plans.

Every duck hunter has his own ideas about a boat, so you'll probably redraw her. My only admonition is, if you do, I'd suggest you loft her final lines full size on paper as described in the section on how to build a scullboat. An additional virtue of this boat, besides all its virtues as the perfect duckboat, is that it will plane with fairly little power. If you make her large, say 14 feet, and wish to use a 10 to 20 horsepower, you'll have to beef her up considerably with heavier planking and transom knees. The flat-bottom shape is the simplest of all to build, and with any carpentry skill at all you should be able to produce the boat of your dreams.

As designed, she is a boat for the ponds. Weight is about eighty pounds, and with a maximum width of 44'', she slides inside a standard station wagon's usual 45'' horizontal clearance. If you drive a minicar, she'll ride on top in high style, and the ducks will tremble at your coming.

Best of all, she employs the classic johnboat shape that is the simplest, cheapest, and quickest to build. Since today you can tape the seams and thus avoid the necessity of making a true watertight connection, I wouldn't hesitate to say that if you can pound a nail into a board, saw a straight line, and read a ruler, you can put this boat together. I think the cost would come in around a hundred dollars.

There are some exciting features about her that aren't readily apparent. Waterline beam at 38'' is a nice compromise. It floats the boat in around five or six inches of water with you in it, which is important in so many ducking spots where the water gets thin, yet the beam is enough to handle the power of a small outboard. A 3 hp would be about tops and the little 1½ hp is perfect and light as a feather. I'm stressing lightness here because this is the kind of boat you drag across a field or a marsh. For that, you need a flat bottom and a weight of less than a hundred pounds. I'd guess speed at 3 or 4 mph with the 1½ hp, maybe 5 or 6 with the 3 hp.

This boat's virtue is her small size. She isn't made for doing any rough-water work, though her deck and spray shield will help if you do have to come home against a bad blow. The sled bow will make her throw water like a firehose, but you can sit on the floor to keep her center of gravity low and hide behind the spray shield. If you are running in a following sea, sit on the floor and lean back against the after coaming so your back and arms will help turn any waves that want to join the party. It's better not to put her to any such tests, however, and use her in sheltered bays, rivers, and ponds.

This little rascal will row. Tucking up her stern helps that, but with no roundness to her bottom and her short length she'll be cranky—okay for picking up decoys but not so hot for chasing down cripples. The motor would be a wise partner for her.

You can slide this boat in a gooey mud ditch, and she'll disappear. Let me dig this boat into a sandbar or shoreline (or a cornfield, for that matter) and I'll bet you ten bucks you won't be able to spot it at fifty yards. You don't even have to dig her in, because her curved sides throw the ends of grass down over the side, hiding it. Grass this boat with reeds, willows, marsh grass, seaweed—anything natural to the area— and you won't have any problems fooling ducks and geese.

How to Build Her

You set this boat up with forms that you throw away, except for the transom. First lay out two straight, sturdy stringers, block them at right angles, and brace with two-by-fours. Lay out the molds with great care. It's best to draw them on construction paper and use these as templates. Draw the lines on 5/8" plywood to avoid warping, and carefully saw. Notch each mold to take a 3/4-by-3/4-inch gunwale and chine (bottom) batten. Don't notch the transom for these, however. Screw a block on the transom and screw the batten ends to it. (You'll throw these battens away. They are used only to scribe [draw] the gunwale and chine lines to the sides.) This gives the boat her pleasing shape and sheer (curve). Molds attach to stringers upside down. You build the boat bottom first, then turn her over. Transom arcs (the round tops of bow and stern) extend over stringers at either end.

The transom should be cut from 1/2" plywood. The arc for it and the deck beams is from a circle with a radius of 43 1/8". Cut the sides using the four-to-one ratio (or taking measurements off the scaled plans). Then screw 3/4" X 2" oak or mahogany pads along bottom and sides as shown in the drawings. Fasten the transom temporarily on the stringers, like the molds, placing them carefully at right angles.

The sides are made from 3/4" spruce or cedar, two planks 10' long, 12" wide. Clamp the planks to the transom at the stern, then make a Spanish rope windlass at the bow to draw the planks in. Soaking the planks will make them bend more easily. This, incidentally, is a compound curve, and plywood won't bend to it. Be careful you don't pull the molds out of true. With the planks flat, scribe the side contours from the previously laid battens. Saw planks to shape, leaving an extra 1/4" for planing true (fairing). Shape the bow according to "Section at A-B," locate points X and Z and saw sides to this line. Both sides should be identical. Place a straightedge across the ends and plane them fair to receive bow transom.

Bow transom is 1/2" plywood. Draw it directly from the boat, not the lines, to compensate for any errors. Cut it slightly larger than the distance between the sides and about fifteen inches top to bottom. Draw the arc at top to a 34" radius. Deck arc is 43 1/8", but pitching the bow forward requires a different curvature for bow transom. Temporarily fasten to sides (transom overlaps them), scribe, and cut to fit. Leave about an eighth-inch extra at top to plane flat to receive the deck. Remove bow transom and screw-glue oak or mahogany pads as shown, then screw-glue bow transom to sides. Now go to the stern, unclamp stern transom, and screw-glue it to sides.

Turn the hull over and plane the sides flat to receive the flat bottom. Remove the chine batten. You are ready to frame. Make frames (ribs) of light cedar or spruce.

Nail or screw and glue, using 1/4" plywood gussets on one side only. (You don't need double gussets.) You'll have to plane the ribs at top and bottom to compensate for the side angle. Don't forget to put limber holes in the bottom ribs.

You can use 3/8" plywood for the bottom, as called for in the original design, but I would prefer to use 1/4" and glass it. My pond box is 1/4" throughout and has served for five seasons and is still in good shape, despite hard use and no care. I did punch a hole in the bow, but this boat is not fully glassed; only the seams are taped for waterproofing. If it were covered with lightweight glass or Dynel, it would be much stronger.

Temporarily fasten the bottom sheet to the sides, scribe the shape, remove, and saw. Fasten with glue and nails on 2" centers on the side and 6" centers into the frames.

Unscrew molds from stringers and turn the boat over. Fair sides level with gunwale batten, then remove the batten and all the molds. Saw out the nine deck frames to the 43 1/8" radius, as described. They'll cut out of a 3/4" plank 1½" thick. Use spruce or cedar. Double the frames at cockpit ends and where the side deck next to the cockpit is installed. Screw-glue arcs at transom tops. Leave frames across cockpit uncut until you install deck braces, then fair all surfaces with a plane, using a long straightedge so that all surfaces butt neatly, and sides are angled to take deck. Put in the oak knee at transom. Cut the cockpit frames and install cockpit liner. Save frames cut away to use for building hatch. Fasten 1/2" X 2¼" coaming to cockpit liners.

Deck goes on in four pieces. Temporarily screw deck panels in place, scribe, remove, and cut. Glue and nail deck beams on 2" centers on sides, 6" centers on deck frames. Put a 1" rub rail at gunwale. Plans show a galvanized eyebolt at deck top, but the boat will tow and come up a trailer more easily if you install it low just above waterline on bow. Plans show oak runners on bottom. If you will be dragging the boat much, don't install these or skeg. Keep skeg, though, if you can, as it will make boat track better towing or rowed. Cockpit floor is 1/4" but you had better double-support it where you step in the boat, as I broke mine. Don't extend it beyond where you sit.

The rest is incidental. Hatch is easily fashioned using the sawed frames of cockpit. Build up oarlocks as shown. Add decoy racks if wanted. (I find them very handy to store blocks temporarily when putting out or picking up decoys.) Oars should be 7-footers. Cut the spray canvas and tack to deck. Sew in pocket or install grommet at top to hold erect on stick. I found that with shock cord I could hold almost all decoys inside a cup made from the spray shield. This little shelf inside is indispensable for holding shells, calls, hip flask, *Know Your Ducks*, etc. I found with my sneakbox I couldn't keep the bottom dry (you track in water and mud, getting in and out), and my regular canvas bag full of essentials got so cruddy I made a special plywood box to fit under the transom, and my gear stays clean and dry. The hatch is important, as you can leave the boat in the rain without its filling and, of course, it locks. Thieves can't get the hatch off so they take the whole boat instead. Note the hatch device that slides under deck. Make it from bar aluminum if you can't find brass.

There you have it. I sometimes think that all the words describing how to build a boat scare many people off. They make it sound so complicated. And they make it sound as though everything must be done only a certain way. In truth, it doesn't work this way. You see what's required as you go along, and if you make an error, there are many ways you can correct it. You can glue extra pieces on or saw them off. Plenty of boats have been built by squint and pound. I remember a stool boat I watched two guys building down in Havre de Grace, Maryland. "How high shall we make the cabin, Charley?" one asked. Charley got a kitchen chair, sat in it, drew a line on the side of the plywood cabin side a few inches higher than his head. "Cut her off right there," he commanded. So much for plans.

COFFIN BOX

There are plenty of reasons—some new, some old—why gunning from a coffin-box blind is one of the smartest, easiest, and deadliest ways to kill ducks and geese. Here are some of the old reasons the coffin box offers all the advantages that sneakbox gunning affords.

A boat can be taken from one place to another, according to where the birds are trading.

The low profile of a boat (in which, of course, the gunner lies flat) makes it easy and simple to hide almost anywhere.

Being a relatively small watertight and airtight space, the boat is warm and dry under the severest conditions.

Closed tight with a hatch and moored securely, the boat is relatively safe in storms that could sweep a blind away. Decoys can be locked inside when not in use.

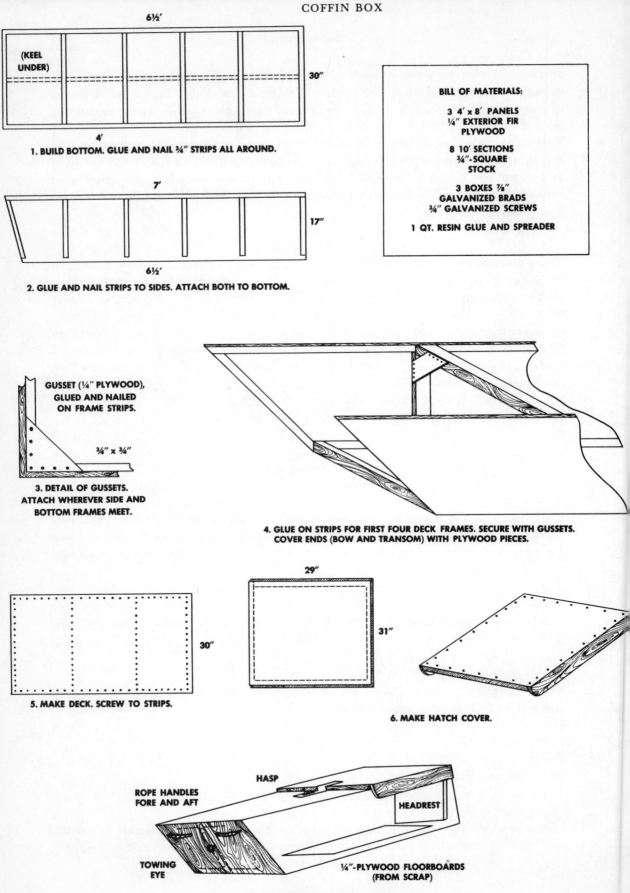

6½'

4'

(KEEL UNDER)

30"

1. BUILD BOTTOM. GLUE AND NAIL ¾" STRIPS ALL AROUND.

7'

17"

6½'

2. GLUE AND NAIL STRIPS TO SIDES. ATTACH BOTH TO BOTTOM.

BILL OF MATERIALS:

3 4' x 8' PANELS
¼" EXTERIOR FIR
PLYWOOD

8 10' SECTIONS
¾"-SQUARE
STOCK

3 BOXES ⅞"
GALVANIZED BRADS
¾" GALVANIZED SCREWS

1 QT. RESIN GLUE AND SPREADER

GUSSET (¼" PLYWOOD),
GLUED AND NAILED
ON FRAME STRIPS.

¾" x ¾"

3. DETAIL OF GUSSETS.
ATTACH WHEREVER SIDE AND
BOTTOM FRAMES MEET.

4. GLUE ON STRIPS FOR FIRST FOUR DECK FRAMES. SECURE WITH GUSSETS.
COVER ENDS (BOW AND TRANSOM) WITH PLYWOOD PIECES.

30"

29"

31"

5. MAKE DECK. SCREW TO STRIPS.

6. MAKE HATCH COVER.

ROPE HANDLES
FORE AND AFT

HASP

HEADREST

TOWING
EYE

¼"-PLYWOOD FLOORBOARDS
(FROM SCRAP)

7. FINISHED BOX WITH INTERIOR DETAIL.

If the marsh floods, the boat can be floated to higher ground and disguised in minutes. You can still gun.

When you consider each of these duck-shooting essentials, you'll see that a coffin box does just as well as the fanciest sneakbox ever built. Of course, it can't get to and from the shooting grounds under its own power, and it isn't at all seaworthy. A sneakbox hunting skiff has it beat hollow there.

However, there are some dismal realities to hunting from a sneakbox-type boat. The little boats have complicated designs, are hard to build and expensive to buy. And they're heavy. A twelve-foot sneakbox may weigh two hundred pounds and cost three hundred dollars.

The better the little duckboat, the more attractive it is to thieves, and boat theft is a growing problem everywhere. It is impossible to guard against completely if the boat is left in lonely places.

Severe storms are often powerful enough to wrench any boat loose from its moorings. Unless you trailer the boat home, loss is a definite risk.

The little ducking skiff also requires its own trailer (or auto-top carrier) and must be licensed in most states. There's upkeep. And since the outboard from your summer boat will overpower it, you need a smaller motor strictly for the little guy. So no matter how you slice it, a good duckboat can be costly and bothersome.

Many sportsmen today are making use of their larger summer boats for their duck hunting. No reason why not. For years, building a blind has been a traditional preseason chore of duck shooting. But, alas, it too presents problems, problems, however, that a coffin-box blind solves. Consider:

A blind hastily thrown together is almost worse than no blind at all. It is cold, ill concealed, and more likely to frighten waterfowl than not. Coffin boxes are blinds in themselves, always warm, dry, and easily hidden.

A permanent blind represents an investment in time and money pretty much commensurate with its worth. If you make it tight and warm, well built to survive storms and damage, well hidden with grass or reeds, somebody's dollars and/or hours have to go into it in not inconsiderable numbers. A coffin box that lasts five years costs ten dollars a year.

A permanent blind sits unattended ten months of the year, subject to weather damage and the possibility that sliding ice floes will tear it apart. Worst of all, many ducking areas are also summer-vacationing spots, and local kids then often destroy a blind, presumably thinking it is of no value. A coffin box comes home after the season. It's safe where you store it.

A permanent blind usually requires some arrangement with the landowner. It would be foolish to build an elaborate spread on an unposted bit of marsh, only to be informed at the last minute that the owner has leased it. If you find that a landowner doesn't like where you gun your coffin box, move it.

A coffin-box blind is not perfect, of course. Lying down for long periods of time can be uncomfortable. You can't see as much as when sitting. This box as designed is the worst object to tow I've ever found. They leap and jump and dive. I thought that putting a keel on them would stop this, but it doesn't. The best way is to bridle them on two lines so they are right behind the outboard.

Building the Coffin Box

The coffin box is very nearly a nonboat, so there's no need to build it like a conventional boat. Cut the bottom and frame. Then cut the two sides. Glue and nail these sides to the bottom. Then add side frames and gussets for each. Now frame the stern to receive the transom. Add transom. Turn the box over and glue a double-frame size across the bottom where the bow meets the bottom. Cut bow section and plane this to fit by placing the bow section against it. After this, turn the boat over and add the deck and make a hatch.

The dimensions are deliberate to permit building out of two sheets of standard 4' X 8' exterior plywood. Sides are 17" so your booted foot will slide in and out easily and you can gun with feet straight up and down. When you dig the box in half its height, the profile is so low the boat practically disappears.

If you plan to use your coffin box more as a boat than as a blind, it would be well to broaden the beam. I've found the 30" beam too tippy to be safe under all conditions, and have extended it to 36". And if you plan to float the boat extensively (rather than dig it into sand or mud), extend the length 6" or a foot and add an afterdeck. This has the effect of centering your weight in the boat, keeping it on a more even keel when floating.

The little coffin box is simple to build. This shows the light frame construction, using the 3/4-inch strips and 1/4-inch plywood throughout. The boat is nailed and glued.

This is the way to "dig in" a coffin box or, for that matter, any other kind of boat. Taylor slogging around in the mud again.

The next step is to grass the boat. Any raw mud areas should be covered with marsh grass from the surrounding area.

ZT at work. As you can see, there isn't much of the boat showing. Lying down flat in the box, the shooter is almost invisible.

Because the simple coffin box builds quickly (about eight hours) and costs little (about fifty dollars), you can build one or two of them before the season. If they aren't lost or stolen, they should last for years. Two or three can be towed behind an outboard.

At a weight of seventy-odd pounds, coffin boxes can be carried on auto-top racks or resting on the seats of your trailed utility outboard. Since in the eyes of the law they are floating duck blinds, no boat license is required. But in a pinch you can paddle one out to retrieve a duck or decoy.

If you worry about building a watertight seam, glass the bottom. Or you can use fiber glass or Dynel tape on just the seams. Dynel is watertight, resistant to abrasion, and easier to use, since it stretches. It is not as strong as glass, however. The price is about the same, and the same resin is used. Taping with either will add another ten dollars to the cost of the boat.

Rounding the deck makes the box even better, but building curves is difficult. Unless you are proficient at it, it is hardly worth the work involved. Long ends of grass or reeds will droop down eventually.

Use conventional plywood construction. Glue is far easier to use than fastenings, although repairing can then be a problem. If you punch a hole in the box, just nail and glue a piece over it. Some epoxy glues will set even in freezing weather if enough hardener is added.

One gunner I know who uses boxes around potholes has fitted them with wheels and handles, so they can be rolled across marshes like a wheelbarrow.

Using The Coffin Box
How you position and hide the box depends on what kind of cover you have in your shooting area. Try to keep the natural look as much as possible. If you want your box on a river sandbar, dig it down well and cover the deck with sand and mud. Pile grass on the hatch so that you can throw it off to shoot.

Coffin boxes are good auxiliary blinds. Let's say you and your pals have a permanent blind that is just right for prevailing conditions, but once or twice a season, good shooting occurs with winds and weather from the direction opposite your blind. Instead of building another permanent blind, throw together a couple of coffin boxes and position them in the secondary spot.

You can build two—even three—coffin boxes together. Place decks between them so the gunners have enough room to sit with elbows extended during duckless spells. As their weight and size expand, however, the advantages of coffin boxes diminish. Unless there are unique circumstances, it is probably better to fit in two separate boxes side by side.

I built two coffin boxes one summer and used them during several seasons with great success, dragging them from one place to another to suit conditions. A sneakbox trick I resurrected was to dig a "slot" in various places. Then I'd haul a box to the spot and slip into a hidden place with little effort.

Although coffin boxes aren't perfect (what is?) I found them to be another useful and helpful addition to the seasoned waterfowler's bag of tricks.

POND BOX

Years ago a partner and I were deep in waterfowl country, admiring a little duckboat a local man had built. "She's a nice little pone box," he said. I can't phonetically spell the way he said pone. Maybe po-oon. About a syllable and a half. Partner and I looked at each other. Neither had any idea what he was talking about. It took us a couple of weeks to figure out he was calling it a pond box.

I built this box when I switched from gunning big water to gunning a little pond. I thought I'd use the boat to set out and pick up decoys and do my gunning out of the sinkbox. After bailing out the box several times, I dug a slot for the boat and gunned out of it if I was alone.

It is a minimum vessel, I'll admit, but it's easy and cheap to build, safely stable, doesn't row as badly as you'd expect, tows okay, and is warm and comfortable to gun from.

You could make it strong enough to take a small motor, but you'd have to beef it up considerably from what I'll describe.

Materials
The boat is designed to utilize 10' sections of exterior grade 1/4" plywood, which are easily available. You'll need three sheets. They'll cost about $8.50 each. One

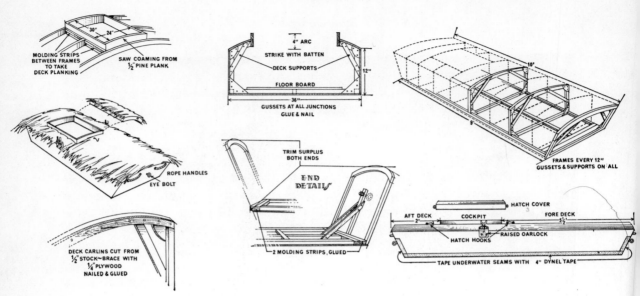

sheet builds the top and side; the other builds the bottom and side; the last builds the ends and hatch cover and provides scrap for gussets and supports. The carlings must be sawed. Get 1/2" stock. Good clear pine is okay, but oak or mahogany is better. All junctures are butted with 3/4"-square molding strips. Glue with Weldwood and nail with 3/4" galvanized nails to hold until the glue dries. A saber saw, plane, hammer, and backing weight, some Dynel tape and resin and a pot of duckboat paint complete the bill of materials. You'll have change from $75 even after you buy oars and a preserver cushion.

Design

Don't make the cockpit smaller than 24" wide and 30" long, or it will be clumsy to get into and out of. You want an afterdeck to position your weight amidships, so the bow doesn't hunker up when you lean back in the water. Stability at 36" beam is okay. You can stand up in her. She'll be cranky to row, especially without an exterior keel. Leaving it off makes it easy to drag in and out of grass. Floorboards aren't needed, since you sit on a preserver cushion. The cover makes it possible to lock the boat with hasps at both ends. You can build decoy racks at either end or, as I do, store the blocks inside her.

How to Build

Use the Boating Editor's can't-go-wrong building method developed at great expense over the years. Start with the bottom. Cut your sheet to 36", then take 12" off one end to provide for the bow and transom angle. Nail and glue the chine strips (of 3/4"-square stock) 1/4" in from either side. The side planking is set on the bottom in this boat. Nail and glue crossribs or frames from side to side on about 12" centers. Put the keel of the same 3/4" stock on the inside or outside, whichever you

I have the little pond box under tow. It makes a neat little boat to gun from. It's light and with the wide beam it's also stable, even if you have to get acrobatic to shoot. It's almost cheap enough to be a throwaway duck boat, but if you build it with care it should last a long time.

prefer. Take two sections of the 3/4″ stock and glue them together. Then glue them in position at bow and stern with enough sticking out so that you can plane in the angle. This part of the job, including building the hatch, can be done in a shop, since everything can be carried through a door.

Put the bottom on horses and cut the sides. Nail and glue to chine strip. Now extend the frames up the sides, and at each junction glue and nail a gusset to strengthen the joint. Leave room for the carlings.

The deck carlings and the hatch coaming must be sawed. Take a pliable batten and strike a 4″ arc. Get 1½″ clear pine in 8″ or 10″ planks. You can saw several frames out of one spot then. Because pine isn't strong, I braced mine with plywood carlings nailed and glued to the pine. I can sit on the deck without worrying. Cut the hatch coaming from the 1/2″ carling at each end so it stands up enough to receive the sides of the hatch above the deck. Cut the sides of the hatch to fit over it generously, as it will swell. Saw a couple of carlings to strengthen the hatch.

Plank the hatch cover. Plywood will bend one way but not the other. I learned this the hard way, even jacking a clamp right through the wood. If you get the right bend, it can be made to bend fairly easily. Put the carlings in the hatch cover after you glue and nail it to the ends.

The deck carlings sit on the ends of the side frames. Remember, you left space for them there. Gusset each at the joint. Then cut plywood strips about 2½″ by 12″ and nail and glue two supports at each carling. Make sure you cut them so that the nonbendable way functions to support. They will make the deck strong. The carling angled at either end by the angle of the transom and bow will have to be made slightly oversize. This way you can rasp the surplus away so it will receive the deck. I forgot this and had to fill the void with a mixture of Weldwood glue and sawdust. You can attach these carlings when you plank the ends.

Turn the boat over and plane the bow and transom angles into the two bottom endpieces that you glued together. Fit the end planking, fiddling with it until you get a good fit. Run a piece of the 3/4" square stock up the middle of the endpieces and out along the bottom. Put supports between so the two bolt is strong. Use a 1/4" galvanized eyebolt for this. While you're drilling for these, drill holes for rope handles. Knot 1/4" nylon line between the holes, to make handling the boat easier.

Turn the boat back and glue and fit the carling at transom and bow end. Cut the deck so the bendable way is from side to side. The deck is fastened with the only screws in the boat; galvanized are fine. The screws make it possible to remove the deck if you ever have to make repairs. Get the deck with the bendable way right and screw down the centerline on each carling and thereafter at 6" toward the sides. The plywood will lie down that way without clamps or cussing.

Once the deck is planked, turn the boat bottom up and round the plywood edges with a rasp. Fill all voids with a mixture of glue and sawdust or plastic putty.

The oarlocks have to be raised to row. Rig locks that fold down like those on a plywood sneakbox, or bolt pieces to the side and mount a galvanized lock to take them. It may look awful, but it works fine. The boat is cranky and horrible to row, probably the worst I've ever experienced, but it doesn't have to go far.

Paint the boat outside and inside where you can reach with duckboat brown paint. Grass it up, and she's ready to go. If you build and use one, drop me a note and tell me about it. If you're not pleased with it, I'll eat a seagull.

GUNNING BARGE

I believe this design represents the greatest breakthrough in the concept of modern waterfowling. Andy Tanner is the man who came up with this revolutionary idea. In fact, as I write these words (on a Saturday) Andy is probably staked out in his barge somewhere. I wish I were with him. Here's the story:

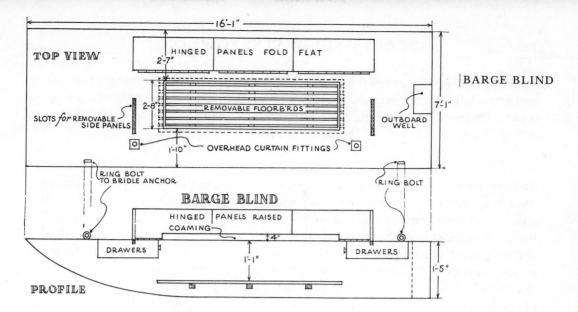

TOP VIEW

16'-1"

HINGED PANELS FOLD FLAT

2'-7"

BARGE BLIND

2'-8" REMOVABLE FLOORB'RDS

7'-1"

SLOTS for REMOVABLE SIDE PANELS

OUTBOARD WELL

1'-10" OVERHEAD CURTAIN FITTINGS

RING BOLT TO BRIDLE ANCHOR

RING BOLT

BARGE BLIND

HINGED PANELS RAISED
COAMING

4"

DRAWERS

DRAWERS

1'-1"

1'-5"

PROFILE

Andy was disgusted. Prime waterfowling land he'd leased had been sold to a developer, and other leasable land was sky-high in price. He and a friend built an elaborate floating blind and moored it off a prime point, but he turned out to be the man whose blind was burned up. This ruined the season for Tanner, but he vowed it would be his last wrecked duck season, because a solution to his problem was taking form in his mind. He was designing a new and unique duckboat.

This new craft had to be fully mobile. No one was going to burn it up, because it would come home every night and sit in the driveway, where it would be safe from storms, vandals, ice damage, and the general ravages of wind and wave. It had to be self-contained. Everything except guns and personal clothes would be stored in it at all times. Tanner liked to hunt the length of his state, and this meant the boat had to be trailerable.

A view from the gunning barge shows that it will fool both Canada geese and black ducks.

Since Tanner always gunned with friends, his craft also had to be big enough to accommodate three men, their gear, and at least two dogs. It also had to be reasonably fast. The good gunning areas always seem to be miles from where you launch.

Tanner drew a design of what he wanted, and the boat emerged from his shop in the spring. No one could figure out what to call it. It was more of a duck blind than a boat. Tanner considered its boxy shape and sledlike bow and dubbed it a gunning barge. It's a most remarkable vessel. It serves as a storage area as well as functioning perfectly as a three-man blind. When grassed up next to a suitable shore, the barge almost disappears. Moreover, being flat-bottomed and beamy, it planes well with relatively little power. Tanner has been using a 20-hp outboard on the latest version of the barge, which weighs approximately six hundred pounds. Empty, the barge will do 25 mph. With three men, two dogs, decoys and assorted gear, the 20-hp outboard isn't enough to bring the barge up on plane, and Tanner is readying a 40-hp for the next season. Another remarkable factor is the boat's shallow draft. Again, because of its great beam, it draws no more than three inches fully loaded. Like any experienced duck hunter, Tanner is cautious about the weather, but if conditions are okay, he regularly works the big water of Raritan Bay and even runs the boat around Sandy Hook to the open Atlantic for scoters and sea ducks. He reports having weathered some fairly hairy stuff with the barge taking it handily.

The plans reproduced show the present barge. Tanner's experience with the first two are instructive, however. The first barge was 10' X 5' X 19''. He felt it was too unstable. The second was 14' X 5' X 12''. It too lacked stability, and the short freeboard, although making the boat slightly easier to hide, was troublesome both in getting in and getting out of the cockpit, and it was uncomfortable because you had to sit with feet splayed apart to fit under the deck. Both these barges were built with square sides—no outward flare. These were a problem. Without flare to throw waves back, they tended to splash aboard. The present barge is just shy of 7' on the deck and is 6' on the bottom, which creates a 6'' flare to the sides. This makes for more of a building problem but is well worth the trouble, according to Tanner.

The front of the blind is a series of hinged plywood panels which conceal the hunters from incoming birds. A push from inside, and the panel falls flat. A canvas overhead cover also helps conceal dogs and men. It works on homemade sliding hinges at the sides. The hinges hold two aluminum rods at the leading edge and at the line where the top meets the side. It's secured by regular canvas snaps on the deck. You can easily make one of these tops using standard awning fixtures or the aluminum rods and fittings that are used on regular boat-cockpit covers. Buy the canvas and sew the pockets to fit the rods and hem the edges. Paint it brown with canvas paint.

Tanner found that ducks coming in from the sides could sometimes see movement inside, so he built a slot on deck to take plywood partitions for additional hide. Another trick barge-blind experts use is to rig fold-up panels and grass them so well that they extend above any seated hunter's head.

There is no keel on the barge. Tanner has found that it controls well enough without one. If you'll be using your barge around rocks or other tough stuff, you might install several shallow oak keels for protection. Notice, too, that the barge's cockpit is off-center. This is to position the gunner's weight more in the center of the vessel, so the side doesn't lift it.

Construction is conventional plywood over oak frames, or you could substitute fir or mahogany. Frames are about 1 X 2 s on 16" centers. You'll have trouble with the curve of the chine. Saw out the long graceful curve, then jack the panel in place with clamps. It might help to wet the plywood with as much boiling water as you can. Planking is 3/8" exterior-grade plywood. The entire boat is fiber-glassed. A hatch cover keeps the boat dry for storage. The outboard well is self-bailing through a small scupper. Make the limber holes extra large (1/2" X 2") so you can pump the barge dry. Make the floorboards removable for easy cleaning. Duckboats collect grass, dirt, feathers, shells, etc., in vast quantities.

Tanner uses no flotation, as 140 plastic decoys under the decks amount to the same thing. However, another ingenious plan is under way. Tanner is building collapsible wire cages to hold the decoys. This will sit in the middle of the cockpit for trailering. When the boat is launched, the cages are put on the vast expanse of deck so men and dogs can go in the cockpit. When the decoys go overboard, the cages are collapsed flat and stowed on deck with a piece of burlap to conceal them.

Obviously, this vessel is for do-it-yourselfers. Any respectable boatbuilder would throw up his hands in horror at the mere sight of her lines. (Beautiful, she ain't.) You'll have to design to your own specifications. Andy's present barge is 10' X 5' X 17"; cockpit is 6' X 27". This barge is wall-sided, and the bow is not curved. It angles up in a straight line to a small bow transom. This is an easy construction method, but the barge does not perform especially well either driving into the wind or with a following sea. On the basis of Tanner's experience, if you went to a two-man barge, I'd suggest you bring it in around 14' X 5½' on the bottom, 6½' on deck X 16". You can put the outboard on a board bolted to the transom to avoid building the well. Just be sure the motor is 15" from the water.

JOHNBOAT BARGE BLIND

Here's a variation on the barge blind that I wish I could take credit for. However, it comes from the drawing board of Bill Phillips, a Norfolk, Virginia, structural engineer. His design utilizes the hull of a regular fourteen-foot aluminum johnboat on which a superstructure is placed. Two men gun side by side as in the barge blind.

Using the commercial boat saves you the problems of building the hull, a job many would not feel competent to tackle anyway. And at today's prices for wood and fastenings, the price of the two would be pretty close. The fourteen-foot aluminum costs about $200, and you'll have to put well over $175 into a comparable wooden hull, especially if you fiber-glass the entire hull.

Aside from the fact that it's professionally built, the aluminum offers added advantages. It is about 150 pounds lighter than a wood boat of equal size, No ice protection is required. And, of course, you have a hull that is shaped to plane easily and can take moderately rough water. And a wood boat (which will probably be plywood) won't be as pleasing a shape as many aluminum johnboats. Bill's boat was a Ouachita (Ouachita Marine, Main Street, Little Rock, Arkansas 72201), but you might check out johnboats from Monark, Appleby, or Sears. If a larger boat is wanted for three-man gunning, both Monark and Ouachita build johnboats in fifteen-, sixteen-, eighteen-, and twenty-foot lengths.

As the plans show, Bill's boat has a three-foot bottom beam. Monark, which offers thirty-four different johnboat models (by far the greatest selection), including one rough-water model with a special "chicken-breasted" bow, has fourteen-footers with forty-eight-inch bottoms that would allow a little more legroom, and some sixteen-footers with forty-eight-inch bottoms that would gun four men easily. Monark's excellent free color catalog shows all their boats as well as placement of seats, frames, etc. Address, Monark Boats, Box 210, Monticello, Arkansas 71655.

Another really neat feature of this rig is that the whole blind superstructure unbolts and can be lifted off when bass-fishing time rolls around!

As you can see, construction is simple. You bolt frames to the johnboat sides. Bill's Ouachita has a round pipe at the gunwale, and the frame must be recessed to receive this. Then the side decking mounts on a chine piece that sits on top and runs the length of the gunwale and on carlings attached to the frames. This, incidentally, is basically how you'd proceed to mount a cabin on the cabin johnboat. The sides of

JOHNBOAT BARGE BLIND

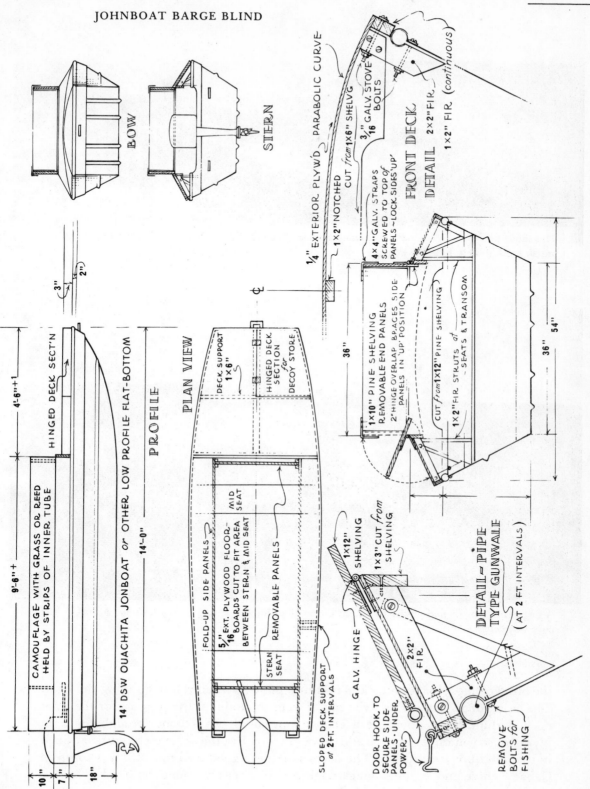

BOW

STERN

¼" EXTERIOR PLYW'D PARABOLIC CURVE

1×2" NOTCHED

CUT from 1×6" SHELV'G

³⁄₁₆" GALV. STOVE BOLTS

4×4" GALV. STRAPS SCREWED TO TOP OF PANELS ~ LOCK SIDES 'UP'

FRONT DECK DETAIL 2×2" FIR.
1×2" FIR. (continuous)

1×10" PINE SHELVING REMOVABLE END PANELS

2" HINGE OVERLAP BRACES SIDE PANELS IN 'UP' POSITION

cut from 1×12" PINE SHELVING

1×2" FIR. STRUTS at SEATS & TRANSOM

36"

54"

36"

3"

2"

4'-6"+1

9'-6"+

HINGED DECK SECT'N

CAMOUFLAGE WITH GRASS OR REED HELD BY STRIPS OF INNER TUBE

14' DSW OUACHITA JONBOAT or OTHER LOW PROFILE FLAT-BOTTOM

14'-0"

PROFILE

DECK SUPPORT 1×6"

HINGED DECK SECTION for DECOY STORE

PLAN VIEW

FOLD-UP SIDE PANELS

MID SEAT

5⁄16" EXT. PLYWOOD FLOOR-BOARDS CUT TO FIT AREA BETWEEN STERN & MID SEAT

REMOVABLE PANELS

STERN SEAT

SLOPED DECK SUPPORT at 2 FT. INTERVALS

1×12" SHELVING

1×3" CUT from SHELVING

2×2" FIR

GALV. HINGE

DOOR HOOK TO SECURE SIDE PANELS ~ UNDER POWER

DETAIL~PIPE TYPE GUNWALE
(AT 2 FT. INTERVALS)

REMOVE BOLTS for FISHING

10"

7"

18"

This shows how the barge blind is positioned against the bank. Notice that a "slot" has been dug in the marsh bank to help hide the boat.

A dog sitting on the middle thwart stands higher than hunters sitting on the bottom. A burlap bag covers the engine.

the blind collapse for running and fold into position when you're gunning the boat. The only thing I can see that you might want to modify is the support for the front deck. I think there would be a chance you could put a boot through the light plywood, so you might want to add extra bracing. Use the same techniques outlined in the pond-box description. The decoy hatch is a good idea too. Bill says eighteen Canada goose and eighteen black duck decoys fit easily under the hatch.

You may want to make some modifications, depending on how your aluminum hull is built. For example, if the side top is flat, the chine piece could sit on it. Exactly how the forward deck fits into the bow also depends on how your bow is shaped. A transom piece might be bolted on the boat and the deck brought out to sit flush on this.

Another innovation would be to support the blind-side panels in a different fashion with braces, hooks, or clamps, and to hinge them so they would fold flat into the center of the boat. Then an additional one-by-twelve plank could be inserted between the two (held in place with slotted holders, perhaps) to create a cover for the boat when it's not in use.

Bill's original hull weighed 160 pounds. The deck and blind panels added eighty-five pounds, reducing the boat's carrying capacity from six hundred to five hundred pounds. Two men can gun comfortably from it, however, with a retriever between them. Loaded, the boat does thirty miles an hour with one man aboard, twenty-five with two and all gear, powered with only a twenty horsepower. Bill reports he has to cross open water to get to his favority spots, and the several times the boat has been in rough water it performed well.

Bill was inspired to write to me in the first place when he took issue with a statement of mine that goose-hunting posed waterfowling's greatest challenge. After twenty years of gunning both black ducks and geese, Bill gives the nod to the black as the smarter. He also feels that they can smell people. He adds, "I agree with you and Andy Tanner that the gunning boat is the shape of the future. I might add that it probably would have been the shape of the past if other methods were not so easy and inexpensive." I'm sure he is right.

MATERIALS

Here is some general information on boatbuilding materials generally available today:

Wood. Plans call for plywood construction, sometimes with pine sides. Use exterior-grade plywood. Boatbuilding grade is not required. If you can't buy 10′ sheets, cut two 8-footers, scarf them together with a diagonal cut, and glue and fiber-glass-tape the joint. Oak is called for where strength is needed. Mahogany is a good substitute and more readily available. Plenty of good boats have been built with fir. If extremely light weight is wanted, use spruce throughout except for the motor pad.

Fiber Glass.   If you figure on dragging the boat much or using it in ice, plan to fiber-glass it. Use about a 7.5-oz. glass cloth, and don't spare the resin. Slightly round chine edges with a wood rasp. If you make errors, fill with fiber glass putty. This will work on all underwater seams. To waterproof only, cover underwater seams with Dynel tape. It stretches and lies over edges and curves better than glass.

Fastenings.   If you follow tradition, you should use brass screws and Weldwood glue. Bronze isn't needed on these little boats. Although the glue is still reasonable to buy, brass isn't. I wouldn't hesitate to go to galvanized screws, especially for use in fresh water. Bronze nails are available with ridges for extra holding power. These are good for building. They hold well while glue sets but can't be taken out easily. I nail and glue sides and bottoms of my boats but screw the decks so I can repair the boats without tearing things apart. Galvanized wire brads can also be used. I have a couple of small boats built (sloppily) with these and Weldwood, and they are holding up fairly well. The nails deteriorate, but the glue holds. Note: Resin glues need 70° temperature to set well. If you are building a really good boat, go to a resorcinol two-part glue.

Tools.   Hand tools can build the boat, but a saber saw is almost a requirement for following curved sides and cutting to many contours, and an electric drill for opening screw holes will ease the job. Besides these, hammer, square, mortar box, and saw are needed. An automatic screwdriver is a delight.

Another boatbuilding item that is indispensable is what my old pal H.I. Chapelle calls (in his classic *Boat Building*) the Groaning Chair. When you make a horrible mistake you go sit in the chair and groan.

Where to Buy.   You can buy a fancy boat lamp anywhere in the United States, but try to find boat fittings. I once shopped every hardware store in Front Royal, Virginia — at some sixty miles out of Washington, D.C., hardly the frontier — vainly attempting to purchase some galvanized screws. They looked at me as though I was a crazy Yankee. The honest ones did. The rest tried to tell me that cheap cadmium plating was as corrosion-resistant as hot-dipped galvanized. There are three mail-order houses, good ones, that list everything I've talked about (except wood) and more: James Bliss, 100 Route 128, Dedham, Massachusetts 022026; Goldbergs, 202 Market Street, Philadelphia, Pennsylvania 19106; or Defender Industries, 255 Main Street, New Rochelle, New York 10801. (Defender has a very helpful article on fiber-glassing techniques.) Catalogs, $1 for the first two, 50¢ for the last. Tell James Bliss you know me, and they'll give you a discount. The others are discount houses. M. L. Condon, 268 Ferris Avenue, White Plains, New York 10603 is a mail-order house specializing in boat woods.

BOAT TIPS AND SAFETY

There are some things I've learned the hard way, knocking around in duckboats. The first is about anchors. I was on the marsh one evening right about dark. The temperature was about thirty degrees. I was taking a coffin box to high ground. My stool boat at the time was a twelve-foot Grumman car-topper. I pulled the boat up on the bank, then started manhandling the box. I turned around and, to my horror, saw that the stool boat had drifted away and was hung on the end of a small sandbar perhaps forty feet away. I started racing up the gut to where I could wade across but instantly decided I did not have the luxury of time. The tide was ebbing out. At any second the boat could slip away and go right on out to sea, stranding me. I whipped back, peeled down to the buff, and swam to the boat, breaking the world's forty-foot record in the process. I slithered instantly aboard, brought her back, and jumped back into my clothes.

If you ever have to go in ice water, it won't be too bad if you have dry clothes to come back to. If you ever have to swim in icy water, strip naked. After I did it, I ran up and down the beach for a minute or two and never even felt the effects of the swim. I learned another water trick when I was lifeguarding. If any of us had to make a rescue when the water was very cold, we never put our heads under. Immersing gives you a headache.

Anyway, since that time I always rig a little Danforth anchor on the forward deck of all my duckboats. I hold it in place with shock cord or rubber rope. Anytime I leave the boat the anchor goes down. Haven't been swimming since.

The guys who know the most about what to do after going into cold water are the canoe experts. Canoeists often go out on nice sunny spring days, never realizing the water temperature is near freezing. Brad Angier and I go into this subject at length in our *Introduction to Canoeing* (Stackpole). In typical 32.5-degree water you have fifteen minutes before exhaustion sets in. In your warm duck clothes, survival time immersed is probably around twenty minutes. Salt water freezes at twenty-eight degrees. Typical winter salt water is about thirty degrees.

I always leave a note if I'm gunning any faraway spot. I tell where I am and what time I expect to return, and I ask if I'm not back by then for the reader to notify the game warden. So far I've always made it.

If one of your pals goes into cold water, get him out as quickly as possible. Don't listen to assurances that he is okay. His body strength is being sapped faster than he can realize, as immersion hypothermia, the lowering of body temperature, masks sensation. Keep this in mind if you fall in yourself. If body temperature is lowered twenty degrees, you've cashed in.

If you are a long way from anywhere, start a fire—use gas from your gas tank—and strip. Wring and warm your clothes and put them back on. Put on anything dry, of course. Just wringing clothes out without a fire will possibly save life. Get a victim as warm as possible. Hold him against your body or between two men. Warm at two small fires so front and back are warmed. The very best way to warm is to put the victim in a hot bath. Don't give the guy whisky if he's at all cold, as it will dilate the skin capillaries and speed the heat loss. We didn't fall overboard one gunning day, but we might as well have because of pelting rain. We ran into town for lunch and put all our stuff through the local drier. Now that's smart.

Another duckboat trick I do concerns the painter. You want it as long as possible. I measure it off and stop it just short of where it would foul the prop if it goes overboard (which it will).

The effects of ice on hull material have been discussed. Cold weather won't affect your outboard beyond having to let it warm up more. Store an outboard straight up and down so water will run out of it. If you tip the motor up or take it off and leave it lying, water could be trapped inside and freeze. If you have starting problems, buy a can of ether. If you use an inboard, or stern drive, the motor has to be drained every night. I rigged the Chrysler Crown of the old *Wanderer* with drains on three-inch extensions and painted them red. It was a two-minute job to drain her. To make sure the drains aren't silted closed, run the engine with them open. The pressure will free them.

Boats can get locked in ice and it won't hurt them. A storm half sank my skiff, and by the time I got to her she was locked in ice, decoys and all, and stayed that way for a week. I was a wreck worrying about her, but the boat and decoys were fine.

Here's another safety tip that, fortunately, I didn't learn the hard way. If you're wading unfamiliar waters, wade so you can fall on the boat if the bottom disappears. I gunned a spot for two seasons, thinking the sandy bottom was all shallow. To my horror, I discovered a section down from where I'd been walking around had been dredged to twelve feet! If I'd hit that slope to the deep, I'd never have made it back to shoal water. Now unless I can see the bottom I do all my wading leaning on the boat.

Another boating tip involves your car and your pocketbook more than your life. In any tidal area or in river locales where water levels change, look over parking spots for your car very carefully. Most will have high and low places. You can park at low tide never thinking that you'll gun a tide or more. At high tides in storms or during equinoctial tides, parking lots are often flooded. If your car is on high ground, you're okay, but on low spots the hubs, maybe even the motor, can go under and you've got expensive problems. I see this happen at least once a season.

Federal law has recently been changed — and many state laws have followed suit — to allow you to hunt with the motor left on the boat, provided the boat and motor are stopped. You are permitted to retrieve dead or crippled birds with a boat under power but are not allowed to shoot cripples from a boat thus powered. But anyone who has ever chased a broken-wing goose knows you have to. Next to citizen-band radio laws, this is the most frequently ignored statute I know of. Any boat is legal that doesn't offer the hunter a method of concealment beneath the water. You could put watertight chambers in a gunning barge and really take her down, but the Feds say, No. It is also illegal to "stir up" migratory waterfowl with a boat, another law frequently flouted. We see big concentrations of brant just sitting out in the bay, not moving. Suddenly we have to run over and see how our buddies elsewhere are faring. That it happened to jump all the brant wasn't our fault, was it, Judge?

This law talk suggests one of Ray Camp's brant stories. Seems the warden threw back a tarp in old Sedge's garvey and there were 112 brant.

"Yes, Judge, I shot them birds," said Sedge in as honest a tone as he could muster, "but it warn't my fault."

"Why not?" the judge asked.

"Wall, them brant come in. And, Judge, you know how brant bunch up. I shot and right at that second they bunched. The next thing I know the sky was raining brant. Now you didn't want me to let all them birds go to waste, did you, Judge?"

"Thirty days. Next case."

12

Blinds for Ducks and Geese

Even though the successful waterfowler depends to a large degree on his boat for getting him to good shooting areas and concealing him once there, there will be times when some kind of blind is required. A "hide," the old fellows used to call it. There are all kinds of waterfowling situations, of course, and various methods of dealing with them. Traditionally, though, a blind should accomplish three purposes. Obviously, it shouldn't scare ducks or geese; it should conceal one to four hunters well enough so even if they squirm around, waterfowl cannot see the movement; and it should offer some kind of protection from bad weather. It should keep the wind off and be capable of being warmed to some reasonable temperature with a heater of some sort. If you hunt in the South, another thing to keep in mind is that the blind shouldn't offer any places for snakes to hide. I once queried a group of Louisiana duck hunters and, somewhat to everyone's dismay, found that half the group had been bitten by moccasins.

BASIC PRINCIPLES

Basically, you kill waterfowl by going where they are and hiding until they fly within range. Under certain conditions, this doesn't require any blind at all. You find a sky highway that ducks like. You go there and set up your rocket launcher. When the birds show on radar, you hunker down, and when they get in range you let fly. Under these conditions the birds will accept minimum concealment because they feel far enough away from you to be safe.

Sometimes you don't need any kind of a blind at all. Natural cover is enough. Every afternoon, let's say, around three o'clock you see birds pitching into a certain lake or river pool. You go there, conceal yourself in the natural cover, toss out a few decoys, and wait. The first time the ducks see the decoys they'll drop in. Maybe you can feel them a few more times. Sooner or later, however, they will get wary.

If you gun areas thick with natural cover, you can bask in glory. For example, ducks using the area may be used to big black rocks along the shore or thick scary-looking evergreens or suspiciously man-sized shocks of corn. When you rearrange this cover to suit your convenience, you've built the best blind there is — which, of course, is no blind at all. But take big black rocks, thick evergreens, or cornstalks to places where

Two gunners prepare to slide their boat up the bank. When it's well grassed, ducks should come to it. That's a horrible-looking decoy, though. *Evinrude Motors.*

they are foreign objects and the wary three and Canada geese, at least, will have no part of it. They may look over your decoys, or even pitch in out of range, but they won't get close to the scary unnatural-looking things.

Another tip is to carry a compass when you build a permanent blind and never face it either due east or due west. If you do, mornings and evenings when the sun in low, the light will be in your eyes and tend to reflect off your face.

Since waterfowling is such an old sport, a number of relatively standard blind types have evolved. Let's discuss each.

CAMOUFLAGE NET

The easiest way to hide is with a camouflage net. They often work surprisingly well. You can drape them over your boat. I've seen guys drive four stakes and string the net around them. The nets won't keep you very warm, and they're a mess when there's a high wind blowing, but they are cheap and easy, portable as all get-out, of course, and they can conceal you

HEAD NET

The thing that scares waterfowl most is movement. They can all detect it and are usually suspicious enough around decoys during the season to interpret any movement as a man waiting to attack them. The second most common tip-off is your face. When you look up, it's like a big headlight shining. *Sports Afield*'s Jerry Robinson made some tests with black ducks. He lay out on a rock island, wearing a camouflage suit complete with a head net and camouflage gloves. As long as he stayed motionless the blacks would decoy to him and fly right over him without the least suspicion that a man was there. There's a good lesson for us all here. Unless you happen to be colored duckboat brown by nature, you should wear a head net or some face paint, or barring that, be darned careful about keeping your face low and peering out from under a hatbrim.

HEADBOARD BLIND

This is the simplest kind of blind and should be in wider use than it is. It is merely a rest for your head or support for your back. With this device you can lie out full length comfortably. A tarp covered with grass goes over your body to make the

This is what I call a "headboard blind." You can't comfortably lie out flat without having someplace to rest your head. Try it. Your neck kills you without support. This headboard just sticks in anywhere. Note that the bottom is serrated.

I got fancy here and used a tarp. In cold weather it helps keep you warm. Make a sandwich and slide in from the open side. Now it's a question of gathering grass and throwing it over yourself or the tarp.

Lying out like this, no duck or goose will spot you if you keep still. The board makes it comfortable for all day if you want to gun that long. This is a good device for field shooters in the Midwest for ducks and geese.

blind. If the grass where you must conceal yourself is high enough, you can sit up, and for this a back support is required. Without support for the head or back, you can't maintain the position for any length of time. The advantages are obvious—the blind goes anywhere, is cheap and fully portable. But on the opposite side of the coin, the blind offers no warmth and not much comfort.

INDIAN BLINDS

In the Far North, Indian guides create natural blinds around hunters, and variations of this technique are in wide practice everywhere. On the muskeg marshes a form of low willow bush is common. The Indians cut these and stake them into the ground around the hunters. Since brush clumps are natural, the birds aren't wary of the clumps until they see the men. I've noticed that these don't often fool Canada geese, however. You must kneel to shoot and rest sitting on your heels, and this becomes extremely uncomfortable after a time. You may be able to fashion your own version out of evergreens, willows, or cornstalks.

Step 1. The fast way to grass up a boat or blind as perfected by the author after years of training. The first thing you need is a sharp machete to cut a big pile of grass.

Step 2. Take two sections of light baling wire. Twist ends together and attach both so you can maintain tension on the strands. Grab a handful of grass and lay it between the two wires.

Step 3.   Pull the wires taut and twist one around the other a couple of times. Vary the leafy ends, first on one side, then the other.

The result: You wind up with mats of grass that look like this. These are then tacked in place on your boat or blind. Grass stays in place remarkably well, even after winds and storms.

PIANO-BOX BLIND

This is the most common kind of blind. At its best, it is a big, rectangular bottomless box, just like a piano box. Two or more gunners sit on a bench with the box sides projecting slightly higher than head level. You stand up to shoot. The outside of the box is concealed with cover natural to the area, usually wired on or held in place with laths. The wooden box is usually dispensed with. Stakes are driven into the ground at the four corners and crosspieces are nailed or wired to them. Natural cover is then wired to the cross-stakes. This cover can be cattails, reeds, evergreen boughs, marsh grass, camouflage cloth, cornstalks, tules, scrub brush, water or willow bush or trees—whatever is found in the immediate vicinity that grows in places near water. The more natural it looks, the better. A piano box is best placed against a background of high growth or in places where natural covers sticks up as high as the box does. If the blind sticks up and stands out—as on a sandy point or flat marsh—it becomes less effective.

There are a lot of good things to be said about a wooden piano-box blind. With sides, it is warm. You can put a back and top on it and increase its warmth. A tarp inside can hold the wind out of sideless versions. A back and top also help if the blind happens to be silhouetted by the rising or setting sun so its shadow is stark. In this case, you might want to stick a lot of natural brush around the box, so the heavy shadow resembles a clump of cover rather than one big single black object.

The box blind is also comfortable. You wait in a natural sitting position and stand to shoot. In a pinch, you can throw a box blind together in a half hour or so with no more tools than a hatchet and roll of wire. It is also good for peering out of and gives some concealment when you get the itch.

Far out on a point, and with no background to soften its outline, this piano box would be all right for divers, principally broadbills—but you'd have difficulty pulling the wary three or geese into it.

A roofed piano box makes a good shelter for the men inside, and the grass blends the blind well with the background. Birds shot here are mostly broadbills. Blacks and mallards would usually shy away from this hide except in bad weather.

The whiteness of raw wood silhouettes your body and head, particularly if you build a back and top on the piano box. The interior surfaces should be painted with flat duckboat-brown paint.

A more sophisticated version lowers the silhouette by making the seat right on the ground. A pit is dug for your feet. The sides of a regular box blind must be around five feet high. The pit lowers this to three feet, which would pay off in some areas.

STAKE BLINDS

If you build a piano box with a floor in it and stick it on pilings about a hundred feet from shore, it's called a stake blind or booby blind, the latter because a lot of open-water ducks are called boobies.

Stake blinds violate all the rules of blind-making. Though it is true they draw the less wary species like broadbills, canvasbacks, and redheads better than they do mallards or black ducks, these last two, and even Canada geese, will at times pitch in as though the high-rise apartment wasn't even there. Two possible (feeble) explanations for this have been advanced. The first is that in the aras where stake blinds are common, they've been a part of the landscape so long the ducks have become used to them. A second, more reasonable theory is that waterfowl aren't as suspicious of something actually out in the water away from shore. Open water is their safest refuge, and they feel more secure on it, which is why they are so vulnerable to the old floating sinkbox. Although stake blinds aren't as good as a sinkbox or even a good floating blind, I think they should be in far wider use than they are. In places where stake blinds are not known they'd scare hell out of the other duck hunters, but I suspect the ducks wouldn't mind them one bit.

The disadvantages of these complicated contraptions are obvious. It is a substantial effort to build one. In areas where ice forms, the blinds are subject to damage, and everywhere storms bust them up. Vandalism would be a factor in many places. A boat is needed to get to one, and the blind must be big enough so that the boat can

This is a huge permanent blind built on Maryland's Choptank River and used by a commercial guide. The covering is cedar trees, renewed every year. As you can see, the blind can hold six or eight shooters.

Why ducks aren't frightened of this kind of offshore piano box, I can't imagine. I found this one far out in the bay shallows at Ocracoke, North Carolina. The blind would be covered by cedars before the season began, though I'm told some blinds are left natural like this.

be hidden somewhat behind it. Generally, strict amateurs lack the equipment needed to transport piling and lumber to a given area, and sinking pilings requires some knowledge of bottoms and methods. And at least the passive acceptance of the landowner is needed to put one out, even in those areas where he does not, in fact, own the river bottom. The blind won't last very long if someone wants it out of there.

On the other hand, a well-made booby blind is generally good for years if undisturbed. It can be made warm and comfortable. (In the Chesapeake, diehards spend the night in them.) And most important of all, they work.

PIT BLINDS

An inland favorite is the pit blind. It is easy to build in fields and offers the best-possible concealment combined with good visibility as well as full protection from the weather. Grass, stubble cornstalks, or hay camouflage the resulting dirt pile. Often a ditch can be used as a portion of the blind to save the shoveler some work. A quck way to build one (the only way in sandy soils) is to dig it out just deep enough to lie down in. You lie until the birds come in, then sit up to shoot. Any pit blind is good because it fits so naturally into the surrounding terrain without disturbing it much.

Pits are especially associated with Canada-goose shooting. Here no dirt pile should be left, and you want to be sure there aren't any tire marks from tractors or pick-ups in the blind area.

The disadvantages of pits are that they fill with water, cave in unless lined with wood, are hard work to dig, and usually must be filled in at the season's end.

You pay $50 a day for the privilege of gunning out of a commercial goose pit like this one. And after you limit out, other hunters come into the blind. The cornstalks make a perfect cover for eager hunters who can't sit still.

SINKBOXES

These are a version of the pit blind that goes into marsh areas and proves as effective there as a pit, though they're a lot more work to build. A watertight box is built, then sunk into the marsh next to a likely pothole or on a good point. This is easier said than done as the hole keeps filling with water and has to be bailed and dug simultaneously. The top of the box sticks up twelve to eighteen inches above the march, so the box won't flood on normal over-the-marsh tides. Dirt from the hole is spread around to create a low mound. The best material is exterior plywood (3/8-inch for a two-man box, 1/2-inch for three). You had better fiber-glass it. A well-built box should last for years. One of the problems with boxes is having them pop out on high tides. Stringers must be bolted to the bottom to form a kind of shoe. Another trick is to drive pilings in an X on each side and drill and bolt these to a box. Most blinds get put in the marsh in the fall when waterfowl fever strikes hardest. It is far better to put them in during the summer. You fill them with water and let the earth around them settle before fall. Then there is much less chance they'll pop out.

The sinkbox, or sink blind as it is sometimes called, is a deadly device. On river sandbars, or in marshes on which the grass does not grow high, it is the only really

A good example of a two-man sinkbox. Although the man's face is conspicuous here, when birds are in the air you can hunker down and hide your face with the brim of your hat. Grass around the blind's edge breaks up any outline.

Standing up in the sinkbox puts gunners in business. I took this shot years ago and said at the time that when they rose up and I clicked the shutter the picture would make the cover of *Life*. It didn't. But it has been reproduced dozens of times.

good permanent blind. An easier version uses big wooden barrels, one barrel per man. If you can get good waterproof barrels, it is a good idea to fiber-glass the top, as the hoops exposed to water and air will soon rust away, while the wood and glass will last indefinitely. Down in the earth the rusting is much slower, and the pressure holds the barrel together anyway.

You'll have to take my word for it, but back of Barnegat is surely the darndest sinkbox ever made. When I saw it, I couldn't believe my eyes. It is a huge box and is so deep that gunners have to step up on a seat to shoot. Some commercial guide must have got so mad at having his sports twitch around while ducks were decoying that he sank them so far in the earth it was impossible for anything to see them. But can you imagine sitting down there staring at the blind wall all day with the sky a tiny hole in the top of the box!

The drawbacks of sinkboxes are the torturous work of digging in, the fact that they flood and have to be pumped out, and their expense. Heavy ice late in winter can also bust them up. A top helps, but few use one.

Anyone who volunteers for this job should have his head examined. You can see the black ooy gunk you have to work in. By this point the blind has been bucketed full of water. Right below my knee is an extension on the bottom to keep the blind in. Once you could hire somebody to do this job — but not any more.

FLOATING BLINDS

These work for the same reasons that stake blinds work. They are far more susceptible to storm damage, however, and are almost goners for sure if caught in the ice. But they don't cost anywhere near as much in time or money, and you can easily build one yourself.

Most hunters build a raft and put a piano box on it. Fiber-glass-covered plywood is a good material for the hull, or you can use Styrofoam logs. Most gunners use a small boat to tow the blind to a likely spot, then anchor there on two anchors, so the blind stays facing the right way.

My feeling is that if you're going to build a floating blind, you should go all the way and make it a gunning barge. You should consider the box blind on a float only if you must stand up to shoot.

All floating blinds should be grassed up. The more they look like natural humps out there in the water, the better the ducks will decoy to them. You may occasionally get a few of the wary three and Canada geese to decoy to a floating blind, but generally you won't.

The main disadvantage with floating blinds is that the hunters who use them usually aren't boatmen enough to anchor them securely to stand winter storms. High and ungainly, they are vulnerable to wind and need such heavy weights on the bottom as an auto-engine block, Danforth anchors in the eighteen-pound category, or railroad-car wheels in the one-hundred-pound weight class, depending on the size and weight of the blind. These should be secured with chain and 1/2-inch nylon rodes at least five times the maximum water depth. Remember when the wind howls, you may be able to stay ashore but the blind can't.

OUTER BANKS CURTAIN BLIND

A unique blind is used along the outer banks of the Carolinas. Although it requires some elaborate procedures to build, it makes up for it by being one of the effective blinds possible.

Along the banks a sandbar stands well offshore, the length of Pamlico and Albemarle sounds. This bar bares on extreme low tides. Normal depth of the water

Here's a good example of a floating blind, somewhat casually grassed up. If you can anchor them so they last through fierce December storms, floating blinds made good hides.

might be one or two feet. Stake blinds serve in some places, but the curtain blind is preferred for its effectiveness.

First, a cement box is constructed, usually of cinder block, though reinforced poured cement is better. Brass bolts are sunk in the wet cement along the top of the box. The box is then transported to the blind site, which is no small feat but possible on the banks, since workboats and watermen abound. The box is sunk into the sandbar, either by digging or pumping or both, so it is just under water at an average low tide.

A wooden frame the exact size to fit the inner dimensions of the cement box is then built. This is almost like a plywood inner lining but without a floor. Canvas is then sewn in a rectangle to fit around this inner liner. Along the bottom, the canvas is wrapped around wooden pieces which are then drilled and bolted onto the brass bolts extending from the cement box top. The canvas, in effect, makes a watertight seal flexible enough to allow the inner shell to be raised or lowered over a range of several feet. As the tide rises, the shell lifts up; as it declines, the shell sinks farther in the box. At all times the gunners sitting in the cement box are fully hidden. Since nothing sticks above the surface of the water except the buoyant rim of the "curtain," both ducks and geese come in readily to the decoys that are spread around the box. The gunners are tended and ducks retrieved by a large boat standing off a half mile or so.

BODY BOOTING

I'm saving the most bizarre blinds for last and certainly body booting tops that list. This is practiced on the Susquehanna Flats of Maryland and no place else that I know of, though variations with waders or wet suits would work anywhere. All that is required is a wet suit that fully protects the wearer up to the neck. U.S. Navy surplus suits were generally used; now I suspect frogmen wet suits are worn. The shooter stands among several silhouette decoys and hides behind them when ducks and geese come over. Water depth on the flats is about five feet. Special silhouettes are required that can slide up and down their anchoring poles and adjusted to correspond to the tide's rise and fall. Shell boxes are built on the backs and some have racks to take the weight of the guns. In cold water the sport is not for weaklings, and even the "hardest" shooters, as they say on the flats, can take only a half-hour or so at a time. A tender boat stands by at all times. I've always been amused by the fact that a large mental hospital overlooks the area. The "crazy" patients can sit in their warm, cozy rooms and watch the "sane" waterfowlers standing up to their necks in ice water.

BLIND HOUSEKEEPING

At all times, with any kind of blind, it is good practice to police the area. A piece of aluminum foil from a sandwich wrapper, a tin can, or even the shiny brass bases of empty shells can spook waterfowl. Heaters go into duck blinds. I use a catalytic heater. A friend prefers charcoal, which admittedly throws out more heat and permits cooking on the top. A kerosene lantern was standard on old-time sneakboxes for both heat and light. The seats in blinds are invariably muddy and wet. Dress accordingly.

It is fitting to leave so engrossing a subject as blinds with a word from the president of the Old Duck Hunters' Society Inc. (The Inc. stands for incorrigible.) The president's desperation measure to lure ducks within range was to stand up in the blind. Any duck flying by, so theorized the president, would instantly spot this action, immediately decide that only a damn fool would stand up in a duck blind, then fly back to make sure.

This is as good a place as any to say that when you sight waterfowl it's good form to announce the fact to your buddies by saying "Mark," rather than "Look out," "Hot damn," or "Jazus, here they come!" although I have heard, and probably said, all these things on occasion. I've tried without success to track down where the expression "Mark" originated. I wouldn't be surprised if it went back to game-keepers hollering at the break of a stag. You usually say "Mark, left" or "Mark, right" to position the bird.

It took me about ten years to learn not to wheel my head around to see them for myself, when somebody spotted ducks before I did, the resulting motion spooking hell out of the birds, of course. This is why you should try to keep the announcement as unexciting as possible, to avoid causing heads to spin and demands of "Where? Where?" The proper technique is to freeze at the word "Mark," and to stay perfectly still, moving only your eyes to determine where the bird is and if it can spot any motion.

It's a lot easier to get a conch out of his shell than to slither out of a wet suit. These suits were worn by navy lookouts in World War II. The man inside is wholly dry. But even dry and heavily clothed, a man has to be "hard," as they say on the flats, to stand more than thirty minutes at a time in the water.

Here the men have concealed themselves behind the stake decoys. These have to be adjusted up and down as the tide changes. There are ledges on such stake decoys to hold shells and guns. Most of the body booting rigs are syndicated; several gunners go in together since the cost of decoys, boats, and other equipment is very high.

A body-booting rig on the Susquehanna flats with another "set" behind it. This is the only place in America where such a practice is legal. Gunners anchor out on the flats at 2:00 and 3:00 A.M. to ensure a favored position. The rigs are particularly effective because they're out in open water where the geese don't expect danger.

13

The Fascinating Subject of Decoys

The subject of waterfowl decoys is an area of hunting that can—and often does—become an end in itself. In the days when market hunting flourished, decoy makers turned out wooden decoys in astonishing profusion. Many of them were merely crude representations of the numerous species of ducks, geese, and shorebirds. But the gnarled hands of a surprising number of these carvers of long ago turned out waterfowl reproductions of such delicacy and grace that without even knowing it, they created a treasured American art form. View any of the great collections, the Joel D. Barber, Richard Moeller, Edward Mulliken collections, for instance, in the Shelburne Museum near Burlington, Vermont, the nation's most outstanding exhibit, with over a thousand decoys. Sooner or later one of these little blocks of wood, lead, and paint will reach out to you and astound you that human hands could breathe such life into the inanimate and make you wonder about its creator and where under heaven he acquired the skill to create such a masterpiece.

Some of this aura still clings to the crassest commercial decoys, though they do their job poorly or well as the case may be. How important the difference is between rough and finished decoys comes up as a subject of endless debate, apparently even among the ducks themselves, for they will at times accept crude decoys and other times scorn the best. The debate will continue until men penetrate the minds of waterfowl. What is not debatable is that a waterfowler's decoys are, or should be, cherished possessions, objects of admiration and pride.

Most of all they must be good at their job, which is indeed a demanding one. Who would believe that a handful of decoys could reach out to freeflying waterfowl miles away and lure them within gunshot range? Such a profound subject should be approached with varying emotions, humility not the least among them. We are all students to the last. No one man can hope to know it all about waterfowl decoys. You're doing well, in fact, if you know barely enough.

History

Decoying ducks with artificial representations of the real animals stretches back to dark antiquity. In certain Egyptian wall paintings of duck hunting there are objects in the water that look like decoys woven out of rushes. The ancient Greeks were supposed to have used wooden decoys drawn back and forth from a concealed position to entice ducks and geese within range of a thrown net or arrow shot.

The origins of the word *decoy* seem to stem from the Dutch word for duck trap—*de kooi*. These traps were in use throughout Europe during the Middle Ages. They resemble the fyke nets used in commercial fishing. Long net arms extend in a giant Y. At the point of the Y the net becomes a long tunnel or cage. Wild birds were slowly driven into the trap, then into the cage or tunnel, where they were clubbed. Wild birds would soon get shy of the tunnel and refuse to enter it. To calm the wild birds, live decoys were brought into play, and in medieval England these became know as coy ducks. The word decoy is thought to have evolved from this term. In modern parlance decoys are also called "blocks," apparently since they were carved from blocks of wood, and "dekes ," a contraction. An older synonym is "stool," a word evidently derived from the European practice of setting out wild pigeons on movable perches or stools as live decoys to attract others of their kind. The word "stool" is used as both singular and plural. An old bayman will say, "I put out my stool," i.e., the whole rig, and refer to individual "stools" and to the birds "stooling" to the decoys. Mostly decoy is accented on the first syllable. If you hang out with a fancy crowd you'll hear the second syllable emphasized—deCoy.

It is certain that the American Indians used a variety of decoys. These were woven out of grasses of various.kinds or made of actual duck skins stuffed with grass. This practice was carried on by the white men who made the very earliest decoys known in the colonies. Almost always a duck skin was used to cover a block of wood. Decoys as we know them today probably first came to be made in the early 1800s, with the great days of the art starting in the latter part of the century and continuing right up to the 1930s.

Most professional decoy makers of the 1940s to the present learned their trade as young men in the early years of this century, and as these men die off their skills are rarely handed down to others. With each passing year, the individual commercial decoy carver becomes more and more a relic of the past.

Yet, curiously, the reverse is true of amateur carvers. The great profusion of decoy shows around the country, usually aided and abetted by chapters of Ducks Unlimited, has spurred growing numbers to create decoys to be shown in competition, and their efforts in the working-decoys division arouse envy, and in the ornamental categories, amazement.

Decoys made by machinery appeared after the Civil War. Among the earliest manufacturers were the Dodge and Mason factories, both in Detroit, and the Stevens factory in Weedsport, N.Y. Prices ranged from $2.50 a dozen for crude decoys to $12 a dozen for handsomely painted versions.

All decoyable ducks were imitated both by factories and by individual carvers. Such rare types as old squaw, ruddy ducks, loons, eiders, swans, wood ducks, and even seagulls are now special collector's items. (More about seagulls later.) Most early decoys were carved from wood, but a variety of species were imitated in cork, canvas, tin, and even iron. The birds were positioned in almost every natural resting or feeding position. Tip-up and headless feeders were common. Extended neck dippers were found along with "confidence" decoys. These last are low- or turned-neck decoys that appear to be sleeping and so give decoying birds confidence to come in. Other confidence decoys were seagulls, cranes, mergansers, loons, and coots. These forms have all but disappeared from the selections of commercial decoys offered today, though their importance will be discussed later. About the only body position you will not see in the great decoy collections is the raised-neck position of alarm. (The beginning duck caller's first efforts are usually to imitate the alarm call, since it is the duck cry he hears most. The art of the decoy maker has prevented us from imitating the waterfowl's last position before takeoff, when the bird cranes his neck as high as possible to view approaching danger.)

The Why of Decoys

Most ducks and geese are usually attracted to their own kind when they see them feeding or resting. But by no means will all species decoy, and any waterfowler knows that the birds' sensitivity to decoys varies greatly. When threatened—by bad weather, floating ice, extremely cold weather, impending storms, hunger, separation from the flock or mate—all waterfowl become more sensitive to a decoy rig. In most places gunning pressure is the greatest danger of all, and ducks and geese will become shier and shier of heavily gunned places and more and more wary of decoy sets as the season progresses.

Let me illustrate with an extreme example. I was set up in a local area that is as heavily hunted as any in the country. There is a "slot" there that connects two large bodies of water. Such a spot is usually good because most ducks are suspicious of land. They obviously have to fly over land often, but you'll notice that when they're near a river or stream they'll stick to the water wherever possible. I saw a single mallard coming up the slot. Now, a single bird is the most vulnerable of all, so I was amazed when the bird saw my decoys, turned, and flew around the marsh behind me and back to the slot a hundred yards up from me. The bird was decoy shy. It didn't see me. There wasn't anything amiss about my set. The mallard had been shot at so many times from that spot that a rig there of any kind tripped his alarm bell; just the presence of ducks there spelled danger.

The mallard is America's most popular duck by far and is readily susceptible to decoys. Other popular species like the teal, wood duck, pintail, bluebill, and all the geese can be pulled out of the sky at times by a proper decoy spread. I hunt Atlantic brant a lot. They aren't too bright, but if you gun the same spot hard, say three times a week, even brant will become much more wary. In smaller waters such as creeks, twice-a-week gunning is plenty. This is true everywhere to a certain extent. Waterfowl will be quick to decoy early in the season but become less so as their ranks thin and unpleasant memories thicken. In preferred gunning spots—points, coves, ponds, "slots," passes—that receive heavy gunning pressure, it becomes harder and harder to attract birds as the season advances. This can be countered somewhat by using more and more decoys.

Small ponds and potholes are least able to take gunning pressure. These should be gunned no more than twice a week and once is better. Any shooting at large flocks around a pond will quickly discourage waterfowl from using it.

Decoy Size and Numbers

It's vitally necessary that the waterfowl can easily see your decoys. The set must stand out. Because waterfowl can so instantly spot the motion of a hunter's head or hand, most waterfowlers think that the birds' vision is all-encompassing, that they miss nothing. That's just not so. After all, about the only thing that's going to kill a duck or a goose is a human. Human motion represents death. On the other hand,

On the Susquehanna flats you'll hear the words "stool boat" more than anywhere else — and this is the reason why. In the old days they set out plenty of decoys and they still do. I have a few of these processed paper decoys; they require plenty of work to keep them healthy.

other ducks or your decoys mean companionship, safety, and feeding and resting areas. As such, in terms of relative importance, other ducks or geese aren't all that significant. Many times birds flying swiftly by, keen to reach some other destination, simply won't spot your decoys until it is too much trouble for them to turn around and fly back to them, especially if there's a wind blowing. I've read that commercial gunners for scaup sometimes waved a flag to make the birds look toward the decoy spread.

In former days this problem was met by putting out huge numbers of decoys. To a lesser extent this is still done, especially in goose hunting. As many as two hundred to four hundred decoys are commonly set out for Canadas, specs, blues, and snows. Old pictures of canvasback spreads in the Chesapeake show hundreds of decoys in action.

The trend is away from this nowadays, as hunters have found that, to a varying extent, size can be substituted for numbers. This trend has been carried to outlandish lengths in the Chesapeake, where silhouette Canada-goose decoys six feet high are common. Because of the wind resistance offered by these giant saillike slabs, which are cut from quarter-inch plywood, the silhouettes are bolted to metal fence stakes and driven into the ground with sledgehammers.

There isn't any question that heightened visibility is the factor at work. In the old days swan decoys were common on the Atlantic flyway. One or more of the huge white birds can be seen for miles, and since numbers of ducks feed in among swans, they appear natural in a set. As a matter of fact, I saw a couple of swans in a set on the Miles River just the other day.

Every duck shooter should always set out at least a pair of Canada geese in his rig. You will read that the reason for this is that ducks know Canadas are smart and think they will be safe where they are. This is nonsense. If it were true, ducks would follow geese around, which, of course, they do not. What's involved is visibility. The geese decoys are big and can be seen farther away.

Let me illustrate. I was gunning early in the season in a river so crowded that a spread was offered at almost every possible spot. I put out eight giant black ducks, then tossed out a brant. I would have used a Canada, since my water Canada decoys are bigger than the brant, but Canada geese seldom stray into confined rivers and a brant is more natural there. Two mallards flew over and decoyed beautifully to me, ignoring the others. Why? They saw my rig first because of the brant.

You read sometimes that in the smaller areas you don't need a lot of decoys, that a few will do. This is partly true. If you fill up a small pond with decoys, the birds will think there's too much competition and go where it's easier to fill their stomachs. If you are gunning a river, creek, or lake where ducks normally stay in twos and threes, by all means use a spread of five to seven birds. (Always put out an uneven number of decoys, with one bird off by itself so singles will go for it.)

However, the greater facts of decoy life are blunt. Most places, most times, the guy with the most decoys wins, and the guy with the most and biggest decoys wins biggest. Anything that causes the waterfowl to look your way aids in decoying them. I'm convinced that at least a part of a call's effectiveness comes from the fact that it makes the birds look your way.

Life-sized commercial duck decoys are made with a body about fifteen inches long. Geese are twenty inches. So-called oversized duck decoys average eighteen inches in

One of my decoys has misbehaved and busted his line — and I'm displeased by its behavior. This shows the size of the black duck bodies; they're almost as big as the Canada decoy, which is itself oversize. The bodies are 21 inches long. A standard black or mallard decoy is about 18 inches. Note how the three brant behind have managed to intertwine themselves. I'll have to go out and separate them.

body length, geese about twenty-five inches. I attach black mallard heads to twenty-one-inch goose bodies and often use them simultaneously with eighteen-inchers. I see many different-sized decoys mixed together with no harm done. It may offend the hunter's feelings for precision, but the ducks don't seem to mind. The largest duck decoys I ever saw were on a commercial guide's pond near Barnegat, New Jersey. I didn't get close enough to measure them, but they were immense — over thirty inches long. They looked like privies floating on their sides with heads attached.

It's hard to guess exactly where the use of oversize decoys reaches a point of diminishing returns. I've had the feeling that on smaller ponds my smaller decoys pull better than the big ones. Certainly on big water the big "coaster" blocks are better. It's a sound principle that big waters demand large numbers of big decoys; smaller, more confined spaces require the opposite.

A question that enters the picture in many places is how many decoys should you use when you expect to get only one or two ducks. It's simply too much effort to put out a big spread for so little return. You can pull a few divers a day with ten to fifteen

A commercial guide rearranges decoys that spread in a circle around his pit. In all, about a hundred and fifty decoys are set. These are nice silhouettes with flaps that give them body when viewed from above. The wing flaps fold flat for easy stowage.

birds, and in most places eight to ten divers will often suffice. But get the biggest you can. I doubt that you would have much chance of pulling geese of any variety (except brant) without at least twenty decoys, and twice that is a much better minimum.

Decoy Variety

In these days, and for far into the foreseeable future, owning decoys of a variety of species will be a waterfowling essential. The variety enables you to take advantage of special seasons. Within shouting distance of where I sit I can lay my hands on Canada geese, brant, canvasback, scaup, wigeon, and black duck decoys. And even so, I miss a special early teal season in my state because I'm not rigged for it.

Seagull decoys were once popular. Usually a single gull was positioned on the edge of the set to give it a natural look. I doubt that you could buy a seagull decoy today, and I do not think the trouble of carving one worth the effort. If you're going to use specialty decoys, put out a swan or an oversize Canada or snow goose to heighten your set's visibility.

Sex Ratio

People have questioned me as to what the ratio of the sexes of decoys should be in those species in which the plumage of the sexes is different. The question is not particularly vital, as there is little pairing of the species during hunting season. A rig of all males or all females would probably pull birds of both sexes. Decoy manufacturers usually split an order fifty-fifty or in some cases eight males to four females. I prefer this latter division because in the popular species—pintail, mallard, scaup, canvasback—the male plumage is brighter and more conspicious.

Decoy Patterns and Positioning

Much of the vagueness and generality that accompany the questions of when and why waterfowl will or won't decoy disappears when we discuss the matter of positioning the decoys in your set or rig. Much can be laid down almost as "law."

All species of ducks tend to stick fairly close to one another. You seldom see birds scattered widely. Birds of a flock will usually stay within several feet of one another. This means that while decoys can and often should be split into bunches, individual decoys within the groups should not be far apart—three to five feet at most. Putting them too close to one another decreases the overall size and visibility of your rig.

Decoys should be out in open where they can be seen. Don't hide them in close to a bank.

Ducks never bump into other ducks. Neither should your decoys.

With many exceptions, ducks and geese tend to stick to their own kind. You should certainly separate them if you set both divers and puddle ducks. With other species it is difficult to draw rigid lines. If pintails and mallards are feeding in the same fields, decoys of either species will probably attract both. If they're feeding on different foods, the attraction will be less, maybe nonexistent. Teal, wood ducks, wigeon, and gadwalls will normally come in to mallard decoys. If separated from the flock, the young of most species will decoy to most others. Any port in a storm. Canada geese may come into puddle-duck decoys but probably because they like the spot, not because of the decoys. Generally, birds that show white won't decoy to species that don't. The best way to solve the problem of which species to put out is to observe carefully which birds frequent your area (after the season is best) and duplicate them with your rig.

Land and danger are one and the same to all waterfowl. Positioning decoys close to the blind in the effort to get birds to alight within closer range won't work. If the birds decoy at all, they will probably land out of range and swim it. I once asked an old bayman what was the best size pond for black ducks. "Wal," he said, "it shouldn't be too big. Then again it shouldn't be too small." That seemed reasonable. How deep should the water be? I asked. "Wal," he replied, thinking deeply, "It shouldn't be too deep. Then again, it shouldn't be too shallow." In this way do we learn. Your decoy spread shouldn't be out too far, then again it shouldn't be in too close. Generally, I like to position my inner decoy from twenty to twenty-five yards from the bank. The blind may be another four or five yards inland of this. That puts the nearest decoy about thirty yards from the blind. My farthest decoy will be from five to eight yards beyond the nearest. This means I am going to try to take the birds at thirty-five to forty yards, which is out far enough to allow my pattern to open up but close enough so lead calculations are easier. If birds are wary, set the decoys out another ten yards and shoot at from forty to fifty yards. They can still be hit at this range, especially if they slow down to alight. However, you are approaching maximum duck range, which is sixty to sixty-five yards.

Some experts suggest placing a decoy at maximum gun range, to indicate when the ducks are within range. If you do this, you run the risk that decoying birds will sit down next to this decoy. If a decoy drifts off downwind, as frequently happens during storms, birds will invariably sit down next to it. The reason for this cannot be overemphasized. All waterfowl feel safer out in open water.

Important points to remember are that most diving ducks will fly over their own kind and sit down at the head of the flock. Puddle ducks won't fly low over other puddlers, as the danger of one springing up and causing a midair collision is too great. They sit down behind other puddlers. Geese will do either or both or will land right in among other geese.

Decoys should be positioned to create landing areas in front of the blind. There are generally two ways to do this. The first is the fishhook, which is popular with guys who have a big spread. The decoys are placed in a big C with the open part of the C directly before the blind and the center point some thirty to thirty-five yards out in open water. From the far "tail" of the top of the C, decoys extend out toward open water perhaps as far as sixty to seventy-five yards. For diving ducks, the fishhook is reversed so the birds will pick up the shank, fly down it, and sit down in the open water of the C.

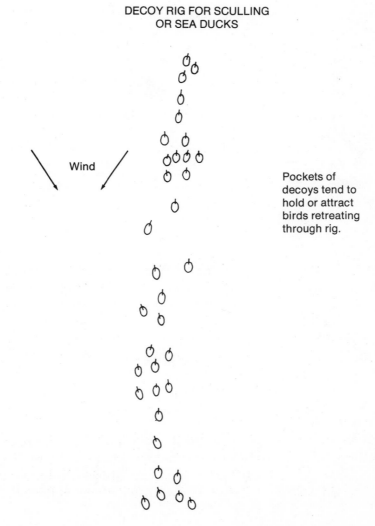

DECOY RIG FOR SCULLING
OR SEA DUCKS

Wind

Pockets of decoys tend to hold or attract birds retreating through rig.

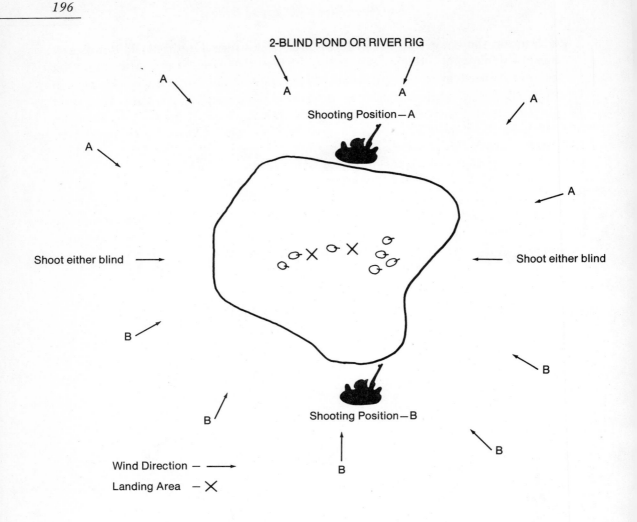

2-BLIND POND OR RIVER RIG

Shooting Position—A

Shoot either blind →

← Shoot either blind

Shooting Position—B

Wind Direction — →

Landing Area — ✕

The double O is the spread I prefer. In this setup two similar-sized groups are created and separated by a landing area of about twenty yards of open water in front of the blind. If you add a goose set to this, you split the bunches in a triple-O arrangement with the landing area on either side of the blind or shooting position. You put the divers to the right so they fly over the decoys and land in the open water. The puddlers land short of their decoys on the left in the same open-water spot.

Decoys in Relation to Wind
Ducks are coming to your decoys for rest or food or both. This means the decoys should be in a sheltered spot, in the lee of land. Like airplanes, waterfowl land into the wind. Although ducks frequently pitch into a spread from every which way, the more usual course is for them to make a somewhat systematic approach. They will

circle around so as to fly up to the decoys from a downwind position. This indicates that you don't want anything downwind of them that looks scary. Above all, you don't want them flying over the blind. With many exceptions, your decoys can, in effect, create an "approach pattern" downwind from your decoys. Birds that enter this pattern are extremely susceptible. Birds far out from it more often than not won't take the trouble to circle and come in. The same is true of very high birds. They are usually going somewhere and couldn't care less about their buddies below. A bird that's flying low is looking for a place to rest.

The best spot to have the wind blowing is against your back. Winds blowing directly across the decoys are okay, and it can even be blowing into shore a slight amount. Where you don't want it is in your face.

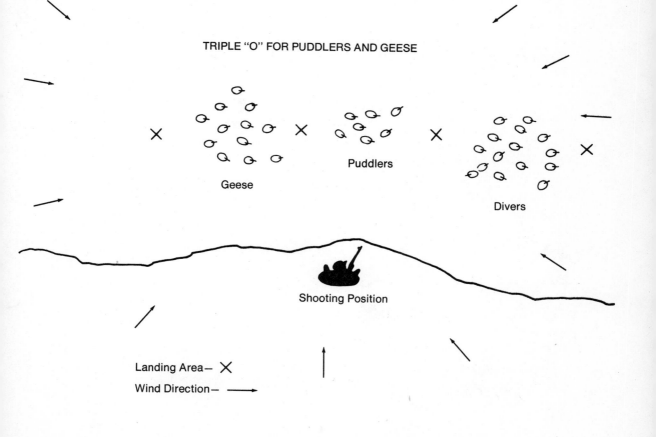

TRIPLE "O" FOR PUDDLERS AND GEESE

Geese

Puddlers

Divers

Shooting Position

Landing Area— X
Wind Direction— ⟶

Modern Commercial Decoys

Today you'll find decoys made in a variety of materials. Rubbber decoys are still available. These can be squeezed together for extreme lightness and portability. They have no place on open water and should be reserved for tiny spots where a long hike in is required. Most rubber decoys ride terribly and will last but a few seasons. Coloring is often subdued or downright poor.

Paper, usually pressed with glues or plastics for added toughness, is a common decoy material, as it is cheap and durable. This material is okay for field shooting but less so if the decoys must be immersed for long periods. Some shell-bodied paper goose decoys of mine require yearly service. Paper decoys often will not last the season without work. Separating or chaffed edges can be restored by saturating with paint or polyester resin. I patch them with Dynel and resin.

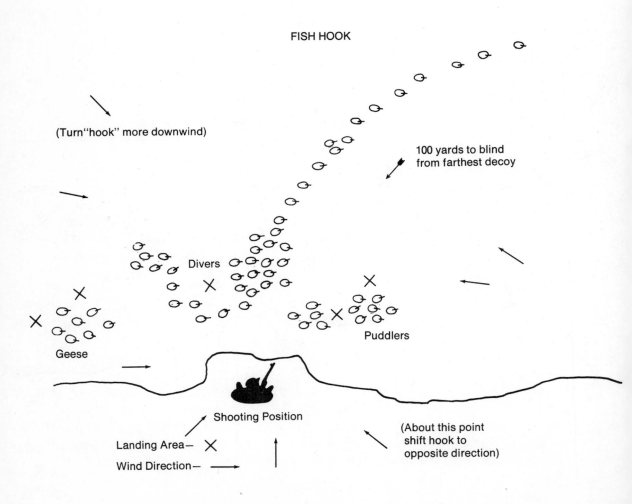

FISH HOOK

(Turn "hook" more downwind)

100 yards to blind from farthest decoy

Divers

Puddlers

Geese

Shooting Position

Landing Area— X

Wind Direction—

(About this point shift hook to opposite direction)

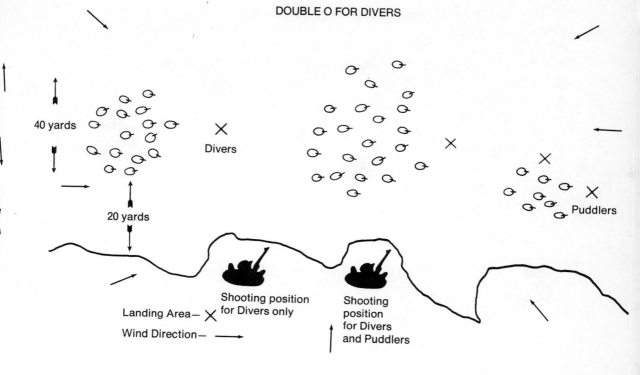

DOUBLE O FOR DIVERS

Plywood is in wide use for making silhouette decoys. These are used primarily for geese, though some are used for field-shooting mallards in the West. These are very satisfactory, though why they are is a mystery to me. What the birds think when the angle closes and they disappear I can't imagine. But the large shapes are easily cut out with a hand saber saw, the plywood takes paint well, is relatively inexpensive (quarter-inch exterior grade is usually used), and large numbers of geese can be stowed in boat or pickup. A variation that adds weight and cost is to add two "wings" as horizontal silhouettes that fold flat for storage but can be opened in the field.

Wood or wood-cork combinations are still popular *if* you can locate a builder and don't mind the expense. Most craftsmen today make decoys as a sideline or as a labor of love. Wood or cork blocks take paint beautifully and last for decades if not centuries and have the added advantage that you can fall in love with them. In Gordon MacQuarrie's delightful Old Duck Hunter stories, Mr. President beamed with pride at old Min and Bill, a couple of his seventy-five-year-old broadbill blocks. Although much fissured and leaded, they had experience, Mr. President insisted. What's more, both were "game to the core." Wood lends itself well to different experimental shapes. A problem today is cost. L. L. Bean of Freeport,

FIELD SET FOR DUCKS OR GEESE

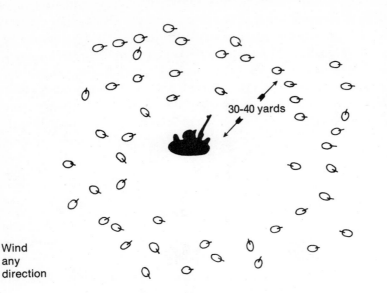

30-40 yards

Don't put
decoys beyond
30-40 yards
as birds often
light at
edge of set.

Wind
any
direction

Maine, still sells wood decoys by mail. Eighteen-inch coasters are $6.90 each, six for $38.40; oversized — nineteen inches long — are $12.35 each, six for $72.50; Canada geese of 20 3/4-inches are $12.25 each, six for $72. These are handsome blocks and, indeed, these days all decoys made by local carvers are minor works of art; each carver stamps his individuality on the blocks. One nice thing is that, if you ever get tired of gunning, you can mount them on a base and with $1.00's worth of fixtures and a shade create $50 lamps.

If you are planning to build your own decoys, cork is the easiest material. Old telephone poles make good raw material for bodies. Carve heads out of pine or cedar. Many good plans for decoys exist.

Plastic is taking over as the most popular material, mostly because it's inexpensive. There are two kinds — solid-body and hollow-shell blocks of molded plastic. The molded decoys are usually available only in certain shapes and sizes. Colors are often molded in. Many of these are fine decoys; anyway, those I've seen are good, considering the cost. They ride well, are tough, and can be repaired easily with patches of light fiber glass or Dynel tape and with plastic putty, either by itself to plug shot holes or in conjunction with tape for strength. Cost is about $3 each, $30 a dozen. Some versions go for $2 each, $20 a dozen.

Decoys with solid but light plastic-foam bodies are also popular. These are used in conjunction with hollow, plastic heads held in place with an eye rod that threads into a reinforced neck slot on the head. The eye receives the anchor line. A weight molded in the body sits the decoy deep in the water. Both head and body take paint well, and the decoys are amazingly strong. My four-year-old son nicknamed an unused pintail "Joe" and dragged it around for several years. During that time he totally destroyed toys of wood, steel, and concrete. "Joe" has miraculously endured and incredibly enough could be restored to workable condition. If heads become cracked, Dynel or light fiber glass tape will cover cracks. Plastic putties quickly restore holed bodies. The great threat to plastic foam is gasoline, which will quickly dissolve it.

The cost is approximately the same as for molded-plastic bodies—$3 per for ducks; geese come in at $4 and $5 each, depending on size, about $50 to $60 a dozen.

Old automobile tires can make excellent field decoys. These are widely used where geese are shot over rigs of four hundred or more decoys. The tire is cut in three slices

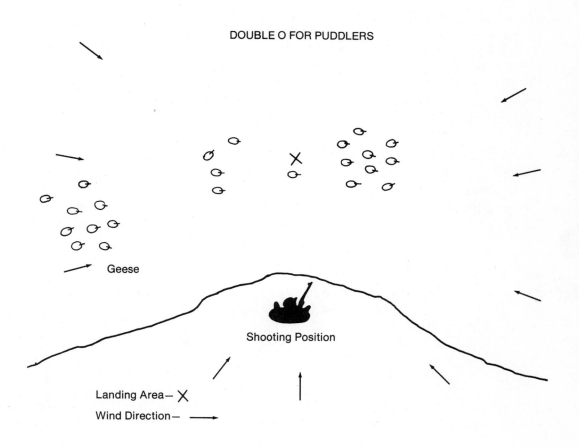

DOUBLE O FOR PUDDLERS

Geese

Shooting Position

Landing Area— X

Wind Direction— ⟶

to resemble the back of a goose. A silhouette head, usually cut with a band saw out of a one-inch pine plank, is attached by a long screw. The head and tire back are then painted. The decoy is propped on a mound or simply set on the earth.

Decoys can be made out of very simple materials. Snow geese will decoy to white newspapers or pieces of sheets. I've also heard of but never seen a series of corks held on long lines, the whole bobbing slightly to create the kind of disturbed water that excitedly feeding diving ducks make. Decoys can be made from previously killed birds whose heads are propped up with Y sticks.

For the record, there are about 25,000 dozen duck decoys sold annually by the large commercial houses. Most of these are mallards. The number made by local carvers is unknown, but is probably fairly small. Goose-decoy sales amount to about 20,000 dozen each year.

Years ago I owned two of the finest decoys I've ever seen, and I've never found anything like them since. They were made about 1950 by a Jersey carver then in his seventies. They were wooden black ducks. The necks and heads were extended straight out and so delicately balanced the blocks that the slightest wave action made the ends of the bills dip in the water. They were made to imitate the premating bill-dipping ritual. We gunned with these plus ten regular blocks and two headless feeders about a hundred yards from a commercial guy with 150 stools out, and this fourteen-decoy rig pulled everything—scaup, blacks, wigeon, teal, brant, and Canada geese. Someone stole them finally. If I had them today, I would sit up all night guarding them.

Herter's now offers an animated mallard and an animated Canada goose. The decoy is positioned on a long rod with wings curled so it looks as though the bird is dropping into the set. The wings can be removed for storage. Price is about $4 for the mallard, $5 for the goose.

A trick I've heard of but never seen used is to throw a handful of pebbles into the decoys on lifeless still days, to stir up the water when birds are looking things over. I don't see how you can throw so the decoying ducks won't see you. You see various Rube Goldberg arrangements for rigging lines so a decoy can be made to bob. If you could fashion the rig so no human motion showed, I'm certain it would add to the set's attraction on calm days. But with the slightest action of wind, wave, or current, it wouldn't be worth the trouble. Homer Circle claims he rigs catfish bait on his decoys and thus gets double duty out of them. When a catfish bites, it animates the decoy, says Homer.

Decoy Lines

What kind of decoy line you use depends to some extent on water depth, the holding power of your anchors, and the strength of the current. In some parts of the Northwest, to mention an extreme example, decoys are set in water that may be four hundred feet deep. This calls for monofilament of about twenty-pound test or better. (A brick is used for an anchor.)

I see lines of every conceivable description being used. No matter what sort of lines you use, they will occasionally get tangled. (Lines are sometimes referred to as leads, an older term stemming from the time when live decoys were tethered on leashes, or leads.) No matter how you wrap the decoys, a few leads will come unwrapped. The thicker the lines, the less likely they are to get tangled and the easier to separate if they do. Braided nylon dyed green makes a good lead. Sash cord and chalk line are traditional lead materials. If you could get monofilament in hundred-pound test, it would be thick enough to avoid tangles. I use tarred codfish line about a quarter-inch thick and secure it to anchors, rings, and even together (when I cut leads in the prop) by wrapping with old-fashioned "tire" tape. It's cheap, fast, shipshape and holds for years.

Wrapping the leads for storage is a matter of personal preference. All kinds of techniques are used. I've seen guys rig notches on the decoy's keel. The line wraps in these, and a turn or two around the head secures it. There are anchors made in a form that permits the lead to be coiled on them. Most gunners wrap the line around the body, then secure it with several turns around the neck. The only dude thing to do is to wrap the line around the neck. It takes too long to wrap and unwrap.

If you gun widely varying depths of water, say a forest pond one day and a reservoir point the next, use brass snaps in your leads. For deep-water work, unsnap the short line and snap in a longer length.

Another trick used by the offshore sea-duck and coot shooters is to set a boat anchor with a long heavy rope—say half-inch—strung from it. The decoys are on short leads with trot line clips on the ends. You just drift down the line and stick the clips through the rope at appropriate spots.

Decoy Anchors

Probably the most common decoy anchor is a wire stuck in a mushroom-shaped piece of lead. These are super-simple to make. You get some heavy wire (brass or copper is best), twist the ends, and stick it in the molten lead in the pouring ladle. Plunge the whole thing into a pan of water. Instant anchor!

What kind and weight anchor you require depends on a number of factors, which are complex out of all proportion to the importance of the problem: current strength, water depth, drift material (grass, driftwood, ice), bottom type, scope (the relationship between length of anchor line to depth; the line should be about three times the depth, holding shape of the anchor, and so on. I mean you need a computer to figure out how to hold a dumb decoy in place.

The commercial anchors I've seen come in ring shapes and mushroom shapes and weigh around ten or twelve ounces. An iron sash weight is a traditional goose-decoy anchor. The best material is lead, as it retains more of its weight underwater than iron. If you can find scrap sheathing from telephone cables, pour your own anchors. Make a string of lead and curve it in an O to slip over the decoy's head.

Iron anchors will rust, and the rust can mark the decoy. I paint my iron anchors every time I'm painting the decoys, and they have such a buildup of paint now that rust is no longer a problem.

A grapple is not an anchor but is similar to one. The old commercial guys always used them to pick up. Get yourself a three- or four-prong grapple hook of the sort used to snag suckers, or make one out of the biggest treble hook you can find. Weight the shank enough so you can throw it. You can use this in a couple of ways. It's easy to anchor your duck boat in the middle of the decoys and throw the grapple over the leads to haul in the decoys. Or, if you are gunning a place where you can't put a boat out, you can position the decoys by heaving them out and collect them with your grapple.

Decoys in Ice and Snow
Keeping the decoys clear of snow and ice is a problem. Generally ice can be knocked off by a sock with an oar. A stern admonition that the decoy must behave better will also help. Snow is a problem only with land decoys, as the water usually melts it on floating decoys. Either way, no real duck or goose ever had snow or ice on him, and keeping decoys clean can be a task when the white stuff is falling.

Making Decoys
You can make your own decoys if you have the time and a knack for carving. The easiest way is to locate a carver and buy rough heads from him. They are turned on a lathe. Then you can smooth and finish the bodies yourself, using wood or cork. Buy a commercial decoy to copy for colors and shape.

My iron anchors have been painted so much they sneer at rust even in the salt water. My method of attaching decoy line with friction tape isn't patented—and it's fast, cheap, holds well, and is neat.

It is now possible to make plastic decoys at home, and numbers of blocks can be made at extremely reasonable prices this way. Decoys Unlimited, Clinton, Iowa, offers molds for mallard, pintail, wigeon, canvasback, redhead, scaup, and Canada goose with upright or feeder heads. I've seen several samples, and they are excellent blocks—oversize, well shaped, and durable.

Here is how the process works. The plastic comes in dry pellet form and is boiled to create a liquid. Once enough for, say, twenty decoys is prepared, the mold is painted with corn oil (for easy release) and a weight, such as several old bolts, is added. The mold is filled with the plastic and the whole is baked, or boiled in water, for about thirty-five minutes. Then the mold is opened and the decoy taken out. Some slight rasping is necessary to smooth the block, which is then ready for painting. Heads are made in a different mold. (A nail goes in the beak for reinforcement.) Head and body are joined with a long eye screw.

DECOY MAKING

Here are the ingredients you'll need to make your own plastic decoys. Resin powder (*at left*) is mixed with water in the bucket. At the lower left front are old bolts and iron scrap that will be used to weight the decoy. The long eyebolt and washer go through the body and then screw into the head. You can see the hole in the body through which the plastic is poured. Finishing nails go in the head to strengthen the bill. You'll need paint and brushes to complete the job.

The molds are filled and boiled in a pot for twenty minutes, then cooled and unbolted. The inside of each mold must be painted with corn oil so the decoy won't stick.

All mold marks and other roughness are smoothed off with a rasp. Any voids are easily filled with plastic putty.

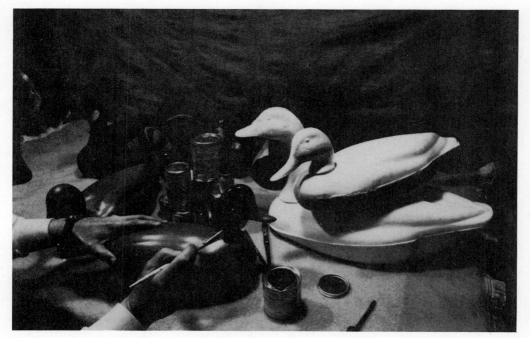

The final task is painting the blocks. Although the paint on the broadie's head looks shiny here, this is only because the flash reflected in the wetness.

There are some complications, not the least of which is devising a way to bring a washtub to a boil, but the great thing is that once the mold has been paid for a complete duck decoy comes in for less than $1. Geese cost perhaps $1.50. Head and body molds cost about $30 for oversize mallard, $50 for goose. If you're interested, Decoy Unlimited's owner, an enthusiastic waterfowler—a sculling man, no less—will send full particulars free and a sample decoy for $5.

Decoy Painting

How realistic a decoy's paint job should be is yet one more matter of controversy. The late Glenn L. Martin had a fancy estate in the heart of prime Canada goose country and gunned with decoys that were taxidermy mounts of real birds. His guides told me he fared no better or worse than other good gunners.

Traditionally, the old baymen were scornful of fancy painting. And considering the numbers of decoys they put out, you can see that they could hardly afford much attention to individual blocks. Things are different today. With our fewer, larger decoys, and with all the leisure time we are supposed to have these days, I don't think you can paint too realistically. Carefully painted decoys can certainly do no harm.

There are two painting guides I know of that will help you. Decoys Unlimited has an excellent four-color guide with all popular species handsomely portrayed. Herter's, Inc., which probably sells more decoys than all other makers combined, also offers decoy paints for all popular species and an excellent painting chart that works like a kid's painting kit. Paint color #1 in area #3, etc. I must have painted a thousand decoys, but I'm not much more skillful now than when I started, having little talent for brush and colors. I've always depended on the Herter guides and with their help produce a credible job. I don't enter any contests, though.

Those fourteen black ducks of mine that pulled so many different species so well were beautifully painted. The dear old man used a feather as a brush to ripple in the feathers on the back. They were beautiful in every other way too. They were perfectly shaped and sat in the water with infinite balance. The regular blocks looked alive, and the animated dippers and headless feeders added even more action and reality. That, of course, is why they pulled so. They put in long hours of overtime and never once demanded time-and-a-half. They were game to the core.

Decoy Don'ts
Decoys should never shine with glossy paint. All paint shines somewhat, even flat paint, so try to paint decoys a month or so before the season, then let them sit in the weather for a while. Another trick I've used when, characteristically, I've not taken my own advice and let everything go until the last minute, is to rub them down with sand or mud out on the marsh—not enough to take paint off but enough to dull it.

Skating is another bad characteristic of some decoys. This can happen when a gust of wind hits a too-light decoy and causes it to suddenly skid sideways in an unnatural fashion. It will flare ducks if it happens when they are coming in. To stop this, put keels on your blocks or weight the body enough so the decoy sits in, not on, the water.

Decoys shouldn't rock excessively. Lead tacked to the bottom of round-bottom wooden decoys will discourage rock and roll. Few modern decoys are built with round bottoms.

Decoy Collecting
Collecting antique decoys makes an interesting hobby for waterfowlers. You tend to it so easily, probably enjoying being around the old-timers and haunting the "byways" of the flyways. It can be a sport in itself, of course, and authenticated antiques, especially those by the famous carvers, command prices in the hundreds

of dollars. All my life I've wanted an iron decoy. They are scarce now but make super doorstops.

I claim no expertise in decoy collecting beyond boundless admiration. Yet I suspect that if you find a local commercial carver, working in wood or cork, his decoys will someday be worth many times what you will pay for them today. Fifteen years ago I ordered a sleeping black duck from the old Wildfowler Company. It cost $5 then. Not now. Some time ago I walked warily into Madison Mitchell's shop in Havre de Grace, Maryland (you always chanced meeting a corpse visiting undertaker Mitchell), and fell in love with a swan decoy, a magnificent work of art. I think it cost $25. Anyone who tries to sail it off the top of my gun cabinet would have to start adding zeros to that purchase price.

If you are at all interested in collecting decoys, Joel Barber's *Waterfowl Decoys* is the classic work on the subject and is itself a masterpiece. Published in 1937, it is long out of print, but copies might be available through bookshops specializing in locating old books. *Duck Decoys*, a classic with much carving and collecting good sense is available at $6.50 from the Stephen Greene Press, 120 Main St., Brattleboro, Vermont 05301. *The Art of the Decoy* is a lush $12.95 opus available from Bramhall House. (Your bookstore can order it.) There is a quarterly, *North American Decoys*, put out by Mr. Bryon Cheever, Box 242, Herber City, Utah 84032 for $8 yearly that lists shows and gives much helpful information.

14

Equipment That Lets You Stick

Nowhere is the waterfowler spared. He must be a boating enthusiast, probably a boatbuilder to boot. He must have the skills of a field naturalist, a weather prophet, wildfowl observer, historian, and (next chapter) long-range ballistics expert. To these accomplishments must be added another. Experience quickly turns every duck hunter worthy of the name into an equipment specialist. The dove hunter needs little besides his camouflage suit and a chair to sit in. Deer hunters purchase their red wool suits, boots, and knives, and go forth. Briarproof pants equip the rabbit hunter. Not so, the waterfowler. Layer upon layer of clothing lie upon him, each performing a specific duty and function, all cooperating in harmonious accord. (If they don't, he can't move.)

Look at what the waterfowler asks! When winds whistle, ice floes form, and snowflakes fly, he breasts the waves, endures the flying spray and is supposed to—indeed, he must!—lie in his boat or sit in his blind warm, dry, snug, and content. I'm always upset during the waterfowl season. In the beginning it's because there are so many guys gunning. At the end of the season, when it really gets good, it bothers me that so few are. I think the reason most hunters pack it in early is that they haven't got gear that leaves them comfortable enough to hang in there when the going gets rough.

You simply can't gun the very best times with the run-of-the-mill gear you usually find at your local cut-rate sporting-goods dealer. You must have good equipment, if not the best, or the weather will put you out of business just as conditions reach their prime. You must have first-quality stuff, be willing to pay for it, and learn how to patch, sew, or piece it back together when snags, splinters, races after cripples, and falls in the mud take their inevitable toll.

You learn in the first week of basic training that equipment should be drab at the least, camouflage at best. You don't want any shiny buttons on your jacket or emblems on your hat. You want to cover your hands, and, as I've mentioned, paint your faces like commandos to blot out that headlight. Today there have been some breakthroughs in foam-lined cold-weather clothes, and camouflage outer coloration is now so commonplace we should probably all wear it. Yet brown-canvas gunning coats have been traditional for centuries, and I gunned for years wearing a black canvas parka procured under suspicious circumstances from the Point Pleasant, New Jersey, Fire Department by my brother-in-law. If you are lucky enough to have a well-stocked sporting-goods store within reach, you can probably build up your outfit from it. But sooner or later the sport will turn you toward the famous mail-order equipment houses, and you will join the rest of us drooling over the new catalogs as they come out. You can make your own list, but I look forward to pursuing the works of Herter's, Inc., Route 2, Mitchell, South Dakota 57301; L.L. Bean, Freeport, Maine 04032; Eddie Bauer, Box 3700, Seattle, Washington 98124; and The Orvis Company, Manchester, Vermont 05254. All of these contribute to my wardrobe with faithful frequency as they do to the great and small of all walks of life from all points of the globe. All their catalogs are free, and comparisons among them can often save you money as well as more perfectly fill your needs.

Clothes, of course, are highly individual. I'll confine my discussion to generalities and personal observations.

Underwear. If nothing else is certain, the second layer is. Over light cotton underwear and a T-shirt, you'll don some form or other of long underwear. There are several kinds. I know some who swear by the fishnet type. Gene Hill prefers silk long johns. He says they impart a high-class warmth and don't inhibit your movement as much as bulky types. Bauer offers an itchy-scratchy suit that keeps you warm by friction if you can stand it. I have a couple of sets of the two-layer cotton-wool Duofolds that hold me through the worst weather. A lot of hunters wear the insulated quilt types or even down underwear. These pad you out some, though. I've found that insulated clothes get too hot if you have to move around much. On the other hand, I once came home with my insulated top soaking wet when my rain gear split, and I didn't even know that I'd sprung a leak, the underwear kept me so warm.

Pants. The best pants I know of for waterfowling are those thick woolen lumberjack pants. You don't need the canvas pants that the upland hunters must have. You want your pants cut narrow, so you can slip them in and out of boots or waders. The thick wool pants deer hunters wear go okay into duck blinds, even the red ones, as you'll probably have a camouflage parka over them. I have a pair of L. L. Bean's Canada gray trousers. The catalog says the cloth weighs almost two pounds a yard, and I believe it. Wearing these, with their splendid baggy knees, supported heroically by my frayed suspenders, sporting a four-day growth of beard (me, that is, not the pants), and topped off with a pint whisky bottle sticking out of my back pocket, hardly anyone ever takes me for a fancy outdoor writer.

Shirts and Sweaters.   Any kind of good, thick shirt will serve you well. I bought a sweater years ago to go tuna fishing in Nova Scotia (caught one too, 240 pounds). It was a turtleneck made with wool that had not been processed to remove the natural oil. It was like a stove. I finally wore it out. When I reached Dover, England, a few years ago, the first place I went to was a shop that catered exclusively to commercial fishermen. There was my sweater, and it cost about $15! They make them in dark blue and white. I see them advertised from time to time in the United States for around $30.

Coats.   Any good warm coat goes into a duck blind. You will probably be wearing a slicker or parka over it anyway, so a red mackinaw type is okay. The new foam-insulated coats are terrific. I once bought secondhand a sheepskin-lined coat that came from Abercrombie & Fitch in the 1940s. It had a collar that turned up almost higher than my head, and the woolly wool was *soooo* cozy. I loved that coat. The years tried to take it from me, and I fought back by gluing hunks of deck canvas to it (the fabric was too worn to sew anything on) and painting the patches duckboat brown. Black defeat came when the sheepskin treacherously gave up the ghost. I had to junk it, and believe me my image changed for the worse. I now wear an Ontario game warden's jacket. It is revoltingly neat and presentable looking, and I would have nothing to do with it were it not for the fact that its buttons can be eaten in an emergency.

My beloved commercial fishing overalls that wouldn't wear out are the stars of this shot. We killed these brant in back of Barnegat Inlet. The sneakbox is a small boat about ten feet long.

Of course, when you think about coats for cold weather, you think of goose down. Down is bulky, I admit, but I have never been cold (except for my feet) inside my Bauer polar light ($191.50). Mine is ten years old — I got the fur collar to remind me of my lost love — and shows not a sign of wear. You can buy cheap down clothes (not from Eddie Bauer, though), and even the cheap down is warmer than most other stuff.

Outer Gear. I've always yearned for that camouflage parka, "not to be confused with ordinary lightweight flimsy camouflage cloth," offered in the Bean catalog for $24, but I've always been too cheap to lay out the cash. What you don't want is flimsy wet-weather gear, as it will quickly be torn. I wear a fairly rugged green vinyl, knee-length wet coat supplemented by many patches. The parka that came from the firehouse was also well tailored to waterfowling. Its value was increased (to me) not only by the fact it was purloined (naturally I erased the coat's origins with duckboat paint) but also because it had galosh-type metal clips totally unsuited for duck shooting to keep it shut. It was warm and dry, and I don't think you could have shot a hole through it with a light gun. Alas, it too went the way of all flesh.

If you gun in waders, you need only the jacket part of a wet-weather top. If you wear hip or field boots, you probably should have both top and bottom. The best foul-weather gear is made by Canor Plastic in Norway. It's what all the commercial fishermen use. Mail-order houses stock it. It's made in green as well as yellow.

Boots.   Any waterfowler who can gun in short boots is lucky. Waders tire me out, and they are a mess to try to work in. I've used Herter's insulated waders for years, and they keep my feet relatively warm. The thing about insulated boots is to find out (if you can) how thick the insulation is. The thicker the better. I once ran a gaff through the foot of my insulated waders, and even though I waterproofed the hole, it felt forever after as though my foot had a wet spot. The cold still came through. I patch my present brown waders with an inner-tube repair kit whose patches are black, and I now look as though someone has patterned his gun on me.

For years I wore hip boots instead of waders. I wore these surf fishing, and over them I pulled a black-rubber commercial-fisherman's open-leg overall with a bib front. I could not wear the overalls out. Until I did I wouldn't buy waders. I like to gun out of hip boots, but boat gunning with these is too sloppy. Your (or at least I) always step on the seat to get in or out, and this leaves a gooey wet spot that you sit in. It's a lot easier to pick up decoys by wading among them, pushing the boat. I rig up suspenders for my waders with light shock cord. It works better than the commercial suspenders.

If you shoot out of a dry blind, such as a goose pit, you can wear leather boots. I have an insulated pair from Canada that are pretty good. I'd think snowmobiler boots with their felt liners would be top-notch for this work.

Socks.   I am not the right man to pontificate on the subject of socks, as my feet are chronically cold except during the months of July and August. I used to experiment. I tried the cotton sock next to the skin. Cold. Tried thermal booties. Cold. I bought Herter's insulated boots 'way oversized and wear two pairs of wool socks, one slightly larger than the other. This I live with, but my toes still get cold. I once knew a gunner who used battery-heated socks, and he loved them. I've never thought they were worth the bother.

Gloves.   If for no other reason I achieve immortality it should be for discovering that skindiver gloves are made to order for waterfowling. Even though your hands get wet, the gloves keep them wonderfully warm. They are magnificent on days when the spray is flying as they let you run the boat or when picking up decoys. The gloves come in two styles, a mitten with single forefinger and a glove with five fingers. Be sure to get them large enough. Too small they are tight getting on and off.

I also carry a pair of plastic gloves in my kit, the orange or yellow ones they sell in hardware stores. I've tried neoprene but found them too slippery. I use the plastics for the wet work when it's not cold enough to break out the skindivers. Incidentally, both of these are slightly too bulky to shoot comfortably with, although it can be done. What I've found best when sitting in the blind are regular woolen finger gloves, some with leather palms and fingers. I have three pairs so I can generally field a dry pair. I wash them regularly too—to get the salt out of them. If it is severely cold weather I have a pair of ski mittens with a split palm to shoot with. I slip these on over the woolens.

Hats. I think you ought to wear a camouflage hat, although it sure isn't necessary. I wore a yellow corduroy hat for years until it fell apart. (Do you get the feeling I'm falling apart?) In cold weather I wear an Eddie Bauer down hat and tuck the flaps down. I like a cap with a bill. The bill keeps the hood on my wet-weather jacket out of my eyes and helps hide my face.

I use this thick cod line for my decoys. It never tangles and will last well (if I don't wrap it up in the propellor). These are my skin diver mittens.

The weirdest cap I've ever seen in a duck blind is the one usually worn by Nelson Bryant, outdoor editor of *The New York Times*. A native Martha's Vineyarder, he habitually sports a long-billed swordfisherman's hat. To pay him back for this outrage, I tell everybody that he wears a duck hunting hat when swordfishing. If you see him, ask him to tell you about the time his Aunt Minny backed her car into the cesspool. I see plenty of guys wear those Robin Hood type camouflage hats, and I even bought one. How do you keep it from blowing off in high winds?

Safety Gear.   In my kit goes a Zippo lighter with spare flints instead of waterproof matches, a compass, a hand warmer, a flashlight; a pair of pliers (I have a screwdriver on my knife), a roll of wire; friction tape, and a bottle of assorted nails for blind building. I'll tell you about those nails. Partner had gunned one Saturday and busted the shear pin when a decoy cord got wrapped in the prop. I headed off alone the next Saturday, and it blew forty miles an hour out of the northwest. I went out to pick up the decoys, picked up a decoy lead, and busted the spare pin, having (of course) neglected to get another spare. I quickly threw over the anchor, and though I was only about fifty feet from shore I might as well have been fifty miles in that wind. I pulled the motor in the boat, as the skiff was leaping around, and took out the pin. It was not the kind you could reverse. Then I took a nail from my nail assortment and bent it back and forth with the pliers until it snapped exactly at the length of an intact pin. I stuck it in, put the motor back on, and headed for shore at about two miles an hour, holding my breath. The nail brought me home.

A lot of hunters use walkie-talkies to find out what's doing. I have never used one but see no harm in the practice. The radios also have a certain safety value.

Some hunters carry a pair of binoculars. I happen to have good eyes and don't need any assistance in the long-range vision department. The problem with the glasses, aside from keeping them out of the water, is that you're likely to be moving around too much with them. Don't forget a Canada goose is looking at you with binoculars too. If you do want to use them, the new Bushnell floating plastic types would be the best. They are big but extremely light.

Booze.   Plenty of waterfowlers think they have to drink whisky all day long to keep warm. I drink. All my friends drink. But I don't drink in duck blinds or aboard fishing boats. I think booze has no place in a duck blind or goose pit, and anyone who gets lightheaded around loaded guns deserves to get shot. I don't mind if a guy brings a flask of brandy (one pal of mine drinks blackberry brandy, awful sweet gooey stuff) and takes a pull on it from time to time to ease the pain of life. But I can tell you, anyone who drank enough to feel any effects of the stuff would lose me as a companion fast. After the shooting day is over I'm all for poker-playing, joke-telling, wine, women, whoopee, and song. That's different.

CALLS

I have to truthfully say that I do not believe I have ever called a duck within range. I have plenty of duck calls, and I use them. I'll call, for example, when a pair of black ducks is about to sit down somewhere other than in my decoys in the hope the sound will flare them and they will decide to come to me. Sometimes it works. Not often.

Yet I know that in many areas ducks are highly susceptible to a call. Every duck hunter should have one and learn how to use it. The best way to do this is to listen to real ducks and imitate them. The next best way is to spend $2 and buy a record of real ducks and imitate it. Calling is an important part of conning geese. Here, again, learning from the real thing is best. Probably the most important thing in calling is practicing until the call you make sounds natural. Herter's has a good recording with both duck and goose calls on it.

15

Guns for Ducks and Geese

For almost ten years I shot all my ducks and geese with a shotgun that any waterfowl expert would dismiss as totally unsuited to the sport. I readily admit it was more of a grouse gun than a waterfowl weapon. It was bought during the 1930s as a lady's fowling piece and was bored full and modified; any recognized grouse authority would be forced to state that it wasn't a very good gun for shooting grouse either. How it functioned so well and for so long for two purposes with dissimilar requirements is at the heart of any discussion about any weapon for any species anywhere.

My gun was (and is) a sixteen-gauge Parker. Now, you know something? No company in this country ever made a better-handling shotgun. I grew up with this weapon, as you may have surmised from the dedication of this book. I have carried it hundreds of miles, shot it thousands of times. The season before last, I hiked six actionless hours looking for grouse. When a bird broke at the end of the day that little gun flashed to my shoulder and downed it almost without conscious effort on my part. The Parker and I are perfectly wed. I don't think at all about where the gun sits on my shoulder, where my cheek goes on the stock, whether or not I am holding the barrels level. All these elements crucial to shooting success just happen, and (all important) they apparently happen the same way almost every time.

There are two reasons why the little sixteen functioned for a decade as an effective duck and goose gun. The first reason is that it shot where I pointed it. I could kill with it. This would seem a basic point. But I constantly see hunters shooting and shooting and never hitting anything except by luck. They should practice. They should throw their guns to their shoulders every day. Here's how. Pick a point. Close your eyes and throw the gun up aimed at the point. If you don't open your eyes looking down the barrel at the point, something's wrong.

You'll hear and read that shooting trap or skeet won't help you in the field because clay targets are declining in speed while wild birds are accelerating. This is one of the most mistaken myths in the outdoor field. The clay-bird experts are crack field shots. It's the reverse that isn't necessarily true. Many excellent game shots are indifferent clay-bird shooters, probably because they don't care and don't concentrate. Any shooting helps your skill. Familiarity with your weapon increases your precision. Go shooting. Start banging at hand-trap targets. I used to go down to the beach in the fall, collect clam shells, put two of them in my hand, fling them as far as I could, and bust them (sometimes). If you really want to become a sharp shot, take up live-pigeon shooting. You'll get used to birds curving away in a wind.

The second reason my sixteen functioned well was as fundamental as the first. I recognized its limitations. I knew I could reach forty-five to fifty yards with it and not a nickel more. Over decoys you are generally taking birds in the twenty-five- to thirty-five-yard range. Okay, I could wait for them to flirt around me and finally come in. When they did, the little Parker—pointed correctly—was deadly. A sixteen-gauge shotgun is certainly not a weapon you'd recommend as a goose gun. But those Canadas I mentioned in the story where I was asleep were goners. Not a wisp of movement would have alerted them. They would have wafted into range. Partner and I would have waited until the moment when all decoying waterfowl are at their most vulnerable, at that last instant when they cup their wings, extend their feet, and hang in the air. Approximately 275 No. 6 shot traveling at some 1,200 feet a second would have lashed into a Canada's head, neck, and breast. My sixteen could kill ducks and geese (or swans, for that matter) all day long under these conditions.

So you see, I have to agree when hunters start recommending light guns for waterfowling. The three-inch twenty-gauge has become a popular duck gun since it was introduced in 1960. I always used the maximum magnum loads in the sixteen—

1 ¼ ounces of shot backed by some thirty-four grains of powder. That's almost exactly the three-inch twenty-gauge load. If you keep barrel length where you should — twenty-eight to thirty inches maximum — this gun gives you both a reasonable duck gun and a superb field weapon.

While I have to admit to the facts presented I am uneasy with them. I once heard a story about a professional elephant hunter who always killed his elephants with a huge .500 (or whatever) cannon. Someone asked him once why he chose this gigantic weapon. "Because I can't get nothin' bigger," was the reply. I feel the gentleman's logic. Much of waterfowling calls for long shots. Many ducks and certainly Canada geese are awesomely tough to kill, extremely tenacious of life. It takes heavy blows to put them down. Despite my romance with the Parker, I would be hard-pressed to suggest to anyone buying a gun strictly for waterfowling that he buy anything smaller than a twelve-gauge. That the twelve-gauge Browning automatic was *the* waterfowling weapon for so many years indicates that others agree with me. The argument is like the prize-fighting adage that a good big man will beat a good little man every time. You may be deadly with your little gun, but you'd be even deadlier with a big gun.

It's in the grand waterfowling tradition to use big guns for waterfowl. The late Nash Buckingham said that monster scatterguns were taken as a matter of course during the Golden Age. Until they were outlawed in 1934, four-, six-, and eight-gauge guns, mostly doubles, were commonplace. What isn't as well known is that the charges commonly loaded for them made the old cannons no more effective than the smaller modern gauges. One old-timer (circa 1900) told Buckingham he loaded his six-gauge with an ounce and a half of shot and five or six drams of black powder, which, incidentally, he "cooked up" on the back of the stove with ingredients bought at the local drugstore for a few pennies. When shooting mallards in timber he'd take them out to sixty or seventy yards, about the same as with one of today's big guns.

Here's a look at what is available to you in twelves and tens with a look at the ballistics of the twenty as a bench mark.

Gauge	Shell size, load, grains	Number of No. 4 pellets	Number of No. 4 pellets in 30" circle at 40 yards	Muzzle velocity (feet per second)
Three-inch 20	3"-1 3/16-35	165	115	1250
Standard 12	2 3/4"-1 1/8-23	169	118	1200
Non-Magnum Magnum	2 3/4"-1 1/2-37	203	140	1320
Three-inch 12	3"-1 3/4-46	250	175	1265
Magnum 10	3 1/2"-2 1/4-58	280	190	1250

Since we are going to talk about what might be called "general waterfowling" and then go on to discuss extreme long-range or "desperation" shooting, let me dramatize the potential of the heavier gauges in the lower register of the chart with another of my amazing true stories.

I was in a duck camp, and we got around to discussing shotgun range. At the time there were ads being run in all the outdoor magazines for a ten-gauge double that handled the 3½-inch shells. The headline on the ad was "Dead Ducks at 100 Yards." An old bayman guide at the club, a great old guy, scoffed at the idea. I can still hear him now. "I'd bar' my ass to any shotgun at 100 yards. Bar' it, hear me?" he cried. I was an associate editor at *Sports Afield* at the time and, not long after, Pete Brown, the magazine's Gun Editor, was in town and I asked him about the subject, repeating the anecdote. Pete likes a good story and laughed at the idea of the old man standing there with drawers lowered, but, as it happened, he'd been running some penetration tests with a ten-gauge Magnum. He strongly advised me not to emulate the bayman. "You mean the shot would sting at that range?" I asked. For an answer Pete pulled out some photographs of what happened when BBs slammed into pine planks at exactly 100 yards. They had disappeared in the planks! They would also disappear in a man's rear end! Probably would wound him severely.

There's no argument anymore that you have killing power at extreme ranges. Putting pellets consistently in birds is another matter, however. Consistent kills come from a combination of penetration potential and pattern. At extremely long ranges, your pattern won't stand up. It develops large gaps, and if the duck or goose you've shot at happens to be lucky enough to be in one of those gaps, he lives to fly another day and you eat beans for dinner. That's if you held correctly on him, which you probably didn't if the range was long.

Pete has run extensive pattern tests with the big bomb. He maintains that you have to hit a bird with four or five pellets to kill it. He found that the maximum range of the two-ounce load (100 pellets) that would hold a pattern of BBs even enough to put five pellets in a goose silhouette was fifty-nine yards, fifty-four yards with an ounce-and-a-half load (75 pellets). Using No. 2 shot (170 pellets) knocked two to three yards off the maximum-range figures.

For the smaller silhouettes of ducks, Pete found No. 4 shot would pattern five shots to a bird at fifty-five yards with the two-ounce (270 pellets), fifty yards with ounce-and-a-half (202 pellets), forty-seven yards with ounce-and-a-quarter shot charges (169 pellets). He also discovered No. 5 and 6 shot size (170 and 220 pellets per ounce respectively) held up nearly as well as No. 5s patterned only a yard and a half short of No. 4s. No. 6s were about three yards shorter.

As the previous chart shows, you can get an ounce-and-a-half load in a standard size twelve using the non-Magnum or "baby" Magnum loads. If you go to the three-inch twelve, you add a quarter ounce or more. Herter's offers a three-inch twelve with 1-7/8s ounces of shot. Alcan, a major reloading company, lists two loads for the three-inch twelve—1-5/8s ounce with 1300-feet-per-second velocity and a 1-3/4-ounce load vacating the premises at 1265 fps. In the 3½-inch Magnum ten, there are two 2-ounce reloads at 1330 and 1335 fps and a whopping 2-¼-ounce charge at 1250 fps.

If you shoot these blockbusters, you are going to be extremely lethal at ranges up to sixty or seventy yards when you are taking birds sizzling over decoys in fast passing shots or twirling in the wind as they wheel to come in.

But to my mind, there is more to the waterfowl gun story, at least, under modern waterfowling conditions. If you are talking about goose shooting, especially refuge shooting where you have to take birds on a lottery basis as they fly in or out of the refuge, you simply will not get many shots that close, except in bad weather. The geese will lift up and sail over you at ninety to a hundred yards. Dave Harbour and his son did a great deal of shooting on western refuges. They made the discovery that the relatively new plastic shot protectors drastically increased the performance of buckshot loads. Formerly the shot sliding down the barrel were flattened on one side. These would sail wild. The plastic prevents this, and fewer of the shot are wasted. As you go up in shot size, the number of pellets decreases, but the individual pellets hold their velocity and penetrating power longer. Here are the comparisons in size and numbers:

Shot Size	Diameter (Inches)	Approx. No. per Ounce
6	.11	220
5	.12	170
4	.13	135
2	.15	85
BB	.18	50
No. 4 buck	.24	21
00 buck (deer load)	.34	8

If you shoot an ounce-and-a-half load of No. 4 buckshot, you are going to put some thirty very lethal pellets up very high. Of course, you are going to have all manner of blown patterns. (The Harbours liked this. Rather than putting nonlethal smaller pellets into birds, they felt they either hit the bird and downed it or missed.)

The rocky, mossy Quebec shooting grounds offer fabulous sport, although often under trying living conditions. The hunter is taking the low-flying fellow at right; from the set of its wings, it appears to have seen the shooters and is flaring. The range is right at maximum.

Now if you start taking fast passing shots at eighty yards or trying to hit birds jumping into the wind at a hundred, the complexities of supercomplicated lead problems coupled with holes in your pattern will reduce the possibility of hitting to pure luck. Fortunately, most pass shots, especially Canada pass shots, aren't difficult, just long. The birds are sailing in a steady, straight line, usually right over you or close to it. You get 'waaay out in front of them and blast. You aren't going to have a high average of connections, but you will score once in a while, and come home with geese when short-range gunners won't. Obviously, if you "desperation" shoot at smaller-sized ducks, the holes in the pattern become more significant. For ducks, you might drop in shot size to BB or No. 2s.

If you are going into long-range work, you should pattern your gun with shells from different manufacturers. Differences in powders and other internal elements can cause one company's load to pattern well, another badly. For example, Alcan's reloads can be made with various powders, the individual characteristics of which will affect your pattern. You should test these through your choke. Hitting at these ranges requires special marking techniques, since the birds are so far away when they fall. You should immediately get a range on the spot where the bird hit by lining up with a distant object. Next, if possible, you should locate an object in the immediate area, a tree or bush, to use as a marker. Failing this, immediately estimate the distance in your mind. The best way is with a two-man retrieve. One man goes running. The other never takes his eyes off where the bird went down and directs as he would a retriever. Of course, if you have a dog, he'll find the bird.

I'll probably receive a lot of criticism for this chapter, as I seem to be encouraging sky busting, even though I've stressed the limitations of lighter weapons. But I doubt if anything I said would either encourage or dissuade sky busting. As long as hope springs eternal, people are going to shoot at waterfowl at unholy ranges. It's such a grand sensation when you score. I carved an impossibly high black duck out of the sky one day while out creek-hopping. It must have been twenty years ago, but I can still remember the feeling of surprise and delight. A lucky pellet found the bird. In recent years I was on the tundra with Cam Currie, an official with the Canadian Wildlife Service. A flock of Canadas went over at least 150 yards high. Cam reared back and let go three shots from standard twelve gauge. Of course, the geese paid absolutely no heed to him at all. Cam looked down at his weapon sternly and said, "This is a good gun, but it lacks killing power." So does a SAM III missile if you shoot it at something too far away. So much for sky busting with anything but a cannon.

It's a fair question to ask now why it is that, if the big tens or three-inch twelves are so deadly, why doesn't every waterfowler use one? To begin with, at ten to twelve pounds, the ten-gauge guns are heavy. You can hunt pheasants with a three-inch twelve, but hardly with a ten-gauge unless you're an iron man. Second, the shells cost an arm and a leg. You almost have to reload. But recoil is the main reason more hunters don't use the monster cannons. Shoot these maximum loads we have been discussing and recoil is somewhere between fifty and sixty pounds. This is the equivalent of having a fifty- to sixty-pound weight dropped against your cheek and shoulder from the height of a foot. To give you some idea of what kind of recoil this is, the kick of the .458 Winchester shooting a 510-grain slug at 2130 fps is sixty pounds. Shooting a ten is like shooting an elephant gun! And you don't shoot elephants over and over again. Only one elephant per customer.

Recoil and the so-called recoil effect (i.e., how much kick you actually feel) are complicated subjects, and shooters vary widely in how much they can absorb. Let me tell you what my experience has been. My partner had the big ten in the blind one day when the brant were flying. He'd empty his standard Browning twelve, then grab the rocket launcher (incidentally, it's illegal to do this). I was studying him carefully from out in the boat, and he was killing in the eighty- to one-hundred-yard range without any question. Now this chap is a strapping six-footer who works at a physical job. He admits that if he fires the ten more than a dozen or so times, it gives him a splitting headache. I flatly refused to fire the monster. It's like getting belted hard on the jaw by a fighter. Who needs it?

There are a lot of these big doubles around, a few over-and-unders, and even some bolt-action goose guns made to take the 3½-inch shell. Ithaca has just introduced a ten-gauge automatic, to my knowledge the first.

In my opinion, the Magnum ten afflicts too much punishment for waterfowling. Shotgunning for deer or fox or wolves, when you could expect only a few shots a season, yes. I've been on enough shotgun deer hunts to know you need all the soup you can get when a buck flashes by. But to sit in a blind and possibly fire a box of shells in a day is to ensure that you are going to come home hurting. When you start hurting, you start flinching, and when that starts you can't hit anything. It's the worst thing that can happen to you as a scattergun shooter.

However, if you rule out the ten and come down to the three-inch twelve, there are interesting possibilities. The Remington 1100, the Browning automatic, and the Winchester 1400 are three extremely successful and popular weapons that are available for the three. Most will shoot both the 2¾- and three-inch shells with little or no adjustment. The Browning works mechanically, the other two are gas-operated. The 1100 was so well received after its introduction that it damn near wrecked the Winchester Company until they could get their own version on the market. What all three do, especially the gas-operated guns, is to change the nature of the recoil. The reason granddaddy could slam away all day with his leviathan four was that black powder burns slower than modern smokeless. Recoil was more of a push than a sharp kick. These modern guns have similar characteristics. The gun is coming back at you as hard but over a longer period of time, and this really makes a difference. I haven't shot the new Ithaca ten-gauge auto but those who have say recoil is reasonable.

I've gone a step further with my 1100 and installed a Poly-Choke. Although there are some who dispute the claim, the manufacturer says that the Poly-Choke reduces recoil by 25 percent. I believe there is a reduction. The other 1100s I've fired have only a light recoil, but mine hands me almost no recoil at all. I can hardly feel the gun. It's comparable to firing a .22 rifle. Even the Parker talks back to me after firing a couple of rounds of skeet in shirt-sleeve weather.

If you are talking strictly ducks, with an occasional goose shoot over decoys, you need no more than the standard twelve. Millions of ducks have been downed by it, of course. When I decided to retire the Parker because it was taking too much of a beating—I once slipped and drove it out of sight in the mud—I went to a standard twelve-gauge pump. I soon found I couldn't remember to pump it when I got excited. Then I went to the Remington 1100, which is certainly a handsome weapon and I love it. I shoot the heaviest 2¾-inch Magnums I can find.

I sent it up to Poly-Choke and had them put a ventilated rib and a variable choke on it. They also installed two sighting beads, the standard one at the barrel tip and the other halfway down the barrel. This has helped my shooting and it will yours too, as you line the two beads up when you shoot. This means you look down the barrel the same way every time and don't get your neck across the barrel or lift your cheek off the stock.

Plenty of beautiful doubles, over-and-unders, and even single-shot guns have gone into duck blinds and will continue to do so. It's a matter of what you can afford and what you like. You'll hear that you don't need the third shot of a pump or automatic, because by the time you're ready to use it the birds are too far away.

Baloney! Not my birds. I use the third shot all the time, often missing with the first, then getting on with the second or third. I also feel that the automatic aids shooting too. You stay right there on the gun, as with a double, and aren't distracted by pumping. On the other hand, some like the pump, using the stroke to re-establish their concentration.

The variable choke helps me too. For most decoy shooting you don't need or want a full choke. Modified or improved cylinder will open your pattern more and will give you more kills. Then, too, I've found that over the course of a season the birds will change in how close to the blind they'll decoy. As they get warier, you have to move the decoys out. With a variable choke you can close down as shots move out. I also use my 1100 rather than the little sixteen on doves, as I find them so hard to hit that I want all the firepower I can muster. Here, again, the choke permits one to adjust to different demands.

The traditional shot sizes for geese have been No. 2 and BB. Standard sizes for ducks are No. 2 and No. 4. I like No. 5s for ducks, and over a pond for teal or wood ducks you might go to 6s or even 7½s. A trick I've used is to load with a lighter size for the first shot, then use the heavier sizes for second and third shots. I hate to keep giving this don't-do-as-I-do, do-as-I-say advice, but you should pattern your gun with different size shot to see which size yours handles best.

Waterfowling shotgun barrels have traditionally been the longest in all shotgunning, except maybe those for trap. This is because of the widespread but mistaken belief that the longer length allows the shot to build up more velocity. Today's modern loads are at full velocity after sixteen inches or so. You want a longer barrel to help smooth out your swing, but certainly nothing like the thirty-six-inch barrel of one gun I see listed. I had my pump chopped off at twenty-eight inches and found that slightly short. My 1100 is thirty inches, and I think that's about perfect. Some prefer thirty-two-inch barrels.

One thing I do as ritual. When I come home, I disconnect the barrel of any gun I've had around the salt water. The barrel goes right under the kitchen faucet and is rinsed inside and out with hot fresh water. I carefully wipe off the action with a rag soaked in fresh water. Then I dry and spray. I started doing this when I took the Parker out of its case a week after I'd used it and there were pits on the barrel despite the fact that I had carefully oiled it before putting it away. I believe the salt lay under the oil, pulled in the moisture, and did the damage. There hasn't been a drop of gun oil on my guns in years. The new silicones, such as CRC or WD-40, are much better. They penetrate water, last even in rain, and can even get under salt particles that may be on the weapon.

If possible, you always want to shoot at waterfowl as they come at you. The head and neck are so vulnerable then. I've spoken of the golden moment when they hang in the air. You can't miss them then. Plenty of ducks get shot going away, but a shot in the intestines probably won't bring them down and will kill them later. What you don't want to do, especially with puddle ducks, is let them come in and sit down. As every jump shooter knows, their initial spring off the water takes them twenty to twenty-five feet in the air, and if any wind is blowing, they know how to get it in their wings fast. You're presented with a curving, going-away shot that is very difficult.

Another thing I've found is that skeet or trap loads are excellent for killing cripples. You can buy them very cheaply at any club. If you've got a bird down, especially on the water, you've very likely got to get a head shot to kill him. You can usually get within reasonable range, and the small-size shot not only saves you money, but also does the job better because of its great number of pellets (around 800) .

Finally, there's the subject of how to hit ducks and geese. The only thing I know about this is that you aren't going to learn it here. You've got to get out and start popping. Learn how to swing, point, and handle your weapon until you start hitting things. Trap or skeet, formally or informally, is a great avenue to skill. Anything that increases your familiarity with the gun, that makes you more comfortable, confident, and at ease shooting it, will make you a better shot. You should know where every shot is going. If you miss, you should know what you did wrong and where your shot went.

The duck without a chance: Two men crack down on a single.

The miss: this duck came in to decoys and survived a barrage of five shots from some surprised shooters. An obvious case of a duck so stupid he didn't realize he was dead.

I see multiple shooting done all the time, and it always riles my gorge. A bird flies into the decoys and four or five guys leap to their feet and blaze away. The duck goes down, but what kind of mass execution has taken place? No one knows who really shot the duck. I think multiple shooting is usually an excuse for lousy shooting. The guys know they couldn't put the bird down individually, so they rely on a cannonade to do it. We designate shooters, and assign backup shooters if the first shooter misses. That way you have the satisfaction of watching your bird fold. Another trick is for the man on the right side of the blind to take right-hand birds, the man on the left, the left-hand birds. That way you don't both pull down on the same bird.

You hear so many tales of people killing every duck they shoot at that there must be some truth to it, but I've never seen anything remotely resembling this kind of skill, and neither has any truthful person I've ever talked to. Probably the greatest game shooter who ever lived was Lord Ripon, an Englishman, who died some fifty years ago. He was also the greatest game hog. He killed over 500,000 birds in his lifetime and once downed twenty-eight pheasants in sixty seconds as bearers handed him one loaded Purdey double after another. Despite being an obsessive, even compulsive, shooter who was in great demand at drives because of his accuracy, he killed only 70 percent of the birds he shot at. I think any waterfowler who kills one out of three is a good shot. One out of two is spectacular. Anyone in Lord Ripon's class is awfully skillful or very lucky or both.

SHOOTER'S SHELL BOX

Most shell boxes sold commercially are for four boxes of shells — too much for a day's gunning. I like to carry two boxes and make up this little box to do so. Here are the ingredients you'll need.

Fasten the box together by using glue and tacking in small brads to hold while the glue sets.

To hold hinges, you'll have to rivet them in. Cut copper nails and peen down with ballpeen hammer.

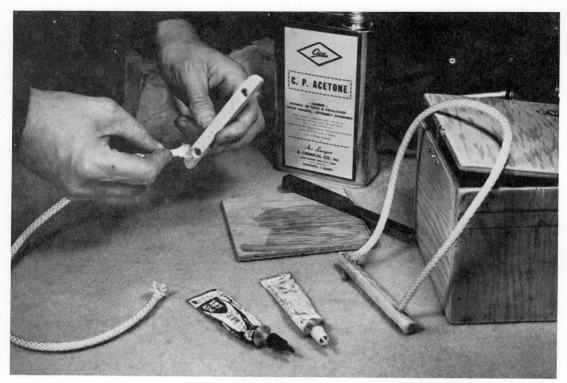

You don't want a handle that won't spill the shells if you forget to lock the hinged lid. I found that setting braided nylon cord in epoxy held perfectly. The handles are then glued onto the sides.

Here's the finished box, nestled among the duck decoys. This keeps the shells dry. The lid prevents them from showing if ducks are overhead.

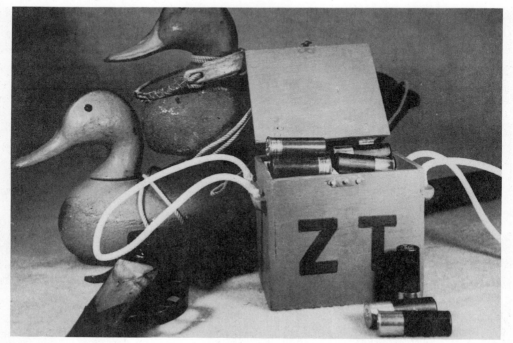

16

The Deadly Art of Sculling

Not many waterfowlers realize that one deadly market method still survives. It is perfectly legal to stalk feeding or resting waterfowl on open water, in a small boat moved by human muscle power. You can't use a motor to chase them, and you can't sail down on them, but you can drift into them or use a boat which (quoting from federal regulations) is manually "propelled by paddle, oars or pole."

Sculling is still practiced. It remains beneath the dignity of a commercial waterman to sit and row a boat in the fashion of a dude with his girl on a park pond. In shallow water he'll stand up and push with a pole or single oar. If the water is too deep to pole, he will stick the oar in a notch cut in the transom and rock it back and forth through the water in a rough figure eight. Once you get the hang of it, you can shove the boat along this way at a good clip.

The reason that the market hunter resorted to the scull oar should start any duck hunter's heart beating faster. They know ducks and geese have no innate fear of boats, blinds, floating objects, or dogs. They are only afraid of the presence of man. Even if you camouflage or conceal yourself completely, if you row a boat down on ducks or geese in a conventional manner, the oars bobbing up and down will be a tip-off. Waterfowl will never allow such a thing to approach them.

Sculling allows you to conceal yourself and the oar too. When you camouflage the boat and conceal the single oar, ducks and geese will take little alarm at what appears to be just another floating object, though eventually they will get uneasy and swim or fly away. (They won't let even a big log get too close.) Exactly how close you can get varies like the dickens. Generally, an expert sculler can expect to approach within twenty to forty yards of the wary three.

Add another fairly common ingredient to the mix and the scales are weighted dramatically in favor of the sculler. If there is floating ice—not skim ice but visible white floes—a white scullboat is practically invisible to the birds. They can no more readily distinguish the white boat among the white floes than they can discern that decoys are not in fact brethren.

Scullers will tell you that in drifting ice, waterfowl are virtually at the hunter's mercy. One reason sculling is seldom employed is that, with seasons coming earlier and earlier, scullers are robbed of this late-season advantage. In most places, heavy ice has no time to form before the season closes. Scullers must content themselves with stalking wild, hard-hunted, suspicious birds on a fifty-fifty basis. Without the advantage of ice to tip the scales in his favor, the sculler still has to prove his prowess with gun as well as boat.

Scullers can reflect on the fact that this is precisely why their method was never declared illegal. Unlike night shooting or shooting over bait, sculling by no means puts the birds at a disadvantage. Federal and state authorities recognize that sculling is not a dangerously easy way to kill waterfowl. It isn't even a better way to hunt. It is simply another way.

But it is a method worthy of revival. Sculling for ducks is very nearly a lost art. It would be senseless, for example, to publish this chapter without the accompanying plans. Almost none are available commercially, and the boats in use where sculling survives are generations old.

The sport needs revival because of the changing nature of waterfowling. Duck hunters don't need to be told that as massive new artificial lakes, reservoirs, and impoundments have proliferated, ducks and geese have been quick to take advantage of them. Migratory patterns have changed. In many cases, especially with Canada geese, resident populations have developed. Although these giant impoundments have attracted ducks and geese to areas where none existed before, that isn't to say hunters are harvesting them. Most impoundments are difficult to hunt by current techniques. More often than not, the birds use these waters only for resting, and feed elsewhere.

Definite handicaps for the impoundment hunters are the high banks and steep drops into deep water. Waterfowl shy away from high shorelines. In most impoundments they raft in open water, far from shore.

Sculling is the perfect solution. It's made to order for this situation. The sculler needn't care whether birds are feeding or resting. Nor must he wait until birds come to him, with all the dependence on wind and weather that this implies. He goes to the birds. If the birds sit in the open far from the shore and stubbornly refuse to move, all the better to drift down on them.

There are a number of ways in which the basic sculling technique can be modified and improved. Probably the most common way is by adding decoys. This works when ducks are trading in a particular area. For example, you might have observed them using a certain cove or resting over a certain bar. You put out your decoy spread in the cove or on the bar, and wait for birds to pitch in. When they do, you scull down on them. One of sculling's incidental advantages is that you don't have to sit there and freeze to death, as when shooting from a blind. Between stalks you can retreat with field glasses and stay snug in cabin or car.

Sometimes you may want to attack upwind, surprising the birds from behind. More customary is a downwind scull, since it seems more natural. You'll·be helped if floating junk is common on the waters. Another great help is stumps, islands, or points, anything that helps hide your stalk.

In those areas where sculling has kept a weak but lingering hold, scullers make good use of vegetation. In the tule marshes of the West, the thick grass helps conceal the boat. In Maine's Merrymeeting Bay, black ducks are the quarry. Scullers account these as the wariest of ducks, as even more skittish than Canada geese. You can be sure if you come down in open water that a black duck will start taking a keen interest in the odd-looking object at least a hundred yards away. Merrymeeting

Intent on sculling. Note the strings of rope at the bow to break any suggestion of a bow wave and to prevent the bow from slapping on the water. In this side sculling, the boat must be pointed in the direction to hide the man's arm and oar. In inside-boat sculling you can come straight down on a duck.

scullers put their decoys along the edges of wild rice. The blacks land, then usually swim in the rice, where they can't see as much. Then the scullers attack.

Another common form of sculling is almost like woodchucking. You drive along the waterways with your boat in tow or atop your car. When you see ducks, you launch and stalk.

Like a canoe or johnboat, a scullboat can, of course, be used to float creeks and rivers and jump ducks. The important difference between floating and sculling is that when you round a bend, ducks a hundred yards away won't immediately spook. When they can't see the hunters they pay no attention to the boat—until you rise to shoot.

The key to sculling is in concealing all signs of man. Depending on what's most comfortable for you, you can kneel low or lie flat with head forward, market style. In the Connecticut scullboats the hunter lies head aft and sculls with an oar that comes in over his shoulder. This almost dictates a downwind drift, as not much power can be generated. The Delaware River scullers kneel and use a high rowlock secured to the side of the boat. With your arm well over the oar you can really stroke the boat along, but the ducks must be approached obliquely so the boat conceals the movement of the oar.

You can see the varieties are endless, and you'll want to be bold and innovative if you decide to build this boat. The basic scull movement is easy to learn. Just moving the oar back and forth will propel you, and the rolling figure eight will soon come quite naturally. You can scull with any oar, but you'll probably soon have the plane out, shaving a regular commercial ash oar to a thinner, bendable shape and experimenting with blade design.

Although it is illegal to approach birds under power, most scullers tuck a midget outboard motor aboard for the trek back to home base.

Experimentation will be called for in deck shape and camouflage. You can use shock cord, wire, lath, or net to hold grass in place around the bow and sides of the boat.

Most old-time scullboats had round bottoms that really slid through the water. The boat shown here is flat-bottom for ease in building, and she is fashioned to be easily drivable as well. But the hull is a displacement hull and can't be powered at more than five to seven miles an hour.

One thing you must keep in mind with a scullboat with a long bow like this is to position weight so the tip of the bow is in the water. If not, the slap or even the shadow below a raised bow can spook the birds.

Scullers using decoys tend to take a sharp interest in painting them accurately, feeling that the closer to nature they are the more comfortable a resting duck will feel among them. They set decoys in a string of little pods. As the boat approaches, the ducks will swim away from it, retreating from pod to pod and tending to linger in each new group for perhaps a fatal moment too long.

Accepting the widely varying nature of all wildlife under various conditions, scullers rate black brant and the scaups the easiest to approach. You can get right in among them, in the center of the flock. The other diving ducks—canvasbacks, redheads, shovelers—are probably next on the scale and probably blue and snow geese fall somewhere in the same range. The divers don't like to fly if they can avoid it and will swim away from the boat rather than make their run into the air, unless the boat is hot on their tails.

The puddle ducks and Canada geese present the greatest challenge. Mallards, pintails, blacks, the teals, and wood ducks will all start swimming away from you out of the decoys at forty to sixty yards. They won't usually jump right away. At first they seem just distrustful of this thing coming at them but aren't sure that it represents grave danger. At thirty yards, however, they will usually jump. As with decoy shooting, singles, doubles, and young birds are most vulnerable.

This is the scull boat shooting technique. Both bow and stern men shoot. Frank's gun is an 1100 with a three-inch shell. Sixty or seventy yards out it commands the field. Notice the nice black duck decoys.

This rear shot shows how low in the water the scull boat sits. This boat was built along the Delaware River; it's over a hundred years old.

Frank Astambranski cracks down on a bunch of pintails he has sculled down on in the Delaware River. The Delaware has always been a center of sculling activity. Gunners would ride the tide downriver until it turned, then ride it back. Frank carries a little 3 hp outboard that he tucks between the legs of the bow hunter for return trips.

These pintails come down the Delaware River and winter in the Chesapeake. Few if any gunners get them there, but Frank gets them sculling. You can see here that the "grass" is really strands of manila rope that stands up better than grass.

HOW TO BUILD A SCULLBOAT

This little duckboat is designed with long, flat straight sections that make it about the easiest kind of boat to build for a man with a yen to go sculling. If you can handle a saw and a plane and take measurements, you can put her together by orthodox boat-building methods and have a boat of professional quality.

Sculling is a hunter's art that should be practiced more, but with perhaps a few local exceptions no scullboats are available. I was lucky enough to get Bill Oakly, one of the country's top naval architects, interested in the project. Bill had studied dozens of different scullboats of the past and, with easy-building requirements paramount in his mind, came up with this two-man vessel. I'd estimate it will cost you less than $200 to build her. I'd guess the weight of the finished boat at 160 to 180 pounds.

Materials and Tools

You'll need mahogany planks in 2" X 3/4" by 15' sizes. Mahogany is expensive, and you could substitute spruce or long-leaf yellow pine for this; bow and stern transoms are 3/4" exterior grade plywood. Marine plywood comes in 15' X 4' lengths; regular exterior grade (which is okay if it's without voids) comes in 10' and 12' X 4' lengths. You can scale the plans down to 12 feet by reducing beam by a couple of inches to make a one-man boat (but only if you loft it; more about this later) or scarf two sheets, making sure you get the bendy sides butting. To scarf, you plane identical long angles into both planks, glue them together, and reinforce with a butt block (also glued). You'll need some screws and bolts. These can be hot-dipped galvanized, but brass is better. For the rest of the construction I'd use bronze boat nails.

Lofting

Go to a lumberyard or housebuilder and buy 45' of construction paper. Scotch tape two 15' lengths to the floor. Draw the boat full-size, looking at it sideways. Draw a straight baseline. Go to the table of offsets and measure off the "height above baseline" for each of the eight stations. You have the bottom line that is practically coexistent with the baseline at stations 4, 5, and 6. Then draw the sheer line; then the deck. The "6" buttocks" line is to give you an idea of the flare (outward angle) of the sides. Draw it in lightly. Now draw the lines, looking down on the boat. Use the "half-breadths"; from a center line, mark the chine, waterline, and sheer. Measure off, using a square, at the stations, then draw the lines with a long bendy stick held in place by weights. You haven't finished drawing yet. Draw the frames.

These show a head-on profile at stations 0 to 4 and a stern-on from 5 to 8. Take these off the half-breadths. Draw a center line, measure out to chine, then the sheer, then the 6″ waterline, which should be in a true line from sheer to chine. Make frames on both sides, i.e., a full frame at each station. Finally, draw bow and stern transoms. These show as dotted lines on the profile view. Take measurements off these rather than from the construction detail, because photoengraving in printing could cause distortion. The transoms are almost like frame stations 0 and 8.

You now have your boat drawn to full-scale lines. If you want to scale it down to 12′, this is the time and way to do it, as you can see your "redesign" form before your eyes. From now on, take all measurements from the full-scale drawings, not the plans. Also, you'll want to scissor out drawings whenever possible, to use as patterns just as a seamstress does.

Building

First cut out the bow and stern transoms from 3/4″ plywood, using your drawings as a pattern. In similar fashion, make each frame. Cut space for keel, chine, mid-batten, sheer batten, and limber holes, leaving projections on battens at chine and sheer, to plane flush, later, to receive planking. Plans call for laminated deck beams. These must be laid against a cut mold and glued. The result is light and strong. Or you can saw them out of 3/4″ mahogany. Note that end of deck beams sit against inside of sheer batten, not on planking.

Out of a 3/4″ X 6″ by 16′ piece of scrap (laminating to build it up if necessary) draw in the curve of the bottom using full-scale plans as a pattern. Cut the keel to this measurement, and temporarily screw it to this "backbone." Your boat will be built on this. You might want to lift it up from the floor on horses. Draw bow knee carefully and attach. Although no stern transom knee shows on plans, if you intend to use an outboard bracket, by all means include one, drawing it on your full-size profile. Build and use to set proper angle of stern transom. You must fit carefully at the bow; everything comes down to a 3/4″ point, so the keel must be planed severely.

Following your full-size patterns, fit the frames together. (Double-check measurements again from table of offsets.) Follow building procedure shown on drawings, keeping center line of keel and 6″ waterline plainly marked. Your boat is about to take shape. Mark off frame station centers on keel and drill a hole for 1/8″ galvanized (or brass) bolt. Drill exact center of frame and fit each to proper station. With your knife, slightly bevel top of keel socket so frames 1, 2, and 7 are not thrown out of 90° true by the keel's curve. Draw bolts tight.

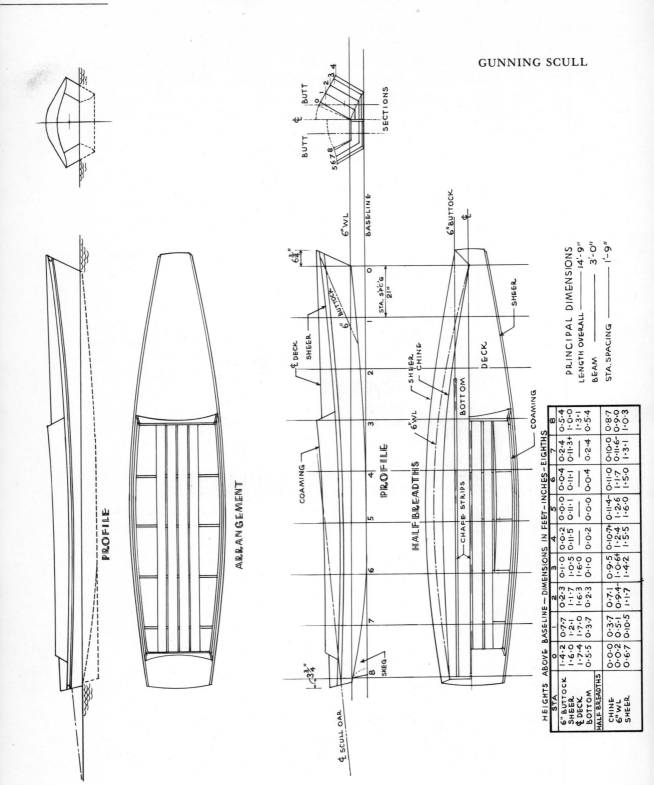

GUNNING SCULL

PROFILE

ARRANGEMENT

PROFILE

HALF BREADTHS

PRINCIPAL DIMENSIONS

LENGTH OVERALL —— 14'-9"

BEAM —— 3'-0"

STA. SPACING —— 1'-9"

HEIGHTS ABOVE BASELINE—DIMENSIONS IN FEET-INCHES-EIGHTHS

STA.	0	1	2	3	4	5	6	7	8
6" BUTTOCK	1-4-2	0-7-7	0-2-3	0-1-0	0-0-2	0-0-0	0-0-4	0-2-4	0-5-4
SHEER	1-6-0	1-2-1	1-1-7	1-1-5	0-11-5	0-11-1	0-11-1	0-11-3+	1-0-0
₵ DECK	1-7-4	1-7-0	1-6-3	1-6-0					1-3-1
BOTTOM	0-5-5	0-3-7	0-2-3	0-1-0	0-0-2	0-0-0	0-0-4	0-2-4	0-5-4
HALF-BREADTHS									
CHINE	0-0-0	0-3-7	0-7-1	0-9-5	0-10-7+	0-11-4-	0-11-0	0-10-0	0-8-7
6" WL	0-0-2	0-5-1	0-9-4-	1-0-6+	1-2-4	1-2-6	1-1-7	0-11-6-	0-9-0
SHEER	0-6-7	0-10-5	1-1-7	1-4-2	1-5-5	1-6-0	1-5-0	1-3-1	1-0-3

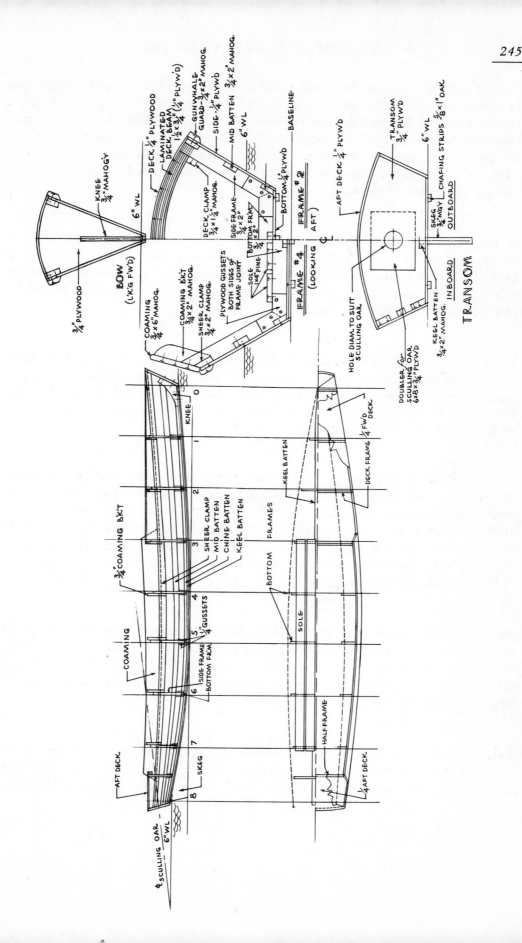

Now fit in the midbatten, sheer, and chine strips. The midbatten will fit snugly, but you must leave excess on sheer and chine to permit them to be planed flush to receive planking. All butt against transom. When all is fair, drill a pilot hole to avoid splitting, glue, and nail. At this point, plane the bottom of the chine strip to receive bottom planking. You'll have to do this awkwardly, upside down, but you can't do it later, as side planking fits outside bottom planking at chine. When all's fair you are ready to plank.

Scissor your drawing side profile at sheer and lines on plywood sheet. Scotch tape to frames to check fit. If all's well, draw out on plywood piece, leaving 1/4'' excess all around — first with your eye, then by fitting the planking plane frames and battens where necessary so planking lies flush. (If you goof, use plastic putty.) Attach by glueing and nailing with boat nails on 2'' centers.

You can release boat from backbone now, as side planks will hold curve. Plug holes in keel with plastic putty. Turn the boat over. Scissor out bottom profile, check it against the actual bottom, and cut out, leaving 1/4'' excess. Lay bottom and fit. You should be sanding and slicing. Fill any voids with plastic putty. Glue and nail on 2'' centers to frames and keel.

It's all over but the shouting. Turn the boat, plane sheer batten, and fit deck. I like to screw decks on my little boats, so if I punch a hole in them, I can repair it more easily. Attach brackets to receive coaming and install coaming. A side deck just adds work, but you will want to retain the afterdeck for several reasons. It's a handy place to stow gear and engine. You can sit on it and curse fate on bluebird days. Most important, it keeps your weight out of the extreme end of the boat, which in a little fellow like this lifts the bow.

You have built yourself a fine little duckboat that will row or paddle beautifully and last for years. If you are worried about a few nonprofessional spots that might leak, fill all voids with plastic putty, round sharp edges of planking with wood rasp, and tape with Dynel tape or a four-ounce-per-square-yard (006) or six-ounce (0085) fiber-glass or Dynel tape.

Last to go on is the skeg. It should be bolted through the keel in at least three places. Whether or not you add the chaffing strips depends on your use. The skeg will track the boat okay. Attach outboard bracket to hold motor 15'' above bottom.

Sculling Oar

You'll have to make your own sculling oar. Get the longest ash oar you can find (7' probably) and plane it down until it is light and bendy. Pro scullers shape the blade like a scimitar with the curve on the bottom. They make oars from surplus lifeboat oars, but I couldn't tell you where they find them. You'll have to decide where and how to mount the oar. I'd suggest trying an outside transom mount to begin with. Bolt a rowlock to the stern. You may want to lie forward and scull behind you. Or you might prefer the Connecticut technique of lying feet first and sculling over your shoulder. The outside Jersey mount is powerful. Any welding shop can rig a bracket to your design. Paint and camouflage to suit.

17

Other Hunting Methods

FLOAT HUNTING

A sporty, often scenic, and always exciting way of putting ducks in the freezer is to float rivers or streams. Ducks, and sometimes, but not often, geese, are surprised as you round bends or pop out from behind natural cover. There isn't much to tell about how to do it. Here's what not to do: First, don't shoot your bow man; second, don't tip the boat over in your excitement. This would seem to be rather obvious advice, but as we will see, it is astonishingly easy to cause either disaster.

Canoes or johnboats are generally the vessels employed on floats. Some gunners go to the trouble of camouflaging them with grass on the bow; others simply rely on the element of surprise. A lot depends on the water you hunt. If it's a big river and the ducks are out in the open, you'll have to resort to some scullboat techniques to get within range. If you are floating a small, brushy stream, the natural conceal-ment may be such that no camouflage is necessary.

All kinds of different techniques can be used, depending on the streams or river and the access points to it. Some make several floats a day, setting out decoys on the first float, picking them up on the last. The strategically placed decoys draw birds and tend to position them in spots where natural configurations favor surprise.

Another trick is to float partway downstream until you find a particularly good spot. Then you build a makeshift blind or settle into natural cover, put out a dozen decoys or less, and let the ducks come to you. In the afternoon, you pick up and continue the float. As you become familiar with the streams, you'll find the spots where the ducks like to rest, probably because of an abundance of cover, and the places where lush river grasses draw the birds to feed.

Most people think you need two cars for floats. This really isn't true. I lived in a canoe last summer and floated almost every day. The trick is to pick good put-in and take-out spots along a road. You launch the canoe. One man stays with it (to guard the gear) and the other man drives the car to the take-out point. Then, carrying a canoe paddle and life preserver, the driver hitchhikes back to the other man and the boat. The trappings of the trade — the paddle and preserver — instantly identify your purpose. I don't think more than four or five cars ever went by me before I was picked up.

Floats have several nice attributes. Most streams are navigable, so you don't need anyone's permission to float them. If you want to come ashore, permission may be required, but the water is free to all. You can float in bluebird weather and still have a good crack at birds. It helps if they are moving around, but even on calm days you still have a good chance. And you don't have to die at dawn. Oftentimes there are morning and evening flights along streams and rivers, and you'd want to set up for them if possible. However, the birds that settle in for the day after the morning flight are probably going to be there for the lazy gunners that round the bend at high noon.

Weather can help the float hunter. When storms slash, ducks tend to leave big water and settle in sheltered spots. They'll leave the open water on, say, the Mississippi or Ohio and head for smaller streams where you can get a crack at them. Another good time to float is when there is enough of a freeze to ice over ponds and lakes. If these still waters are frozen and the motion of your stream keeps it open, that's good. Every flock of birds in the neighborhood will be on your stream.

If you are just starting in floating, it is best for only the bow man to shoot. You switch positions after each jump by turning around in your seat. As you get more experienced, the stern man can help out with crossing shots. I advise you to pick your stern man with caution. Some guys get excited in the presence of game and seem to lose all sense. You don't want a man like this shooting over your shoulder. A trick to aid in overcoming the excitement is to tie lines to the paddle handles and attach them to the boat. When the birds break, you can drop the paddle and lose no time going for your shooting iron.

Here's how boats get capsized on floats. You're sliding down a river and suddenly a flock of mallards bursts off to one side. You don't think about anything but spiking a few, so both men wheel and fire. The simultaneous recoil on the same side can spill you. Van and I were gunning out of a pram one day in a northeaster. The marsh was flooded, and we pulled the pram into some reeds. A flock of ducks came in fast and went over our heads. We both swung back for them and rolled the pram right over. One instant we were dry, the next we were sitting on a marsh in about two feet of water. The water was warm, so we could laugh about our mistake. But if you capsize in cold water or in fast-moving rapids, the mishap could have serious consequences. If you plan to do a lot of floats, consider rigging your canoe with pontoons. Any Grumman dealer has them. They are outrigger floats that don't detract much from the canoe's handling characteristics but make it almost impossible to capsize.

You should make a realistic assessment of your canoeing ability. Winter streams are at their height in flow, and as more water goes down the rapids they become more dangerous. You want to pick streams and rivers with a minimum of white-water danger. You may have to portage or line through rapids you could easily run during summer. Rapids are extremely treacherous, but deceptively so. A sheer rock wall presents itself plainly to would-be climbers. The higher, the scarier. Not so the rapids. Often canoeists don't know that rapids or even waterfalls are there! Inexcusable, but terribly common. Once you enter a rapid there is no turning back, no chance even that others in your party can come to your aid if you get in trouble. I go into all this in *Introduction to Canoeing* and include a chapter of how to learn white-water skills. If you plan to do a lot of floats, you might look it up.

Finally, you should have some sort of survival kit. A plastic garbage can makes an inexpensive waterproof container. It would be well for you to have one and keep dry clothes, fire-starting equipment, and an axe in it. If I'm running water where the possibility of a capsize exists, I tend to lash things down. Plastic garbage bags are handy items for this kind of thing. They are rugged, cheap, and keep stuff dry.

JUMP SHOOTING

Walking along stream or river banks or across marshes, and shooting at ducks that you scare from their hiding places is another common waterfowling technique and one that can be successful for many of the reasons that floats pay off. If possible, you try to spot the birds from a distance. Binoculars are a definite aid, and the new plastic Bushnells are a perfect pair for the job. If there are hills and dales, you're off to a good start. You can get to high ground and glass the whole area. Often you just hike quietly down the bank of a stream. If there's a canal near you, the towpath makes for fine jump-shooting strolls that combine a welcome tramp outdoors with the possibility of a squawker or two. After you locate the birds, you craftily plan an approach that puts you within minimum range. You use as much natural concealment as possible—bushes, brush, tall grass or reeds, a hill or big rock. Try to make your final approach upwind if possible. The old-timers swear that blacks and mallards can smell you. I've put in plenty of hours creek hopping—"crik" hopping, it's pronounced down the bay—and while I never felt black ducks actually smelled me, I've had plenty jump because they heard me coming from far off. At times I jumped birds that I felt sensed me coming through tremors in the marsh. I'd sure pussyfoot the last fifty yards. I'd be the last to swear they couldn't smell. If you gun tidal marshes, it's always best to jump shoot at low tide, as the lowered water level sinks the bird down deeper out of sight. On high water on a flat marsh they stick up far enough to see you coming a long way off.

Another trick you want to pull when you are hunting with buddies is to come in wide apart and from opposite directions on the spot where you think birds are holding. Ducks don't stick in the same spot, and if they've roamed from where you last saw them, at least one man will get some shooting.

It's a big help to have a dog when you're out hoppin'. You can send your retriever after a downed bird. Lacking a dog, you have to go yourself. I've swum a few creeks in my time, feeling awfully foolish stripping down to the buff out on thě marsh. And I wish I had a dollar for every time I've gone over my boot tops trying to wade a creek for a cripple.

BAITING

When mechanical harvesters replaced hand reaping in grainfields, a great deal more grain was left in the fields. This changed the nature of waterfowling and will continue to do so, as ducks, geese, and swans have just recently turned from feeding in water areas and gone to grazing on leftover field grains.

More than likely this shooter is after railbirds that can't fly when the marsh is flooded like this. But you'll jump ducks this way, and when the seasons for both are open plenty of ducks are shot this way.
Joel Arrington, North Carolina Department of Conservation and Development.

Now how much grain should properly be left in a field is a subject for debate. Not a few of these debates take place before a judge. Let's say the guide has baited the field but has told you he didn't — if you bothered to ask. You go in before dawn and are sitting there, and the game warden nails you just as hard as he does the guide. Some very prominent and very embarrassed sportsmen have wound up with fines this way. Farmers are allowed as much grain as is left by "valid agricultural operations or procedures," and you sure see some awful sloppy harvesting in fields that have blinds on them.

You can legally bait in a variety of ways. Flooding croplands is probably the most favored. In the Sacramento Valley the crops are harvested, and right before the season the fields are flooded. The key phrase says "harvested cropland or grain crops properly shocked." If you have control over duck-shooting areas, you can plant crops that ducks and geese like. The Agriculture Department has a free booklet on the subject. Just write to Agriculture Department, Washington, D.C. If you want to pursue this line, two firms specialize in it: Bill Kester, Game Food Nurseries, Box 371, Oshkosh, Wisconsin 54901 and John Lemberger, Wildlife Nurseries, Box 399, Oshkosh, Wisconsin 54901. Both offer booklets for twenty-five cents that describe the subject in detail. Both gentlemen will offer advice on the subject, including analyzing samples of your soil and suggesting what will grow best in it.

I've heard of guys painting Coke bottles yellow and scattering them around the blind to resemble ears of corn. Whether this will attract waterfowl is problematical, but you better have your licenses in order as it will attract game wardens, especially those in helicopters.

I heard about a tricky way of baiting in Currituck. A guy spent a couple of weeks before the season baiting a small sandbar in the area of a lone pine tree he stuck in the bottom. The birds learned to key on the pine. The night before the season, he moved the tree a couple hundred yards away, right in front of his blind. Pretty sneaky.

I shouldn't admit to such a foul deed, but I once tried baiting. I bought a sack of corn and scattered it in a pond we leased. Then somebody stole our little pond box and our beloved hand-carved decoys, and we abandoned the pond and the baiting project. To bait successfully, you must be consistent — the bait must go out every night. Also, it's hellishly expensive. Ducks and geese can easily clean up several bushels a night. And it is dangerous. I know a commercial goose guide, a pleasant, honest fellow who rears his family, pays his bills, values his friends, and baits. He got caught and was fined. He went on baiting and got caught and fined again. The third time he got caught, the judge sentenced him to jail—then suspended the sentence. He told me that standing there and thinking that he was actually going to prison along with the rapists, robbers, and muggers was the lowest point of his life. He felt disgraced, felt he'd let his family down. "What would my kids think of their old man a jailbird?" he said. Baiting is just something many waterfowlers, and most guides, simply don't take seriously. They don't equate it with sawing off both ends of a shotgun and holding up a gas station. But it is a crime.

And it should be. It's the one thing ducks and geese are helpless against. Their lives are in such constant jeopardy they cannot resist succulent food. They will take almost any risks to get it. It's cheating, taking advantage of them. They deserve fairer play. If you bait, don't smart aleck to me about it, because I'll tell the warden.

Retrievers I Have Known

Regrettably this chapter, which should be one of the strongest in the book, must be the weakest and I am the loser. My gunning has been mostly over open water where we retrieved ducks in a boat. As you may have figured out by now, for me the boating aspects of waterfowling are a large part of the sport. If I bought a dog, I'd be out of a job as a boat jockey. Unthinkable!

But my recognition of the importance of a dog is dramatized by this experience. I spent all one season "casing" ponds to find out the best for next season. After I found it, I went to the expense of building a sinkbox and the agony of digging it in. Then I found to my horror that I could not retrieve the ducks I shot. Unless I made a cold stone kill, the birds would sail down in the grass and be lost. On one bleak day I was on my feet and running toward them even before they hit the ground. It was for naught. The birds eluded me. Losing cripples ruined it for me. I have never gunned the pond from that day to this. The box is there, waiting for somebody to use it. Somebody with a retriever.

Although I can offer no expertise, I can share stories of dogs I have known. My earliest moment with ducking dogs was delightful. As a boy, I went with my pal Irv and his dad to a gunning club near Rock Hall, Maryland. When the lights went on in the clubhouse, two Chesapeake Bay retrievers bounded in. After that, further sleep was impossible. If you didn't get out of bed, one of the dogs would grab your blankets and pull them off you.

It was Irv's Labrador retriever, Squire, that first showed me the amazing stamina and power a good waterfowl dog possesses. Squire was in the line of the famous King Buck. We were building a blind on a big marsh. I'd look up, and there would be Squire on the horizon to the east. What seemed like only a moment later, I'd pause again and there was Squire on the western horizon. This went on all day. The dog raced across the marsh all day, swimming rivers, back and forth, never seeming to tire. (That's about all Squire was good for, too, that and looking handsome. Irv never taught him to hunt.)

The Labrador is such a popular dog that when you say retriever that's really what you are talking about. I'll bet that at least 80 percent of all the retrievers in the country are Labs, and at field trials the figure is more like 99 percent. The Lab combines so many wonderful traits. He's affable. You almost never see a mean Lab. Tractability is above par. You can easily train one yourself. They long to please, and they are tough. Joe Linduska at one time managed Remington Farms. He had a young Lab that he'd trained all summer. On one of his first days on the job, Joe put a Canada down. Out went the Lab. As it happened the bird was a tough old gander still full of beans, and when the dog got in range the gander reared back with its wing and socked the dog across the nose. Joe winced in horror. "There goes my pup," he thought. Nope. The youngster shook his head, ploughed in, and grabbed the old bird by the neck. In they came.

To be certified, Labs have to show no distaste for entering ice-cold water. I used to be a member of a retriever club and go to the trials. If you've followed the circuit at all, you know that they attract a special type of millionaire sportswomen that are almost stereotypes. They are very mannish, these ladies, always decked out in leather-fronted field britches, and usually accompanied by milk-toast husbands. One of these gals was trying to get her Lab to retrieve a dead mallard she'd tossed out into the center of a little practice pond. She'd shout "Go!" and point with her outstretched hand. The dog would start to leap, then cringe at the water's edge. Finally, the gal could stand it no longer. "Go," she screamed and planted a hard

If you want to make a retriever happy, give him a job like this. The light that shows in a dog's eyes when he's pleased is a great sight.

kick on the dog's rear with her booted foot. "To hell!" she added, as the astonished retriever hit the water.

Although Labs are everybody's favorites, let me tell you about two golden retrievers it has been my pleasure to hunt over and watch shine. My pal John Gardella raised Sherry from a pup and taught her everything himself. He had a job that allowed him to train her every day. Sherry was good. And since John hunted her hard on ducks and pheasants, she became a first-class meat dog as well, though this accomplishment once lost her a field trial. A dead pheasant had been thrown, then a live pheasant was released and shot. Sherry was instructed to retrieve the first bird, which she did, bounding out and grabbing it. On her return she was carrying the dead bird when the just shot and supposedly dead other pheasant got to its feet and started to take off. Being a meat hunter, Sherry knew what to do. She immediately dropped the dead bird and went for the cripple before it got too far away. This was smart retrieving under hunting conditions, but Sherry got marked down by the judges for dropping a bird.

John always felt Sherry went into a field trial with two strikes against her because she was a golden, and he was right. The Lab fanciers looked down their noses at her. Although smart, eager, and charming (she had a delightful, typically sweet golden nature), she didn't have the powerful flash of the Labs. Field-trial judges like to see a dog start a retrieve like a pro football player coming off the line at the snap of the ball. Sherry tried, but her gusto couldn't match that of the bigger, stronger breed.

John bred her. As luck would have it, one of the dogs of the litter was a strapping thing, as sunny and bright as his mother, but brute-sized and really rugged. John sent him away to the finest trainers, and the young feller really took to it. To make a long story short, John cleaned up with him. He was so handsome, stylish, and smart that the judges had to rule for him, Lab lovers though they were. And he was a powerhouse. He hit the water like a bomb, drove through cover like a tank, had his mother's magnificent nose but didn't learn her bad habits. He wound up a champion.

Retriever field trials aren't as bad as quail trials, which turn the dogs into racehorses. Anyone who can handle a dog under field-trial conditions has obviously got to be mighty sharp in hunting conditions. On the other hand, the slavish obedience required of a dog to win field trials tends to rob it of its initiative when it has to hunt on its own. Plenty of retrievers who couldn't tell a hand signal from a friendly wave bring home ducks because they are smart and have developed a fine-honed game sense. A field-trial dog often can't do this.

I think the average hunter has it in him to train one retriever. After that, most of the duck hunters I know go to outside professionals, if they can get up the scratch, at least for the fundamentals. It's an excellent way to get a new young dog off on the right foot. Then you can kind of fortify the lesson plan from there.

A poor dog is worse than no retriever at all. He'll spook birds and get you sore hollering at him. You'll find yourself working at the dog all day instead of enjoying the hunting. I hunted with a Lab named Negra in Mexico, and she was something. A nice thing, but every time we fired she'd hurl herself into the water whether we'd hit anything or not. After that, she'd swim around in the decoys until she satisfied herself that nothing was down. Of course, while she was out there nothing would come in. One time a flock of teal shot past, and the two of us cracked off pretty good and five of them lay on the water. Negra was off at the shot. She grabbed the first bird, then instead of hauling that in, went to the second and grabbed it. Would she bring the two in? Not our Negra. The third duck went into her by now gapping jaws. Then as we watched, amazed and amused, she swam over to the fourth bird and added it to the pack. Still churning along, she headed for the fifth teal. This one gave her trouble. She had so many birds in her mouth now that every time she tried to bite down on the last bird, one of the other four fell out. She finally figured that she was making nothing on the exchange and came ashore with the four, then went out again after the fifth.

The curly-coated Chesapeake Bay retrievers, "bay dogs," you call them if you're fancy, are handsome fellows, and just the look of them spells duck shooting. Trouble is, they are contrary, bull-headed beasts at best. They say you train a golden with kisses, pats, and reassurances of affection. To get the job done on a Lab requires shouting, swearing, and a cut or two from time to time with a lease. A Chesapeake is like a mule. You crack him over the head with a hickory club to get his attention. Then to the mat with every lesson. And so many of them are mean. I remember one that lay under a skiff alongside a boat I was refinishing. His owner was rebuilding the skiff. All day the dog would lie there, and if anyone approached the skiff it would growl. I believe if a child had come up and touched that boat the dog would have gone for it. The ultimate in Chesapeake dog stories happened to Gene Hill. He was heading out to the blind and noticed that the Chesapeake retriever rode in a boat behind. It bit everybody, even its owner. "He don't mind it none back there," the guide said, "and it's a lot easier on the rest of us, believe me." Gene believed him.

Retrievers, especially Labs and goldens, make good upland dogs for pheasants and even for grouse. Some guys also use them with great success to retrieve on dove hunts.

With that yellow Lab for company, this gunner can afford to take the trouble to grass his boat so well. If he had to use the *boat* to retrieve, I'll bet he wouldn't take such pains. When he's down inside, no duck or goose on earth could ever figure out there was danger here.

19

Waterfowl Cookery

I don't pretend to comprehend the tangled web of mystery that is hunting. One thing I am pretty sure of, though, is that you cannot be a complete hunter or grasp all the satisfaction and enjoyment of the sport without looking forward eagerly to cooking and eating the game you kill. It is priceless stuff, of course. Most game you can't buy legally. Pen-reared mallards have to be carefully marked before they can be sold, and except for these anyone who offers you any duck or goose in return for money is committing an illegal act. There are two levels to this game-cookery question. We've touched on the mystic level. In the Canada goose story I used the line, "the hunter in you hungers." I don't know if other hunters react in the same way, but my eyes follow a fat mallard like a cat watching a bird. There is hunger in my look. I want to kill that mallard because I know that it can make me a memorable dinner. We were sitting around camp once and got on the subject of the ethereal nature of the Canada's cry and how we loved to hear them calling, especially in the night. My boss was unimpressed. "The sound Canadas make I like best is that plop when they hit the ground." I used to regard his outlook as crass, but now I'm not so sure. Somewhere back in the dark reaches of our brain there is an echo of the past telling us that to live we must hunt. When you hunt successfully, something dies. But, if this act serves as a vehicle for joining with your friends in an evening of pleasure, the sting is softened. We all have our purpose in the scheme of things. That it is the purpose of a few ducks and geese to slide down my gullet would seem to do no harm as long as the conservation crews do their job.

That brings us to the second level, the gut level. The old canard that you cook waterfowl on a plank, then throw away the bird and eat the plank is absurd. Most ducks, geese, and even (I'm told) swans are more than delicious eating when properly selected and prepared—they are matchless. I've never had a better meal at the best restaurants in Paris than the wildfowl served up at my table. The table qualities of all game, waterfowl included, vary considerably, but by keeping a wary eye out for selection and obeying the preparation rules, many, if not most duck or goose dinners can turn out to be everything you could hope for in the way of a gourmet meal.

The flavor of any game animal depends on what it has been feeding on. In the Northwest many otherwise fine-tasting ducks—mallards and pintails, for instance—start feeding on rotten salmon carcasses and become inedible. Similarly, American brant that normally feed on eelgrass, which imparts a hauntingly delicate flavor, become rank and inedible when they start feeding on leafy sea cabbage or lettuce on the Atlantic coast. Herring-spawn on the eelgrass ruins flavor in the West. The main diet of ducks and geese is known, and you can get some idea of what kind of flavor you can expect from wildfowl from knowing what they eat. Those that eat grains or corn will have the best flavor. The grass eaters will have a wilder, "gamier" taste, which is a sort of oniony flavor. Those that feed on animal matter will be fishy, and of course the fish-eating ducks' flesh will taste strongly fishy. Here's how Kortright rates waterfowl feeding preferences. Canadas, "largely vegetable"—wheat, barley, corn, oats. Brant, "eelgrass." White-fronts, "essentially a vegetarian"—nuts, acorns, berries, but mostly grasses and grains. Snow geese, "largely vegetable"—winter wheat, sprouting grains and grasses. Blue geese, "wholly vegetable"—tundra grasses. Mallard, "9/10s vegetable"—wheat, barley, corn, buckwheat, acorns. Black duck, "three-quarters vegetable"—pondweed, grasses, sedges, smartweed, seeds; animal food consumed consists of mollusks and crustaceans. Gadwall, "entirely vegetable"—wheat, barley, buckwheat, corn, nuts, and acorns. Baldpate, "9/10s vegetable"—pondweed, grasses, algae, sedges, wild celery, and waterweed. Pintail, "9/10s vegetable"—pondweed, grasses, sedges, smartweeds, and docks. (I have the impression pintails have turned in recent years to the wheats and corn preferred by the mallards.) Green-winged teal, "9/10s vegetable"—sedges, pondweeds, grasses, algae, duck weed, water milfoil. Blue-winged teal, "7/10s vegetable"—wild rice, wheat, barley (rarely), sedges, grasses, smartweed, algae, mollusks, insects. Wood ducks, "9/10s vegetable" — grapes, berries, chestnuts, beechnuts, acorns, burrs of pin oaks, duck weed, cypress cones and galls, sedges, tubers, grasses, and grass seed. Woodies are also fond of spiders. Redhead, "90 percent vegetable" — pondweed, muskgrass sedges, grasses, wild celery. Canvasback, "4/5s vegetable" — pondweed, wild celery, delta duck potato, water milfoils and muskgrass, mollusks. Scaup, "60 percent vegetable" — pondweed, grasses, sedges, wild celery, muskgrass, mollusks, insects, and crustaceans. To get an idea of why other ducks taste fishy, look at the following diet examinations: Goldeneye, "3/4s animal matter" — crustaceans (including crabs), insects (including caddis flies), mollusks, fish. Scoter, "food entirely from the animal kingdom" — mollusks (including rock clams), oysters, blue mussels, scallops, crustaceans, fish. Red-breasted mergansers, "food is principally fish."

This is an interesting guide, but that's all it is. All sorts of things affect game flavor, not the least of which today is polluted waters. Waterfowl that spend any time in waters that are oily, for example, pick up the flavor quickly. And although this has never happened to me, you hear stories all the time of people raving over a duck dinner only to be informed what they just ate was merganser, or some other duck generally considered unfit. I can attest to the edibility of coot. I'd been out body-booting on the Susquehanna flats, and on the way in one of the guys cut loose on a flock of coot. "What's that for?" I asked. "We eat 'em," was the startling reply. I got an immediate demonstration. One of the boys peeled the body right out of the coot, then fried it up on the stove below. There's an old French saying that "hunger makes the best sauce." I'll admit I was half starved from being out at 5:00 A.M., and with no breakfast, but it was awfully tasty.

You haven't any control over what the duck or goose you shot has been feeding on, but there are some considerations you can control. First, you want young birds rather than old. If a goose family comes in (and you can keep cool enough to do so), pick one of the trailing birds. The leader is likely to be older. You can tell the age of waterfowl by their feet. If the nails are worn, the bird is old and tough. Young birds have soft legs and feet, bright eyes, and a flexible wing tip and breastbone.

Proper preparation starts in the field. I once read that birds should be drawn on hot days in the field and the cavity stuffed with grass. I tried it, and the result was terrible. You should try to keep the birds as cool as possible, but drawing or plucking speeds spoilage before tenderization sets in.

When you arrive home the birds should be hung. How long they should hang depends on several factors. Older birds should hang longer than young. The weather comes into it. In mild weather tenderization is accelerated. You can usually tell when wildfowl have hung long enough by observing a bluish tinge to the skin of the abdomen. I don't pay much attention to hanging time. I've eaten plenty of birds the night of the day I shot them. Others I've let hang a week. If the weather is hot, keep birds in the refrigerator. And don't let them freeze then thaw later.

The birds should be dry plucked. The books say you should not scald or soak them to make this job easier. I dry pluck them in a paper bag in the kitchen if it's too cold to do the job outside into the garbage can. I have an old pot used exclusively for paraffin. I strip the bird of its primaries, the thick feathers of the back and breast, chop off its head, neck, and feet (with a hatchet on a fence post handy to the back door). Then I dip the bodies in the wax. You don't want to sear the flesh doing this. Do it quickly, immersing as little as possible. (The proper way is to brush the wax on.) When you peel the paraffin off, the job should be done.

Next, I gut them. The books tell you not to wash them under water, because it tends to extract the blood, which you want to keep the flesh juicy. I do it anyway, pull the guts, chop off the oil gland on the tail, and wash the exterior and interior. Any shot holes should be cleaned out. The bird is now ready for cooking.

There is a shortcut cleaning method—the breast fillet. You can do this in the field. You pluck only a row of feathers, right down the ridge of the breastbone. Then you take a sharp knife and cut the skin, trimming back to separate the fatty tissue under the skin from the meat. When the skin is trimmed back as far as it will go by pulling the two sides, almost as though you were popping the breast out, you cut carefully down the breastbone, then along the bone of the chest, the same way you'd fillet a fish. The result is two fine pieces of breast, no plucking and drawing. I can fillet a duck in about ten minutes.

ROAST DUCK OR GOOSE

The basic method of cooking ducks or geese is to roast them. How long to roast is the question. Waterfowl lack the fat of domestic ducks and geese and are somewhat dry. People like to eat them with "the blood following the knife," to keep them as juicy as possible. If you prefer meat well done, there are ways to counter the dryness. The classic way is larding. You thread bacon or salt pork through the breast about a half-inch deep with an oversized needle. An easier way is to drape strips of bacon over the breast. (Ducks and geese are usually cooked breast up except in France.) As the fat melts, it lubricates the meat. I dislike both of these methods, as the bacon or pork flavor overpowers the more subtle waterfowl taste. I prefer basting them with various basting recipes, most of them built around wine or butter or both. The basting combines with the cooking juices to form a sauce that further reduces any suggestion of dryness. Another trick used in our kitchen is to put a layer of cheesecloth over the breast and pour the basting over it. The cloth holds the moisture.

As you roast, you can test to see how well done the birds are. With all the size range possible, from a large goose to a small teal, it's best to keep an eye on them. For an average mallard, black, or pintail, preheat the oven at 500° for ten minutes or so, then set it at 350 degrees, put in the bird, and baste every three minutes for fifteen to twenty minutes. For goose, figure about twenty to twenty-five minutes to a pound.

Wild rice is the classic vegetable to accompany wildfowl. It's delicious if you can find it and stand the expense. Good substitutes are the newer rough rices, like Uncle Ben's. Combined with a gravy sauce or tart sweet-wine-and-juice sauce, it's mighty fine.

Understand that you're not required by law to roast your birds. As you'll see, tough old birds should be treated differently. You can split ducks or geese and broil them, either in the oven or over charcoal. They can be cooked on a spit. As with other meats, the turning continually keeps the juices flowing over the meat.

We sauté breast fillets in butter and white wine, which then makes the sauce. Many a brant has been filleted, sauted, and eaten at our table almost before it realized it was in serious trouble.

The heart, liver, and gizzard—the giblets—of wildfowl are as edible as those of their domestic counterparts and are prepared the same way.

How many birds per person depends on the size of the birds. Two little teal make a meal for a hungry man. A single mallard or pintail is usually served for each person, often split in half if they are exceptionally large birds. Goose is generally carved and served like turkey. Smaller birds can be split and served. A good-sized goose feeds two.

If you wind up with a lean, old ancient mariner instead of a fat, young goose or duck, you should cook it by some "moist" method. A pressure cooker is probably best for this. Another method is to simmer the bird. Here's a recipe for that. (This would be a good way to cook a young goose too. Less cooking time is needed.)

SIMMERED DUCK OR GOOSE

Get a good roasting pan with a cover and make a stock by melting a quarter pound of butter. Fry diced salt pork and add fat and pork to butter. To this, add a dozen whole white onions. Cook until onions are done, then lift out pork and onions. Now fry pieces of the cut-up bird quickly until they are brown. At this point, add whatever herbs you might want—a bay leaf is good, garlic always a must. Put the cover on the pan, add two cups of red wine, and adjust the heat at just under the boiling point. Let simmer for about an hour, longer if a particularly big or tough bird is involved. Use the cooking stock for gravy.

Another trick you can try with birds that aren't absolutely first class is to marinate them in a marinade of red wine to which you've added onion, bay leaf, garlic, and any other herbs you prefer. How long you marinate depends on how much you want them to taste like red wine, onions, bay leaves, etc., and how much like ducks. From ten to twenty-four hours is the usual time. Keep in refrigerator while marinating. I must confess I've tried this several times with broadbills without much success.

Another thing I've tried, again with little discernible benefit, is to roast the bird with an apple, carrot, pieces of celery—any or all of these—in the body cavity. The theory is that the stuffing "draws" out the bad flavors. It is discarded and the bird eaten.

CLASSIC RECIPES

I am no gourmet cook. I am reminded of the incomparable Jimmy Robinson, who when asked what recipes for ducks and geese he preferred, replied, glasses bobbing on the end of his nose, "Recipes? Recipes? Who needs recipes? Just throw them in the stove till they're done." Nonetheless, with my wife looking over my shoulder (she is a gourmet cook and a good one), I can offer some of the better-known ways to prepare these sumptuous birds.

PRESSED DUCK

I give this recipe more as a matter of interest than as practical cooking advice. I doubt if you could order pressed duck anywhere but in France. It's more a piece of showmanship than cooking. First, slightly underroast your duck or goose. Then carve off all the meat and place it in chafing dishes. The carcasses of the ducks are then put in the press, which (on the only one I've ever seen) is like a silver tureen, holed in the bottom. The top is pressed down on a worm gear worked by a turning wheel. All the juices are mechanically squeezed out of the carcasses. To these juices are added shallots, garlic, lemon juice, sherry, the diced livers of the fowl (browned) , and whatever else you have handy. A sauce is concocted. The sauce is then poured into the chafing dish and the meat is cooked for a slight additional time at the table.

As you can see, the whole thing is a very elaborate affair, something you should buy a ticket to watch, though I have no doubt the results are scrumptious.

I've never had a duck press, but I bear the remarkable distinction of knowing a man who actually owns one. Sam Bonnell's press sits proudly on his sideboard and, according to Sam, it has been sitting there for about forty years. He said cleaning the damn thing was the second-most miserable experience he's had in seventy years of gunning. First most miserable was lying in three inches of water in a leaky battery.

BROILED WILDFOWL

This works best on ducks. Split the birds down the backbone and pound them until they lie flat. Salt and pepper and cook about four inches over a hot charcoal fire until done to your taste. They should be continuously turned and basted with a roasting sauce of butter, wine, and herbs, or butter to which brandy has been added. An oven can be substituted for the charcoal. Preheat and slide the split birds under the broiler, some four inches from the flame. Turn and baste frequently until done.

BOILED DUCK

This is another recipe that serves admirably with the lesser species, as you can add flavor as you please. It is also a superb meal with first-rate species. Clean ducks and boil for ten to fifteen minutes. Take out and carve as much meat off the birds as you can. Put meat aside in warming pan. Now cut the carcasses in pieces and put in stewing pan along with two cups of chicken stock, bay leaves, lemon juice, herbs to suit, garlic, wine, or brandy if preferred. Simmer in closed-lid pot for approximately two and a half hours. Just before serving, add the meat and stir in carefully (so it won't curdle) a cup or more of sour cream until the whole acquires a thick, creamy consistency. Serve over rice or toast.

STEWED DUCK

The little buffleheads, ruddies, rails, coots, scoters, and so forth, are all edible and, in the hands of a country cooking master, become a treat. Improperly prepared, the meat is coarse and tough and the flavor "strong," i.e., fishy.

Here is a way to deal with these. Fillet out the breasts and allow them to soak for eight to ten hours in a marinade of small whole onions, bay leaves, salt, pepper, garlic clove, and two cups of dry white wine. (Prepare them in the morning for evening cooking.) When you're ready to start cooking, dry and flour the breasts and lightly brown by frying in bacon fat. Next put them back in the marinade and stew for approximately two hours. You can add potatoes, tomatoes, and carrots to the stew.

DUCK SOUP

Yes, there is such a thing as duck soup, and the simplicity of its making must have given rise to the saying.

You start out with duck carcasses from which the breasts have been removed. Then you make a vegetable soup stock of onions, tomatoes, carrots, diced celery, and cabbage, and toss in the carcasses. Add seasoning, bay leaf, a can of chicken consommé, and two quarts of water. Bring to a boil then reduce heat and let simmer for about two hours. After one hour, you may want to take out the carcasses and carve whatever meat you can off and add it later. Or the meat may just fall away from the bone. After two hours, skim any fat off, strain, and serve.

SAUCES AND STUFFINGS

There are no special considerations for sauces and stuffings for waterfowl. The familiar ones used with domestic poultry, ducks, and turkeys work in the same way for wildfowl. Fill your goose or mallard with the same chestnut or oyster stuffing that goes into your Thanksgiving turkey, and use the same recipe. The orange sauce that goes so well on domestic duck is even better when poured over wildfowl. We make a shortcut Cumberland sauce out of equal parts of catsup, currant jelly, and sherry. The three combine in a tart flavor that so wonderfully complements the duck flavor that when we went to the trouble of following a complicated Cumberland-sauce recipe, we found we liked the simple one better. The only additional thing I know about sauces is that they all taste better if you put a lot of brandy in them.

WINES

Nothing sets off the delicate flavors of waterfowl like a good wine. If you don't know anything about wine, stick with the better American wines, such as Inglenook, Almadén, Taylor, or Louis Martini. Gallo wines are found everywhere, and though they're not absolutely first rate, they are far better than no wine at all. Gallo Hearty Burgundy is the best of them, to my taste.

Anyone who tells you what kind of wine goes best with waterfowl is talking baloney. It is entirely a matter of personal preference. Some evenings you may opt for a chilled dry white wine, maybe a Chablis or Riesling. Other evenings, you may want a sweeter white wine. We've served room-temperature dry Burgundy with roast goose and never had any trouble emptying the bottle. A good Beaujolais makes an eminently suitable companion for a waterfowl dinner. The ultimate compromise, of course, that no one could argue with, is any of the fine domestic rosés. Chilled, they are always correct. Lots of people like beer with waterfowl. Some connoisseurs insist that only a very dry sherry should be drunk with wild duck. I say drink whatever you like. It's your duck.

Index